Named in remembrance of

the onetime *Antioch Review* editor

and longtime Bay Area resident,

the Lawrence Grauman, Jr. Fund

supports books that address

a wide range of human rights,

free speech, and social justice issues.

The publisher and the University of California Press Foundation gratefully acknowledge the generous support of the Lawrence Grauman, Jr. Fund.

Reunion

Reunion

FINDING THE DISAPPEARED CHILDREN
OF EL SALVADOR

Elizabeth Barnert

Foreword by Philippe Bourgois

UNIVERSITY OF CALIFORNIA PRESS

All author proceeds will be donated to Pro-Búsqueda and related causes.

University of California Press
Oakland, California

© 2023 by Elizabeth Barnert

Library of Congress Cataloging-in-Publication Data
Names: Barnert, Elizabeth, 1979– author. | Bourgois, Philippe I., 1956–
    writer of foreword.
Title: Reunion : finding the disappeared children of El Salvador /
    Elizabeth Barnert ; foreword by Philippe Bourgois.
Identifiers: LCCN 2022017152 (print) | LCCN 2022017153 (ebook) |
    ISBN 9780520386143 (cloth) | ISBN 9780520386150 (paperback) |
    ISBN 9780520386167 (epub)
Subjects: LCSH: Family reunification—El Salvador—21st century. |
    Disappeared persons—El Salvador. | Children—El Salvador. | Civil
    war—Social aspects—El Salvador.
Classification: LCC HQ574 .B37 2023 (print) | LCC HQ574 (ebook) |
    DDC 362.82/8097284—dc23/eng/20220611
LC record available at https://lccn.loc.gov/2022017152
LC ebook record available at https://lccn.loc.gov/2022017153

Manufactured in the United States of America

31 30 29 28 27 26 25 24 23 22
10 9 8 7 6 5 4 3 2 1

For Father Jon Cortina, the disappeared Salvadoran children, and their families,

For the people of El Salvador,

And for the migrant children and countless others undergoing forced family separation,

Hopeful for reunion.

Contents

Author's Note

Reunion portrays the family separation and reunification experiences of El Salvador's disappeared children, based on ethnographic observations I gathered for more than fifteen years (2005–20) as a participant-observer with the Salvadoran human rights NGO Asociación Pro-Búsqueda de Niñas y Niños Desaparecidos (Association in Favor of the Search for Disappeared Girls and Boys). I volunteered with Pro-Búsqueda while in medical school to assist with creating a DNA bank to match disappeared children separated from their families during El Salvador's civil war with their biological families. I took five trips to El Salvador from 2005 to 2009 and have maintained contact with Pro-Búsqueda and several of the families over the years.

The chapters of *Reunion* are written in first-person present tense to emphasize bearing witness to the testimonies of war and reunion. The ethnography draws on fifty semi-structured interviews and years of field notes, woven into a nonfiction story. Names have been changed. All other information is related as it was told to me, occasionally supplemented with historical texts to provide additional context on El Salvador. Quotations are from the interviews or field notes, unless denoted otherwise. I published analyses of the interviews with the disappeared children and their families in the scientific journal *Human Rights Quarterly*. *Reunion* is constructed to give readers a deeper understanding of the six stages of separation and reunification identified in the articles (pre-disappearance, disappearance event, initial separation, searching, reunion event, reintegration) through the voices of the families.[1]

To further illustrate the circumstances of the child disappearances, *Reunion* opens with anthropologist Philippe Bourgois's instructive foreword and closes with not-to-be-missed visual testimonies of the war. Appendix A presents Philippe's photo-ethnographic account of enduring a Salvadoran military attack. Appendix B displays drawings that Philippe collected in the Honduran refugee camps in the early 1980s, illustrated by elementary school children who had survived Salvadoran military scorched-earth massacres.

As of 2020, a total of 994 cases of disappeared children have been registered with Pro-Búsqueda; of these, 443 have been resolved.[2] Untold more are out there. The experiences of the disappeared Salvadoran children remain relevant to millions of families worldwide separated today, including because of war, disasters, and forced migration. For many Central American migrants, postwar poverty and violence feed new cycles of separation to survive. Within present-day United States, separations occur at an alarming rate, caused by incarceration, foster care involvement, and other forces that drive families apart. As family separations continue to be a global concern, I hope that readers will apply lessons—about identity and the importance of having the option for reunion—from the disappeared Salvadoran children's long journey home.

Foreword

Historical Accountability for Crimes Against Humanity in El Salvador

Dr. Elizabeth Barnert's powerful book, *Reunion*, documents the struggle for survival, social justice, and historical recognition of the generation of "disappeared children" ripped from their families during El Salvador's prolonged revolutionary civil war, between 1980 and 1992. I met her in 2005, when I was an adviser for her master's thesis in the UCSF medical school, where I was a faculty member at the time. Now, wonderfully, we are colleagues at the UCLA medical school, where she is a pediatrician and researcher dedicated to improving the health and human rights of the poor—and in my opinion a human rights and social justice hero.

In 2005 Liz befriended a network of formerly disappeared children who, like Liz, were just entering young adulthood. They were bravely building an inspiring social movement dedicated to locating their long-lost biological families in the face of government hostility. Liz proactively brought the most advanced genetic software technology available in San Francisco to help Pro-Búsqueda develop and manage on-site its own globally linked DNA database. She helped them create a DNA database to reunite themselves and hundreds of other separated children in El Salvador with their natal families. Liz became part of their struggle for justice, and this book is an inspiring account of youth as protagonists of their own history,

demanding justice. It is an honor to contribute a foreword to this important and deeply moving book that so effectively brings alive the ongoing
struggle for transparency over the demographic crime against humanity
of a "disappeared" generation of poor, mostly rural children. These human
rights activists dared to oppose the ongoing abuse of both the Salvadoran
and US governments, which continue to refuse to open their archives and
fail to take responsibility for their historical crimes against humanity.

The lessons we can learn from the trauma of separations of children
from their families, caregivers, and communities decades ago during the
Salvadoran Civil War are burningly relevant in the 2020s. In 2018 the
US "zero tolerance" family separation and detention policy wrenched
thousands of children from the arms of their parents as they crossed the
US-Mexico border, seeking asylum from violence in their home countries (including El Salvador). Many of those children now suffer from
the trauma of enforced disappearance from their parents because of prolonged detainment in US Homeland Security taxpayer-financed concentration camps (most of them built and run by for-profit corporations with
notoriously predatory histories).[1]

Dr. Barnert has emerged as a go-to expert against coerced family separations, synthesizing what she has learned from documenting the Salvadoran Civil War tragedy. She testifies to state legislatures and advocates
to presidential appointees, key members of Congress, the United Nations,
and the world. She speaks regularly to the press about these ongoing
crimes against humanity. Mind-bogglingly, many of the children separated by US Homeland Security were too young to even know their own
name—let alone their parents' names or address. US government officials
failed to maintain coherent identification records, rendering family reunification difficult, if not impossible, for the youngest children.[2] The history
Liz documents in this book is tragically repeating itself because the public
has failed to learn from history and to demand accountability.

PRO-BÚSQUEDA: IN SEARCH OF ACCOUNTABILITY

Dr. Barnert is no ordinary doctor. Affectionately called "La Lease" by her
Salvadoran compañeros-in-struggle, "Leasie" by her Cuban-exile mother,

and "Liz" by her colleagues in the United States, she is a "juvie [juvenile jail] doc," direct-action human rights activist, and researcher advancing science in the service of human liberation. When Liz first flew to El Salvador in 2005 as a medical student on summer break, the country was (and still is) awash with gang violence, rampant public-sector corruption, and authoritarian political repression. At that time, El Salvador was still under the thumb of its most right-wing, promilitary, authoritarian political party, ARENA (Nationalist Republican Alliance), founded by one of the country's most notorious modern-era war criminals, Major Roberto D'Aubuisson. He was the official coordinator of the infamous Salvadoran death squads. According to his own sister and to historians, as well as to human rights investigative reporters and organizations, D'Aubuisson ordered the assassination of the archbishop of El Salvador, Óscar Arnulfo Romero, while the archbishop was in the midst of officiating a memorial mass on March 24, 1980.[3] Pope Francis elevated the martyred archbishop Romero to sainthood more than thirty years later.

Liz centers the book on the lived experience of suffering imposed on all the poor of El Salvador. She also writes beautifully, crafting an engaging, double coming-of-age story, braiding together her own *concientización* (seizing of political and social justice consciousness) and maturation with that of the child victims. Like her, during the first decade of the 2000s, most of the disappeared children were in the process of becoming young adults and political protagonists of their nation's own conflictive history. They became the founding rank-and-file activists of a remarkable organization called the Association in Favor of the Search for Disappeared Girls and Boys.[4]

It was and still can be dangerous to use the term "disappeared" in public in El Salvador because right-wing politicians consider the word to be subversive. Consequently, the Association diplomatically glosses its awkwardly long formal name in public communications with the euphemistic shorthand, "Pro-Búsqueda" (literally "In Favor of the Search," which politically invokes the organization's search for historical accountability). These delicate nomenclature calisthenics offer objective linguistic proof of the "public secret" of the routinization of repression of free speech in El Salvador.[5] As we go to press (August 2022), the country is in the midst of a new authoritarian repressive and corrupt takeover by a young, wannabe fascist populist, Nayib Bukele. He is conducting a new generational–level crime against humanity in the name of a "war on gangs." In early 2022 he declared a state of emergency and suspended key constitutional civil liberties (legal due process, freedom of the press, etc.), encouraging his security forces via Twitter to torture prisoners and conduct extrajudicial killings. The superannuated right-wing politicians and military leaders of the dictatorship justified their war crimes from the 1980s in the name of "saving Salvadoran democracy" from "communists," "subversives," and "atheist terrorists." Those epithets have been used interchangeably for over a century by cynical warriors in the United States and Latin America to defame, torture, and murder anyone who dares advocate for social justice. Now Bukele has added "gangs" to the list of citizens to incarcerate or kill.

In 2005, with the Pro-Búsqueda activists, Liz scoured remote rural villages and urban shantytowns to collect cheek swabs from aging survivors in former 1980s conflict zones. They simultaneously audio-recorded hundreds of oral history testimonies from parents, nephews, nieces, and siblings who had lost young loved ones to corroborate their genetic-testing results and clarify the historical record. Liz returned to San Francisco with hundreds of cheek swabs in her airplane luggage, each packed in a manila envelope that documented the chain of custody of the samples. She delivered the genetic specimens to a US Department of Justice forensic laboratory, where scientists analyzed the DNA pro bono for potential child-family matches.

Six months later, Liz returned to El Salvador. Gang violence was skyrocketing, and living and working in postrevolutionary El Salvador brought Liz into the personal lives and homes of her Pro-Búsqueda agemates. She wrote beautifully self-reflective ethnographic field notes about their courage in the face of tremendous challenges. A young adult, like them, Liz was falling in love and forming a family of her own. She also reciprocated their trust, introducing her Pro-Búsqueda companions to her new boyfriend (who continues to support her work now, as her husband and the father of their two children).

IRRESOLVABLE GRIEF

In addition to being an inspiring story of revolution and struggle, this book also confronts the pain of betrayals and human failures and the cruel long-term suffering imposed by counterinsurgency terror, as well as the irresolvable raw grief of victims compounded by ongoing historical injustice. Most family separations occurred during Salvadoran military "scorched-earth" operations. In fact, most fathers and many of the mothers of disappeared children were killed during the civil war. Families living in conflict zones generally supported the revolutionary process, and many were political activists or even guerrilla fighters. Some, however, were less politically engaged or may have changed their commitments over time. Prolonged civil wars and postwar transitions are notoriously plagued by internecine political betrayals. Not telling a truth because it is too uncomfortable is not responsible, and Liz does not sanitize history, but she contextualizes it empathetically. She documents the way El Salvador's unending economic chaos imposes an everyday "state of emergency" on the poor that continues to systemically victimize children and mothers.[6] By probing unpleasant truths in solidary accompaniment, Liz elucidates the suffering imposed by the "structural vulnerability" of the protagonists in *Reunion*.[7]

Many disappeared children and biological family members retain their revolutionary commitments today, proud of lifelong struggles for social justice and civil rights. A few, however, were simply caught in the crossfire while humbly working in subsistence slash-and-burn corn and bean fields. At least one older brother to disappeared girls depicted in the book was a government-soldier perpetrator of scorched-earth massacres. He was a member of the nefarious Atlacatl Battalion, which committed the largest massacre of the entire civil war—over nine hundred civilians—on its first full battalion deployment after returning from US military training the month after the Cabañas November 1981 scorched-earth massacre.[8]

Liz documents all these heroisms and betrayals empathetically and objectively, acknowledging the context of their political valences. With her gentle charisma, down-to-earth humor, and comforting common sense, she enabled interviewees, especially those she befriended as a solidary activist and companion, to feel safe. They trusted her, summoning up memories of unspeakably traumatic events, stoically recounting them from beginning to end—some for the first time ever. Many had to pause to wipe away silent tears. Invariably, however, they would resume, determined to finish telling their whole story for the historical record.

Reunited children and biological parents have to wrestle with the trauma that is often exacerbated by the symbolic violence of survivor guilt, the erasure of popular history by the powerful, and the everyday normalization of neoliberal social inequality and scarcity. This is especially true for young people who, after being kidnapped or getting lost, were neglected in orphanages, abused by foster caregivers, and traumatized by fleeting early childhood memories of parents and siblings being tortured and killed right in front of them during scorched-earth operations. Surviving biological parents (and extended relatives) similarly suffer from much-too-vivid traumatic memories of loved ones being brutalized in front of them and grief over not having been able to protect them. For example, Francisca Romero, the cofounder of Pro-Búsqueda, had to watch helplessly silent and immobile while hiding with two of her children as her seven-year-old daughter, Elsy (another Pro-Búsqueda activist), was captured by the military. It was the only way to save her other children and herself. Liz reveals the enduring emotional scars of involuntary survival triages and the dumb luck of survival under fire. This is especially painfully expressed by her Pro-Búsqueda companions who survived the May 1982 Chalatenango scorched-earth operation, dubbed by them (almost poetically) the *Guinda de Mayo* (Flight of May).[9]

Counterinsurgency and economic chaos leave deep wounds. The Pro-Búsqueda survivor activists and Liz, consequently, adroitly help families manage the overwhelming emotions of first reunions occurring after a generation of separation. Liz accompanies genetically matched, formerly disappeared children arriving from the United States and Europe with loving adoptive parents, uncertain, terrified, or excited about what to expect next. The first moment of encounter with long-separated biological relatives explodes with tremendous cathartic relief in prolonged spellbound silent embraces. It is simultaneously flooded by waves of grief, tears, maternal coos, and bursts of nervous and blissed-out laughter, as historical cruelties of separation and loss are suddenly shared collectively. The serendipity of international adoptions spawn particularly mismatched assemblages. Desperate mothers, innocent babies, philanthropic intermediaries, and loving foster parents collide with unscrupulous for-profit lawyers and global North-South inequalities. Cultural and class disjunctures complicated by fraught emotional ambivalences generate awkward miscommunications—even if they eventually enable lifelong empowering solidarities.

Liz emphasizes how unfairly the biological mothers separated from their progeny are scapegoated. The turmoils of civil war are invisibilized. Instead, mothers are criticized for having "abandoned" their babies. Lovers who absconded from paternal responsibilities, unnamed heroic companions killed in combat, and the unrelenting desperation of life-threatening poverty and hunger disappear from the historical memory. Structural forces and unjust cultural ideologies are hard to recognize, and injustice is dangerous to talk about publicly.[10] The forces bearing down on vulnerable mothers, consequently, remain a "bad faith public secret" obscuring the perpetrators who inflicted the cruelty.[11] Perhaps most unfair is the blame heaped on the many mothers who felt a moral duty to the revolutionary movement while being simultaneously pressured by overbearing husbands or other guerrilla fighters demanding they entrust their infant child to a relative or neighbor living in a slightly safer part of the country. It was also the only way to get a child out of danger once a mother was identified as a rebel. Informal foster care arrangements under conditions of desperation too often go sour—generating yet more psycho-dynamic suffering and sometimes physical or sexual abuse.

Powerfully complex wartime psychodynamics are structured by class contradictions, cultural values, and ideologies. They generate the nitty-gritty grist of symbolic violence and oppressive public secrets.[12] Liz and the Pro-Búsqueda activists confront the ongoing suffering from the counterinsurgency war and child disappearances by bringing transparency to El Salvador's historical injustices and working for both personal and collective resolutions to trauma. Like most of the poor of El Salvador, Pro-Búsqueda activists, despite working hard, do not earn enough money to support their families. A few were kidnapped and forced to live at tender ages in the barracks among the same soldier assassins who killed their parents. It is heartening, consequently, when Liz brings us into the households of those child survivors who are in the process of overcoming such traumatic odds by successfully forming supportive loving families of their own in the face of ongoing extreme scarcity.

THE HISTORICAL, POLITICAL, AND ECONOMIC CONTEXT

Liz asked me to present additional historical, political, economic, social, and cultural context of the war, especially the shameful US role. Like most

Central American nations, El Salvador fails to guarantee the minimal physical and economic security for its citizens. Like many, if not most, nations across the Americas (including the United States), it fails to punish egregiously corrupt politicians and notorious perpetrators of crimes against humanity. Nevertheless, the poor of El Salvador have repeatedly heroically resisted oppression, defying torture and murder.

During the past century (and previous ones), rebellious insurrections and revolutionary guerrilla armies clamored for justice, culminating in 1980 in the founding of the Frente Farabundo Marti para la Liberación Nacional (FMLN; Farabundo Martí National Liberation Front). A utopian coalition of peasants, workers, and intellectuals who had seized political consciousness over the prior two decades, the FMLN consisted of multiple Salvadoran guerrilla armies allied with radicalized political and human rights activists, determined to overthrow the country's US-supported military dictatorship. The war and political debates protagonized by the FMLN during the conflict were plagued by dogmatisms, internecine killings, and mutual betrayals on all sides. These are inexcusable realities of civil wars and of revolutionary movements more broadly, especially when these are funded, weaponized, and prolonged by foreign intervention—and, as in the case of El Salvador, drag on for twelve bitter years of counterinsurgency warfare. Wars are also deeply engrained in local racialized and gendered hierarchies. These complex conjugations of violence obscure the elephant in the room: the repeatedly abusive international military-economic interventions. By 2001, for example, El Salvador had become so dependent on US markets and so buffeted by corporate greed that it adopted the US dollar as its national currency. A brief sprint through colonial history helps clarify the roots of extreme violence in El Salvador during the 1980s civil war and its links to gang, criminal, and governmental violence in 2022.

SPANISH COLONIALISM

Latin America suffered catastrophic hemispheric-wide genocide for over two centuries following Spanish and Portuguese conquests after 1492. Indigenous populations had no firearm technology or biological antibodies to European germs. Incalculable massacres, epidemic die-outs, and routinized mass starvation occurred.[13] Central America remained a colonial backwater for the Spanish Empire, lacking easily identifiable gold or silver deposits. More incompetent wannabe feudal lords settled El Salvador, fighting primarily among one another rather than extracting resources for export.

El Salvador's indigenous populations were periodically kidnapped to South America and worked to death in more profitable silver mines.[14] El Salvador's preconquest indigenous communities had always been on the margins of both the Aztec and Maya Empires. Being less centralized made them less accessible as a source of feudal serf labor. It enabled the reconstitution of more semiautonomous indigenous communal villages—especially in the Nahuat-Pipil speaking indigenous heartland of the Western Highlands, where more robust institutions of cultural and civil administrative and economic semiautonomies from European colonial and urban mestizo society flourished. As relatively independent, semi-subsistence small farmers growing coffee for export and selling artisanal products locally, they managed to retain more of their indigenous language, clothing, and rituals. El Salvador had the highest population density of all Central American nations by the 1880s, and its small-farmer agriculturalists were renowned for their work ethic.[15]

US INDUSTRIAL CAPITALISM ACCELERATES ETHNOCIDE AND RURAL DISPOSSESSION

The meteoric industrialization of the United States after the US Civil War propelled it into an imperial superpower over Central America and the Caribbean, prompting an influx of US industrial dollars and military-diplomatic interventions at the turn of the twentieth century. This transformed El Salvador's weak, feuding elites into one of Latin America's greediest and most reactionary oligarchies. Entrenched as the so-called fourteen families, this agro-financial elite controls coffee and sugar processing, and finances: they continue to be entirely dependent on US markets, on military/economic aid, and increasingly on organized crime.

As the size of monocrop coffee-exporting estates mushroomed in the 1800s, so too did laborer demand—especially during the summer coffee-harvest months. Unwilling to pay full-time survival wages for harvest workers, elites passed "vagrancy laws" to force indigenous subsistence farmers to become harvest laborers on demand. Landlords also obtained stabler low-cost part-time workers for maintenance and expansion year-round by inviting mestizos (called *colonos* [settlers]) to settle on fallow land on their sprawling coffee estates. They entrapped landless outsider colonos in quasi-feudal debt-peonage sharecropping arrangements that also required unpaid obligatory days of labor per week as well as additional poorly paid extra days whenever needed.

Large-scale mestizo immigration into the indigenous coffee-growing region worsened the classic Latin American racially hierarchized "divide-and-conquer" segmentation of the rural labor force. It accelerated the slow structural and symbolic violence of shame-based indigenous ethnocide—whereby racist ridicule and abuse impose "voluntary" cultural abandonment and language loss (ethnocide). The poorer, immigrant, mestizo indentured sharecroppers were largely indistinguishable in skin color and appearance. Many were in the process of abandoning their parents' indigenous culture. Ashamed, they espoused a virulent anti-indigenous racism to prove their fragile "higher-caste" status, despite their slavish dependence as indentured sharecroppers on white European estates.

Simultaneously, US industrial imports devastated rural artisanal production, driving starving indigenous artisans into rapidly growing shantytowns. Anonymous, depersonalized, urbanized settings accelerated mestizoization. The remaining semiproletarianized, indigenous farmers in the countryside increasingly lost communal holdings through land swindles by literate court-savvy elites and second-generation mestizoized colonos. Ironically, instead of "modernizing" and "civilizing" the countryside, industrial globalization abusively reenserfed both formerly autonomous, indigenous, small farmers and newly mestizoized colonos sharecroppers. Profit-oriented capitalist logics of maximizing efficient coffee-export production assaulted traditional worker privileges and small farmer autonomies.

In this racist pressure-cooker context, indigenous communities attempted to resist cultural loss and humiliation by reenforcing patriarchal age- and gender-graded rules of endogenous marriage, limiting the right of children to choose marital partners. Daughters were most closely monitored to prevent single, male, mestizo immigrants from marrying into indigenous villages and weakening a community's cultural identity. This generated a more toxic hypermasculinity and in-group patriarchal privilege while simultaneously decreasing the autonomy of wives. This triplicate of capitalism, mestizoization, and control of women and children occurred throughout most of Latin America but became a veritable pressure cooker in El Salvador, augmenting violence against children and wives enduring today in the Salvadoran countryside.

US DEPRESSION AND THE 1932 *MATANZA* (MASSACRE)

The exacerbation of market-driven social inequality in the countryside, rife with hypermasculine abusive relations, fomented popular resistance and hypersensitivity to insults. Dispossessed, recently mestizoized rural and shantytown Salvadorans migrated across Central America as starving day laborers. They became a classic hemispheric-wide "lumpenized" surplus, a disposable, illegalized, undocumented population.[16] Responding in kind to abusive exploitation, they earned a reputation for violent oppositionality and intimidating other Central Americans. A classic thirty-two line "Poem of Love to Salvadorans" by the county's most-famous author, Roque Dalton, evokes the trauma of Salvadoran lumpen vulnerability in the early 1970s with critical affection:

> no one knows where they come from,
> the best artisans of the world
> . . . .
> they died of malaria
> or by the sting of scorpions or yellow fever
> in the hell of banana plantations,
> the drunkards who cried for the national anthem
> . . . .
> the moochers, the beggars, the dope pushers
> . . . .
> the eternal illegals,
> make-all, sell-all, eat-all,
> the first to pull out a knife
> . . . .
> my people, my brothers.[17]

Himself a dedicated revolutionary, Roque Dalton joined an armed-struggle organization in the late 1960s and was tragically killed by dogmatic companions during an internal political debate over revolutionary tactics in the mid-1970s. He argued for mass organizing rather than Leninist vanguardist armed struggle.[18]

I emphasize the populist cultural salience of Salvadoran oppositionality because it helps explain the magnitude of repeated violent political mobilizations throughout Salvadoran history, whereby oppressed sectors formerly alienated from one another mobilize explosively: indigenous with mestizo, small farmers with urban workers and rural day laborers, males with females, and heterosexuals with gender nonconformists. The most iconic and enduringly political seizing of consciousness was the January 1932 general strike and revolutionary uprising.

In 1929 the US Great Depression decimated coffee exports. Landlords slashed wages in half and tightened sharecropper-colono obligations. Urban workshops went bankrupt. A prolabor president, Arturo Araujo, was elected for the first time and legalized leftist political organizing. Multiple communist, socialist, anarchist, anti-imperialist parties; reformist movements; labor unions; and peasant organizations mushroomed. Salvadoran oligarchs and US diplomats, terrified by the radicalization of working-class movements across the world in the 1920s following the 1918 Russian Bolshevik Revolution, denounced the moderate reforms of the democratically elected President Araujo as "communist." An eccentric, opportunistic self-proclaimed "general," Maximiliano Hernández, overthrew Araujo. Popular outrage prompted an unprecedented alliance of previously divided sectors. They were united by the explosive historical conjugation of (1) landlord abuse of indigenous day laborers and mestizoized sharecropper colonos and (2) unemployment among artisans in urban workshops and rural indigenous households.

A quasi-millenarian conjuncture of three charismatic leaders coalesced in the heartland of the Nahuat-Pipil coffee highlands, precipitating an insurrection: (1) José Feliciano de Jesús Ama Trampa, a Pipil indigenous day laborer demanding both cultural dignity and fair wages for rural workers; (2) Francisco Sánchez, a mestizo peasant colono leader; and (3) Farabundo Martí, a revolutionary union organizer rendered politically cosmopolitan by a university education and multiple bouts of exile that exposed him to traditional pro-Soviet socialism as well as to anarchism and solidary populist anti-imperialism.[19]

The military immediately crushed the insurrection and imposed martial law. Following kangaroo trials, the three leaders were executed—Francisco Sánchez and Feliciano Ama lynched and Farabundo Martí shot by firing squad. Consistent with the classic racist divide-and-conquer contradictions plaguing the Americas, Maximiliano Hernández manipulatively reshaped what began as a massacre of populist leftists into a several months-long mestizo rampage against the indigenous population, empowering the most reactionary of the oligarch families. Between ten thousand and thirty thousand primarily indigenous villagers were killed in the coffee highlands. The military organized dependent mestizo colonos into paramilitary rural Defense Leagues. Terrified of being mistaken for indigenous, they mercilessly killed anyone speaking Nahuat-Pipil or dressed in indigenous clothing and ostentatiously spared the lives of fellow mestizo laborers.

Carefully triangulating archival research with oral history interviews with survivors, social historians have documented the toll of the 1932 genocide during these months, which also systemically deployed the war rape of indigenous women.[20] The United States immediately deployed two warships to assist Maximiliano Hernández, convening international diplomatic support for his genocidal dictatorship, which endured twelve long years.

I emphasize the virulence of Salvadoran military repression, charismatic revolutionary leaders, US complicity, and gendered, sexual, and racist brutality because fifty years later the disappearance of a generation of children during the 1980s civil war was shaped by similar forces and logistics: (1) rural paramilitary organizations coordinated by the military; (2) systematic assassination of politicized, mestizo, peasant villagers reracialized as "Indios" and sacrifice of forcibly recruited government soldiers as disposable cannon fodder; (3) routinization of military gang rape; (4) unconditional US diplomatic and economic support for anticommunist repression; and (5) resurrection of Farabundo Martí, the charismatic, revolutionary anti-imperialist organizer (executed during La Matanza) as the namesake of the FMLN, the coalition leading the 1980s revolutionary armed struggle.

JESUIT LIBERATION THEOLOGY AND REVOLUTIONARY RADICALIZATION OF THE COUNTRYSIDE

The 1932 *matanza* crushed the indigenous rights movement and practically extinguished the Nahuat-Pipil language. Indigenous rituals and dress disappeared or went underground. Peasant-worker organizing reinitiated in the 1960s, however, through liberation theology priests (primarily Jesuits) advocating a "preferential option for the poor," referred to as *concientización*.[21] They taught literacy to small farmers by organizing "delegates of the word" to hold Bible study groups in remote villages.[22] Literacy and liberation-theology brainstorming spawned pragmatic, self-help marketing cooperatives to reduce debt dependence on abusive landlords. The military repeated its script of massive repression, recruiting rural spies from demobilized military draftees and dependent colonos to identify and kill delegates of the word and priests. Unlike the 1932 *matanza*, this repression radicalized rural organizing.

US INTERVENTION IN EL SALVADOR— ANOTHER VIETNAM

The United States continues to be the proverbial elephant in the room, dominating virtually all Central American and Caribbean nations— including El Salvador. Since the late 1800s, the region has endured dozens of US military invasions and diplomatic economic sabotages. The United States regularly topples democratically elected presidents who dare advocate for moderate reforms. This occurred in Honduras even when Democrats were in power during President Barack Obama's tenure and Hillary Clinton was secretary of state.[23] The discredited Cold War bogeyman of anticommunism has been replaced by interminable new wars on drugs, terrorism, gangs, and undocumented immigrants, with manipulative propaganda blitzes during local elections.[24]

The Kennedy administration's Alliance for Progress in the mid-1960s technified the brutality of Central American militaries by founding national intelligence agencies across the region. The US Central Intelligence Agency placed dozens of military leaders as well as rank-and-file death-squad members on its payroll, including the notoriously right-wing general, José Alberto Medrano, who used US international aid to found El Salvador's first intelligence agency, ANSESAL (Salvadoran National Security Agency), in 1965. The CIA institutionalized his fledgling, rural-based network of spies into an official, salaried paramilitary death squad, ORDEN (Nationalist Democratic Organization). US Army Special Forces (Green Berets) trained local ORDEN and military scorched-earth operatives on-site. A remarkable 1984 investigative report on the CIA in El Salvador by Allan Nairn interviewed dozens of high-level Salvadoran military officers, US intelligence officials, and diplomats (including former US ambassadors), as well as rank-and-file frontline US military trainers and death-squad personnel. Nairn quotes General Medrano and the equally notorious Colonel Nicolas Carranza marveling at the scale, efficiency, and generosity of US intelligence officials, who regularly provided them with photographs, names, and recordings of "subversives." The CIA dramatically augmented the murderous reach of the Salvadoran dictatorship.[25]

Major Roberto D'Aubuisson (General Medrano's handpicked successor) earned the nickname "Blowtorch Bob" because of his predilection for that grotesque interrogation and torture method. In 1981 he founded the ARENA party, openly advocating fascism and unbridled military repression. He served as president of the nation's Constituent Assembly from 1982 to 1983, the bloodiest years of the civil war, when "disappearances" of children and parents crescendoed. Bolstered by US financial and diplomatic support, ARENA dominated post–civil war politics in El Salvador, controlling the legislature from 1991 to 2006 and the presidency from 1989 to 2004.[26]

Human rights organizations exhaustively documented ORDEN's cruelty and effectiveness. As early as January 1979, a lengthy Inter-American Human Rights Commission report calculated that ORDEN deployed eighty thousand operatives across the country. It listed the names of ninety-nine individuals disappeared by Salvadoran security forces over the past year and described ghoulish interrogation detention centers, in which torture was routinized, calling them "veritable slave prisons." Eyewitnesses described lengthy confinement of prisoners in three-by-three foot cells devoid of light and air circulation that disabled the bodies and minds of victims.[27] The following year, 1980, was a watershed for both military cruelty and popular radicalization. In addition to killing the nation's beloved archbishop, Óscar Romero, while he was officiating mass, National Guardsmen raped and murdered four US Maryknoll nuns.[28] That same year a ragtag coalition of five different guerrilla organizations and civilian opposition movements coalesced into the FMLN and declared war on the dictatorship.

Human rights abuses spiraled during the first five years of the civil war and remained extreme. In 1989 El Salvador's attorney general, Mario Zamora, was killed for unprecedently attempting to uphold the rule of law. That year, uniformed Salvadoran National Guardsmen also assassinated five Jesuit priests, their housekeeper, and the housekeeper's daughter in the rectory where they lived together on the grounds of the Jesuit university. The civil war continued for two more years until the military dictatorship was finally forced to sign a peace treaty with the FMLN in 1992. Extreme by historical measures, El Salvador's violent history since the 1880s has been toxically structurally intertwined with that of the United States, which is also the most violent and militarist of its wealthy postindustrial peer nations.

THE EVER-MORE-VIOLENT POST–COLD WAR "PEACE"

Almost as soon as the United Nations–brokered peace agreement was signed on January 16, 1992, the country's political violence and military repression morphed into opportunistic criminal gang violence over control of neighborhood drug sales, protection rackets, and kidnapping schemes.[29] Murder rates spiraled to levels higher than during the civil war era of massacres of politicized civilians. It was fueled by a toxic mix of (1) rampant unemployment; (2) plentiful discount-priced automatic weapons available on street corners; and (3) US deportations from Los Angeles of Salvadoran-origin youths (many monolingual English speakers) who came of age as refugees in segregated, gang-dominated, poor US neighborhoods. Gangs have been the proximate cause during the postwar decades of the rising rates of criminal and interpersonal "meaningless" violence. The police, politicians, and paramilitary proxies however reap the largest profits and interface closely with gang leadership.[30]

In 2021 the current authoritarian president, Nayib Bukele, took corruption and patronage politics to new heights by declaring cryptocurrencies official national legal tender. International banks and multilateral development and finance credit agencies denounced the move because the lack of transparency facilitated by government promotion of crypto finances rendered it impossible to monitor the Bukele regime's relationships to organized crime.[31] Currently, in 2022, legal businesses are routinely forced to pay protection fees; otherwise, their employees are killed. This even applies to distributors of multinational soft drinks and public bus lines, which have to pay whichever local gang happens to control the neighborhoods, towns, and remote rural hamlets through which they travel. Meanwhile, rank-and-file gangs compete for crumbs to keep from starving. For example, the proprietors of street-corner restaurants and even mobile sidewalk food stands must feed gang members on pain of death.

Liz brings these violent pre– and post–civil war years alive, from the perspective of El Salvador's most vulnerable victims. She also conveys the remarkably effective political agency of Salvadorans resisting repression by the founding of Pro-Búsqueda in 1994. It was the brainchild of Father Jon Cortina and his parishioner, Francisca Romero. Both lost loved ones and witnessed horrendous human rights violations during the civil war. Francisca's husband was killed, and her daughter Elsy was kidnapped in the Guinda de Mayo, and Father Jon narrowly escaped death innumerable times. His parish was devastated by the scorched-earth operation that caused the Guinda de Mayo as well as dozens of subsequent scorched-earth assaults and countless aerial bombardments. He also lived in the Jesuit household massacred in 1989 and survived only because he was away conducting mass that weekend in his rural parish in Chalatenango, where Francisca lived.

Thirteen years later, Francisca was still yearning for Elsy, hoping that she had survived. She was determined to find out. The civil war was over, but criminal violence was spiraling vertiginously, and an increasingly kleptocratic government was dominated by promilitary parties. Nevertheless, she and Father Cortina had the courage to formally confront the hostile government and the military about the demographic public secret of the generation of disappeared poor rural and shantytown children. The dozens of unsung brave activists and beneficiaries of Pro-Búsqueda who, through Liz, share their stories in these pages prevent the perpetrators (Salvadoran military officers, US diplomats, and US military advisers) from being able to erase their crimes against humanity.

This book, and the impressive media attention Liz has drawn to the work of Pro-Búsqueda, helps render the suffering of families brutalized by El Salvador's history and US Cold War counterinsurgency politics less "useless."[32] Liz and her Pro-Búsqueda companions clarify that one of the best ways to keep history from repeating itself brutally in El Salvador is by documenting trauma in the full unsanitized context of the vulnerability and ongoing pain of victims and by demanding transparency and remediation. The book teaches us about the exhilarating and painful psychodynamics of belated family-reunion processes that occur one generation too late. Sadly, this is still relevant today—to US immigration's confiscation of children at borders and to the victimization of children in wars across the globe. Finally, *Reunion* is also an admirable work of science and empathy, linking the technology of genetic matching to love and social justice.

For this reason, the success of the organization Pro-Búsqueda; the dedication of its rank-and-file activists in a poor, dangerously violent, and politically explosive country like El Salvador; and the brilliance of the writing and technical expertise are an inspiration. Pro-Búsqueda's activities, and now Liz's book, will prevent the aging perpetrators from the 1980s Cold War era (Salvador military officers, US diplomats, and US military advisers) from being able to erase their crimes against humanity. Outrageously, both governments continue to impede transparency, despite the passing of four decades and the advanced age of the victims and perpetrators.

PERSONAL HISTORY AND SURVIVOR GUILT

This personal section on survivor guilt has been difficult for me to write and reflect on because I was trapped in a scorched-earth counterinsurgency campaign as one of many civilians in rural El Salvador in November 1981. My grief and the terrified memories evoked when I reflect on those events and my actions often morph into a sense of survivor guilt. Rationally, victims of war crimes and interpersonal brutalities must "forgive" themselves for surviving, but I, like many others, am convinced on a pre-conscious level that I deserve my sense of guilt. At the risk of projecting onto Salvadorans the overdetermined sense of guilt that I have as a citizen of the imperial nation that has most brutalized their people for over three centuries, I recognize similar emotions among some of the protagonists in this book. They are all survivors of scorched-earth massacres and have suffered much more than I. Furthermore, most of them also continue to live in a nation devoid of personal security and with only very limited civil rights.

In 1981 I was, like Liz in 2005, a graduate student in my early to midt-wenties, conducting fieldwork on the struggle for human rights and social justice in El Salvador. In appendix A, "Photo-Ethnographic Testimony of a Salvadoran Military Scorched-Earth Operation," I describe the nightmare of the eleven-day scorched-earth operation I survived along with more than a thousand small farmers and their families—including three-year-old Armando who appears in this book. As a healthy twenty-four-year-old, I was able to jump, dive, climb, and run faster than most people under fire and in flight. In the middle of the night, we ran over and around fallen companions struck down by enemy bullets and grenade explosions. Some were still alive, writhing in pain with body parts missing. I vividly remember passing mothers, brothers, fathers, and good Samaritans car-rying infants and toddlers. Many women and children had only flimsy flip-flops, which often fell apart, forcing them to run in bare bleeding feet over thorns, barbed wire, sharp rocks, and roots. Most of the men had clumsy rubber boots, the standard footwear of impoverished small farmers throughout Central America. I had on a brand new pair of Nike jogging shoes, and the vivid memories of people stumbling in terror and pain haunt me.

Reflecting on these events to write about them accurately stirs up over-whelming memories of terror. For me, survivor guilt is the most disori-enting of those painful emotions. As an anthropologist, I am aware that writing about raw brutality risks shipwrecking on the pornography of violence. Psychoanalysts, historians, anthropologists, philosophers, and survivors of genocides and other historical injustices have written about the inadequacy of words in the face of suffering.[33] Reading multiple drafts of Liz's book and being offered the opportunity to contribute to the historical documentation of a war from the perspective of victims, however, convince me it is irresponsible to sanitize the gory cruelty of repression because it is personally embarrassing.

Truth is inherently fragile over time. The accuracy of the popular record of the experience of war is dominated structurally by the distortions of self-interested powerful perpetrators. Erasing history renders it impossible to hold perpetrators accountable. Worse yet, lack of accountability for crimes against humanity encourages the reproduction of brutality by future sociopathic perpetrators. Documenting the terrifying memories and unwanted emotions victims feel can help us heal—despite the tears and insomnia those memories also provoke. Bearing witness to the suffering of others and recounting in brutal detail the cruelty of the Salvadoran soldiers killing us may contribute another useful grain of sand to a clearer historical record. Testimonies can delegitimize the authoritarian populists, military dictators, and imperial warmongers who violate the rights of civilians demanding human rights, freedom of speech, and social justice or who are brutalized for being in the wrong place at the wrong time.

Liz's book is also a respectful forum for memorializing lost loved ones and companions. She enables still-grieving survivors to communicate the great physical suffering inflicted on those who were killed and cannot tell their stories—especially that of family members and companions who were wounded and died in prolonged agonies. In short, it is a balm for healing survivor guilt. Survival guilt is a dysfunctional reaction on the part of victims rooted in two contradictory objective realities: heroes and good Samaritans often die first, and dumb luck is a big part of survival. Worse yet, counterinsurgency soldiers are trained by the United States in "psychological operations" that exacerbate trauma to break the spirit of "subversives." Liz's empathetic documentation of the atrocity inflicted on three-year-old Armando when his mother was killed during this same scorched-earth invasion that he and I both survived deserves special historical valorization because of its unbearability. In the turmoil of our flight, Armando was captured by a government soldier who forced him to call out *"mamá!"* into the darkness of the night from the tops of surrounding hills. The soldier then killed those who responded in sympathy from their hiding places to the wail of a desperately terrified child. The soldier forced Armando to cry out multiple times. Armando's story grips me because I heard many babies and little boys and girls crying. I did not have the courage to respond. I want to express my deeply felt solidarity to Armando, forty years later, for his suffering, which was incomparably worse than my own. I thank him for his courage in documenting the crime against humanity inflicted on him. I hope that reading this might help him ... a little.

Armando's experience may be too traumatic for him to retell as an adult. He also may have been too young at the age of three to retain a clear, linear memory of that terrifying night. Liz gently elicited his story with the help of his close friend, José, another disappeared child, who was two years older than Armando. They confided in each other forty years ago while growing up in an orphanage where they were confined, yearning for their mothers. Forty years later, through Liz in this book, José helps Armando clarify for the historical record the cruelty of the counterinsurgency crimes against humanity of the scorched-earth training that US military advisors promoted in El Salvador for over twelve years. Sensitively, Liz also highlights Armando's filial solidarity with his uncle. She interviewed that uncle when he was dying of cancer, and he expressed his desire to say goodbye to his beloved sister's son, Armando. Liz brought Armando the audio-recorded request from his uncle, who was his closest living relative. The formerly disappeared child took time off from work to make the trek to his uncle's remote rural village in Santa Marta, Cabañas, just in time to comfort his uncle on his deathbed.

In this delicately empathetic way, Liz brings the past into the present of the lives of Salvadorans still reeling from the civil war and its child disappearances. Presenting Armando's story so respectfully and precisely and in its full context prevents the historical record from erasing the cruelty of a frontline Salvadoran soldier. Revealing an irresolvable trauma is painful, but highlighting the cruelty of perpetrators can be healing because it renders our suffering less solitary and invisibilized.[34]

Human rights activists in El Salvador generally refer to this scorched-earth operation as the "*masacre de* Santa Cruz." But the Santa Cruz massacre was only one night, albeit the deadliest, of our eleven-day ordeal. It occurred during the second of the five phases of the November 1981 military invasion of Cabañas (described in greater detail in my photo-ethnographic account of it in appendix A and in the drawings by the refugee children presented and annotated in appendix B). The five phases were (1) the initial encirclement and aerial bombardment, from sunset of November 10 to the night of November 14; (2) the flight through the military cordon at the massacre of Santa Cruz, predawn to early morning of November 15; (3) hiding and zigzagging in the militarized no-go zone, the morning of November 15 to sunset of November 17; (4) hiding and zigzagging in the military-occupied former FMLN-controlled zone, night of November 17 to sunset of November 19; and (5) escape into Honduras to the refugee camps, night of November 19 to midday of November 20. (See also the map of our flight path on the last page of this foreword.)

The massacre began at 3:00 a.m. on November 15, 1981, and lasted through the early morning. We were trying to sprint through the military cordon's line of fire in the hamlet of Santa Cruz. Enemy soldiers had set up a machine-gun nest in a one-room schoolhouse on a promontory above us and were propelling RPG grenades down onto us. No one knows how many people were killed because a forensic archaeological excavation has not been undertaken at the massacre site. The military immediately burned the bodies in two large pits to hide their crimes.

I tried to estimate how many people were killed, but it was too chaotic to conduct a census. I wrote down the names of a few dozen individuals reported to me by family members, but about 300 to 400 of our companions had run back into the FMLN territory from which we were fleeing to try to hide in small mobile groups, and they were still missing. Furthermore, there were several hundred recently arrived individuals from other FMLN territories for whom no one could account. In 2019 Catholic Church documentarians estimated the Santa Cruz death toll at 270.[35]

Over the next seven days, those of us who had made it through the line of fire into the no-go zone (about 600 or 700 people) zigzagged single file together, desperately trying to find places to hide. We sought orchards, standing crops, and streams to keep from dying of thirst, hunger, and dysentery. Meanwhile, inside the former FMLN zone, the enemy troops killed all the people and farm animals they encountered. They also smashed down and burned all infrastructure. The purpose of counterinsurgency scorched-earth operations is to make a territory unlivable.

US military lingo refers to scorched-earth operations and massacres such as this one as "draining the sea to catch the fish"—the sea being civilians, and the fish being the guerrilla fighters. Aerial bombardment is called "softening" guerrilla or enemy positions. In fact, however, the military was purposefully trying to kill everyone, including the children, elderly, and unarmed adults. All this brutality was cynically legitimated by US officials to the world press and the US public fueled by a paranoid anti-communism. The US press generally reported US military and diplomatic propaganda acritically. In the 1980s the United States was claiming that Russia, Cuba, and Nicaragua were bankrolling so-called Marxist-Leninist revolutionaries and flooding El Salvador with automatic weapons.

As an informed graduate student at the time, I assumed US officials were exaggerating, but I could not believe they could be so blatantly lying. The guerrillas did not have enough guns to give to the healthiest, strongest, and fastest runners among the farming families who supported them. In contrast to the guerrillas, the Salvadoran military units pursuing us were awash with brand-new automatic weapons, and they were supported by a US-funded air force. We were all targeted for extermination, regardless of age, gender, or unarmed status. It was a sitting-duck genocide—certainly not a matched combat between armies. Almost every single one of the Salvadoran military's victims, whether civilian or guerrilla fighter, was a dirt-poor, semi-subsistence, small farmer from the surrounding remote peasant hamlets trying to scrape out an existence close to starvation in a rugged terrain devoid of public infrastructure (no roads, no potable water, no sewers, no electricity). They were—and still are today—small farmers unable to make ends meet. Most have to supplement their meager corn, rice, and bean crops with day labor and piece-rate wage work on coffee and cattle farms, or they migrate undocumented to the United States.

This was the beginning of the civil war and only the second or third scorched-earth operation to integrate cadets from the new, more murderous US-trained special forces battalions, including Atlacatl. In contrast, most rank-and-file government soldiers were forcibly recruited, poor, young men not fully indoctrinated into anticommunism. Scared of guerrilla ambushes and land mines, they refused to patrol after dark. That explains why more of us were not killed. Over the next two years, the elite special forces battalions returned fully trained from Fort Benning, Georgia, and the United States doubled the Salvadoran Air Force's fleet. The size of face-to-face massacres increased dramatically, as did the lethality of the air force.[36] In fact, the massacre I survived was followed six months later by the worse and longer May 1982 scorched-earth invasion that provoked the Guinda de Mayo in neighboring Chalatenango, a seven-hour hike from northern Cabañas. That *guinda* culminated in a six-hundred-person massacre at the Sumpul River. Several of Liz's companions were captured in it. Many of the civilians I was with during the November 1981 Cabañas invasion also endured the Guinda de Mayo because, after fleeing into Honduras, they reentered Chalatenango to continue their revolutionary support in the FMLN-controlled zones around Father Cortina's parish of Guarjila.

What moves me most about *Reunion* is that it is both humane and scientifically rigorous in its documentation of a generation-level crime against humanity. It also accomplishes its historical task gracefully, respecting the dignity of the survivors while diligently recording facts. I thank Liz for this beautiful book, and I hope it will have the same therapeutic effect on the protagonists as it is having on me.

RESOLUTION THROUGH HISTORICAL ACCOUNTABILITY AND REPARATIONS

To me, the most important healing act would be for frontline perpetrators to take responsibility for their acts and lay out in detail exactly what they did so that this tragedy can never be denied, distorted, or lost from history. Government soldiers need to testify and clarify their guilt. The few times that I have confronted former soldiers, they have argued some version of "the guerrillas forced us to kill civilians because they used women and children as a shield." That sociopathic perversion of the historical record outrages me. It is the mirror image of the truth. The only reason so many of us survived in November 1981 was because the guerrillas used their own bodies as shields. In fact, most guerrilla fighters died during the civil war.[37]

Some of the soldiers could not bring themselves to follow orders and instead captured babies and children to avoid killing them when they encountered them face-to-face, separated from their parents. I wish more perpetrator-soldiers had the courage to admit they killed and tortured children in front of parents and could explain the logic for why they sometimes evacuated children in helicopters to orphanages instead of killing them.

It can also be therapeutic for survivors to testify in public. I was able to submit evidence to the United Nations Commission on Human Rights and to testify formally before a US congressional subcommittee on Human Rights in El Salvador just three months after making it out of El Salvador alive.[38] In 2014 the Community of Santa Marta filed a class-action lawsuit accusing Colonel Sigifredo Ochoa, the officer who led the scorched-earth massacres in Cabañas, of crimes against humanity.[39] In contrast, in the early 1980s, US officials cynically celebrated that sociopathic colonel as a model of efficiency and modernization. They claimed he was rejuvenating the corrupt and demoralized Salvadoran military. It was a ploy to persuade US Congress to continue the flow of US military aid, which prolonged the civil war for another bloody decade and more.

The US government sent over $1 billion in military aid and more than $3 billion in economic aid to El Salvador from 1980 to 1992. The tiny country was the largest recipient of US military aid of any nation in Latin America during those years. Nothing would clarify the historical record more than US government official reparations for their massive intervention. Neither the US nor Salvadoran governments have taken responsibility for their crimes against humanity during the 1980s, including for the child disappearances.[40] Formal reparations and a public apology by the US diplomats and military advisers who funded, weaponized, technified, and provided diplomatic cover by lying to the world have yet to occur. Short of that unlikely institutional seizing of consciousness by the United States, a few individual US perpetrators, whether they be diplomats or frontline Green Beret officers, having the courage to admit what they did and apologize to the Salvadoran people would be a historic redemptive act.

For more than a century, the Salvadoran people have endured barbaric repression and extreme violations of their basic human rights, yet they have repeatedly risen up in opposition. In appendix A, I draw from my field notes written under fire as well as from the photographs I took during a military operation, to present a photo-ethnographic day-by-day account as a participant-observer of the Cabañas scorched-earth operation from November 10–20, 1981. I also discuss the ongoing trauma it inflicts on survivors. In appendix B, "Refugee Children's Drawings of the Salvadoran Civil War," Liz gives the children of El Salvador the final word, with a

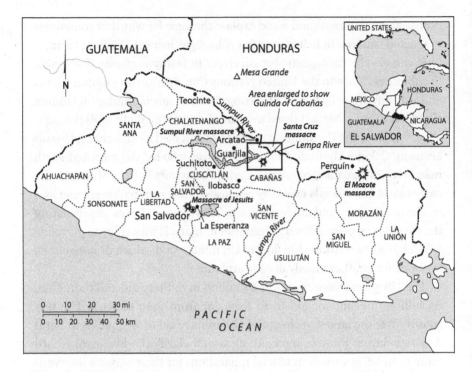

Map of El Salvador, showing the civil war massacres, the rivers, and Honduran refugee camp discussed in *Reunion*.

selection of six drawings I collected in refugee camps during the 1980s with the help of elementary school teachers. The people of the United States need to learn humbly from these children as well as from the heroism of the Salvadoran people in the face of repression to reign in our politicians, corporations, and imperial militarism. Without US military aid, the Salvadoran dictatorships of the 1980s would have been overthrown with much less bloodshed in a couple of years. The US people must prevent the two nations' violent mutual histories of conflict and extreme violence from cruelly repeating over and over again.

In 1992 the US government finally forced the Salvadoran dictatorship to sign a peace treaty. The ongoing atrocious human rights record of the Salvadoran military had become too much of a liability for the US State Department. Pressure from liberal members of the US Congress as well as the international human rights and diplomatic communities had also

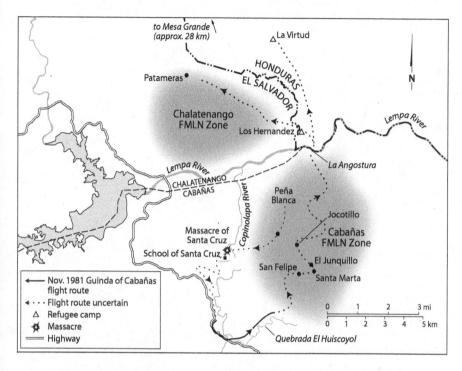

Map of the November 1981 Cabañas scorched-earth military operation and the trajectory of the civilian flight (Guinda of Cabañas) described in appendix A (Philippe Bourgois's photo-ethnographic testimony).

reached a crescendo. Innumerable human rights organizations, the United Nations, communities of faith, and much of the international community also effectively pressured the US government and isolated the Salvadoran military dictatorship. I am in awe of the generosity, courage, and sense of both community and international solidarity of the people of northern Cabañas and the aging rank-and-file revolutionaries who saved my life and the lives of so many other civilians during the November 1981 Cabañas scorched-earth operation. Despite the failures of leadership of the older generation of guerrillas-turned–electoral politicians, the next generation of Santa Marteños continues to struggle for justice, for themselves and for all of El Salvador, with a cosmopolitan sense of self-awareness and of their community's place in history.

Philippe Bourgois

Introduction

In 1979, Francisca Romero, her husband, and their six children were living in the mountains of Chalatenango, El Salvador, as her ancestors had for generations. Like most rural Salvadorans, the Romeros were semi-subsistence farmers, growing crops to feed their family. During harvests, children and parents also worked as day laborers at the ranches of wealthy landowners, earning little pay. In the rainy season, they harvested corn on the ranches; in the dry season, coffee and sugarcane. Francisca's village had no roads for cars; residents traveled by foot. Homes lacked electricity or running water.

Each morning, Francisca would grind corn from the family garden for tortillas and boil beans over an open fire. Using eggs from hens raised on their patio, she baked *pan dulce* (sweet bread) in the outdoor adobe oven and then swept the floor of the mud-walled home. In the afternoons she washed clothes in a ravine with the other women of the village. But their way of life would soon change. Wealthy landowners had amassed most of the arable land, and conditions for *campesinos* (farmers) such as Francisca's family members had become increasingly abusive. The meager wages and small parcels of land were not enough to sustain the families of the villages. As the women gathered to scrub clothes, they spoke of the challenges of getting by on even less—and of the danger mounting in the Salvadoran countryside.

A group of nuns had been coming from a nearby convent to Francisca's village, preaching liberation theology, a Christian ideology that gathered Salvadoran campesinos and other impoverished Latin Americans around the Bible, literacy, and a call for social justice in the name of Christ's teachings. They advocated for better pay for the farmers and land reform—despite violent repression.

The military had controlled El Salvador since the 1932 *matanza* (massacre) of thirty thousand indigenous farmers who had also protested for a living wage and land reform. Throughout the mid-twentieth century, the divide between the wealthy and poor widened as military dominance of the government intensified. By the 1970s, an aristocracy known as the "Fourteen Families" possessed most of the nation's land and wealth. The military had close ties to the wealthy elite and controlled the government. Fraudulent political elections maintained the oligarchy's power.[1]

As resistance grew among a growing base of rural and urban poor, state-sponsored death squads, funded by El Salvador's elite, suppressed votes and then killed civilians protesting electoral fraud.[2] In the late 1970s the Catholic Church documented an increasing pattern of government-ordered civilian murders. Although Francisca's family members weren't rebel fighters, they were under threat, as were millions of Salvadoran civilians who had become targets in a larger global conflict. Within the context of the Cold War, fearing the spread of communism, US president Jimmy Carter's administration backed a coup in El Salvador in October 1979—installing a new military leader to prevent "another Nicaragua or Cuba."[3] The United States also had financial interests in El Salvador's coffee exports and other cash crops.[4]

Francisca recounts that, as Salvadoran military and paramilitary death squads surveilled the countryside, she and her husband joined the nuns. "The armed forces were persecuting us, and we couldn't take it anymore, so we began to organize around the Catholic Bible. In those days, people who had a Bible were persecuted," Francisca tells me.

One morning in 1979, Francisca awoke to find the image of a white hand on her front door. The symbol, representing the Mano Blanca death squad, signified a death threat. Francisca, her husband, and their six children had no choice but to flee. For months, under constant fear of death or torture, Francisca and her family took shelter in the abandoned houses of other displaced families in the area, gathering food from the jungle and deserted farms.

In the country's capital, the archbishop of El Salvador, a Jesuit named Óscar Arnulfo Romero, spoke out against the worsening violence and inequality, calling for an immediate end to government-sanctioned bloodshed. Archbishop Romero had initially sought to be apolitical, but the violence had become too reprehensible to ignore. In February 1980 he sent President Carter a letter pleading for the United States to suspend military aid to El Salvador. "Political power is in the hands of the military," he wrote, and in the face of repression the people are "struggling for fundamental human rights."[5] In March 1980, Romero urged soldiers to disobey commands to murder civilians. The next day, on March 24, when Francisca's family was still on the run, a sniper shot Archbishop Romero while he was performing mass in San Salvador. One week later, government-sponsored snipers killed forty-two mourners at his funeral. Óscar Romero's assassination, ordered by the highest levels of the government, ignited El Salvador's civil war.[6]

Later that year, in December 1980, death squads raped and killed four US Maryknoll sisters who were en route from the San Salvador airport for a Catholic relief mission.[7] Despite public outcry in the United States following the murder of the nuns, US funding to Salvadoran security forces overall increased.

In 1981, five allegedly communist rebel groups united to form the Frente Farabundo Martí para la Liberación Nacional (FMLN) guerrilla force, named after the leader of the 1932 uprising for farmers' rights. Fearful that communism could spread throughout Central America, in 1981, the Reagan administration sent $82 million in aid to back the Salvadoran military-run government. (By 1982 the tiny country became the fourth-highest recipient of US aid dollars.)[8] The Salvadoran military, instructed in counterinsurgency tactics by the United States, sought to isolate the FMLN from the social base that sustained it, using a "scorched earth policy" that deliberately targeted unarmed civilians in rural El Salvador, like Francisca and her family.[9]

Under the policy, the military labeled campesinos as guerrilla sympathizers to justify genocidal tactics of war. US-trained soldiers burned food crops and massacred entire villages, often raping women and children before slaughtering them and placing desecrated bodies in public view to instill terror.[10] Some campesinos may have supported the guerrillas—decades of oppression and death-squad killings had stimulated popular resistance—but many, like Francisca's family, just sought to survive.

Francisca's family was in flight when the military carried out indiscriminate massacres of campesinos in 1980 in her department of Chalatenango. In 1981, slaughters of civilians increased, especially in Chalatenango, adjacent Cabañas, and in Morazán, where the elite US-trained Atlacatl Battalion decimated an entire village in the massacre at El Mozote.[11]

In May 1982, after three years of flight, running from one abandoned village to another and hiding in the jungle, Francisca, her husband, and their four youngest children were caught in the military operation that survivors call the Guinda de Mayo (Flight of May). Thousands of soldiers, including troops from the Atlacatl Battalion, surrounded twenty square kilometers of rural Chalatenango and attacked one thousand civilians. The FMLN sought to protect the unarmed civilians—referred to as *masa*—and lead them to safety.

Francisca and her family hid in bushes from soldiers and from helicopters dropping bombs. She covered the mouth of her two-year-old son to stifle sounds that could draw gunfire, all the while praying that she didn't inadvertently suffocate him. After five days of hiding without eating anything but surrounding vegetation, Francisca's family and several others determined that breaking through the military siege was their only chance of escape. There was "a wall of guerrillas" to defend against military attack and "a wall of soldiers," Francisca says, "and we had to run in between."

By then Francisca's two oldest sons, including a boy who was only twelve years old at the time, had joined the guerrilla force, and her husband had handed over his only rifle to the FMLN. Her husband told his family the plan he'd heard from a friend. "At 1:30 p.m. you will hear our signal: a grenade explosion. When you hear that signal, get up fast and run!" He told them not to stop for anything. "If you see me dead or injured, leave me. Continue ahead."[12]

Moments later, as Francisca was about to bite into a piece of papaya, the only fruit she'd found for days, the grenade sounded. She gathered her children and ran. They sprinted, "not knowing where the bombs and bullets came from." Francisca carried her youngest son while her two daughters held on to her arms. As they raced through the bullets and bombs, Francisca yelled to her husband to take charge of their youngest daughter, seven-year-old Elsy. He grabbed Elsy by the nape of her neck and they ran. When crossing a ditch under a wire fence, Francisca became separated from her husband and Elsy. Her older son had run on ahead.

During a break from the bullets, Francisca hid behind a bush with her toddler and her eleven-year-old daughter. Francisca heard shouting. "Come out comrades! We are the guerrillas." She stayed hidden, covering the two children with her body—and watched as soldiers grabbed emerging civilians by the hair. "The soldiers didn't use bullets to kill," Francisca recalls. "They just got out a knife and cut people's necks, and the people fell, their legs jumping."[13]

Still hiding, Francisca saw from across a bloodstained rice field that soldiers had captured Elsy; she recognized Elsy by her dress. Francisca resisted the urge to run to Elsy—death was near-certain if she did. "The soldiers had taken my girl, and I could do absolutely nothing. That was the hardest for me." Francisca watched the soldiers gather Elsy into a group of dozens of children. "It was two in the afternoon," Francisca says through tears. "They grabbed the children by the hair and put them in helicopters." She could only watch as the helicopter lifted off and faded into the horizon. Francisca surmised that when Elsy was captured, soldiers had likely slain her unarmed husband. She felt listless, but the thought of saving her three remaining children powered her to keep moving toward Honduras, the safest place for them.

The military hunted Francisca and the other survivors of the Guinda de Mayo as they fled toward the Sumpul River, which forms the border with Honduras. Francisca recalls, "There were helicopters and A37 planes that dropped bombs, little planes that we called *la gradilla* [the rack] that just roamed, and helicopters that were shooting machine guns. We had breakfast: bullets; lunch: bullets; dinner: bullets, bombs, and grenades." She continues, "We ran but stayed in the mountains. We didn't brush our hair. We didn't drink water. We didn't eat or sleep. We didn't carry underwear. The only thing I carried was my two-year-old boy. We passed a family—all six of them were dead. Ahead of us, they were dead. Behind, dead. On all sides, dead. Only God saved us." All told, soldiers killed an estimated six hundred civilians during the Guinda de Mayo, which lasted from May 24 to June 10, 1982.[14]

For months Francisca and her remaining children scavenged to survive while hiding to evade the military. Francisca learned to eat the fruit of the cactus with the needles, the shrubbery, and the sticks of the papaya plant. They took refuge in a home occupied by three dead bodies. In November 1982, the military launched a second operation, and the attacks against civilians intensified. Francisca describes, "There were two big piles. The soldiers were so disgraceful. In one pile there were twenty-five heads of children ages zero to about eleven years old. Another pile had the bodies. We hid in a deep gully. You could hear the shouts, and you couldn't come out or they would kill you." Francisca managed to flee. "We didn't stop. When my boy wanted to pee, I had him use a little jar. And when he asked for water, I gave him the urine to drink. When he asked for food, 'a little tortilla,' I covered his mouth so he would stay quiet. All this time," she adds, "I didn't know what happened to Elsy."

At last they reached the Sumpul River. They dodged bullets from both sides of the river, as Honduran soldiers sought to keep out refugees and Salvadoran soldiers continued to chase them. "Many people jumped in, but they couldn't swim. The planes and the armed forces were coming, so the people tried to get away, but they couldn't. Many people died there. By the grace of God, I'd learned to swim in a stream by my home as a child," Francisca says. "I crossed the Sumpul River with my eleven-year-old by my side and the two-year-old boy in my arms. The river was high like the mountain, but we crossed by the great will of God."

Francisca reached the Mesa Grande refugee camp in Honduras. Once there, she approached humanitarian organizations for help locating her missing daughter. She gave her only photograph of Elsy to the Red Cross to assist with the search. The photograph was not returned, and Francisca received no help. Still, she believed that Elsy was alive, and Francisca was determined to find her.

Mesa Grande felt like a concentration camp to Francisca. Honduran refugee camps held twenty thousand Salvadoran families during the war, clustered in tents bordered by barbed wire and Honduran soldiers to prevent escapes.[15] Starvation and disease were rampant. Along with other exiled Salvadorans, Francisca lobbied for repatriation to El Salvador, writing letters to the government and even going on a hunger strike so that she could return to her land and find her daughter.

In 1987, after five years in exile, Francisca relocated to Los Ranchos, a resettlement community in her native department, Chalatenango, El Salvador. The most violent years of the war had passed, though the military still targeted campesinos, especially returning refugees.

There, in a community comprised of hundreds of Salvadorans returned from exile, Francisca first met Father Jon Cortina, a Jesuit priest from Spain. "Father Jon was like an angel for us. As soon as I met him, I felt that I had God there with me," says Francisca. "Everything had been destroyed. We didn't have anything, but with Father Jon we celebrated a mass."

Francisca approached her friend Magdalena Ramos, known as Maida, who'd also been forcibly separated from her child during the war. Soldiers had ripped Maida's six-month-old son from her arms while holding a gun to Maida's head during the Guinda de Mayo. Francisca said, "Maida, let's tell the Father [about our missing children]. He goes to San Salvador. Maybe he'll see them." After mass one day, Francisca kneeled next to Father Jon, who sat before her, and said, "I want you to help us look for our children."

Father Jon responded, "Francisca, how do you know that your daughter has not died?"

"I saw, Father, when they took her. They took so many children that day."

Calm and present, Father Jon told the mothers, "Be patient. One day the war will end." He promised to help when the time was right.

That time came in January 1992, with a United Nations–negotiated ceasefire between the Salvadoran military and FMLN through the Chapultepec Peace Accords, signed in Mexico City. With more than seventy-five thousand people dead, seven thousand reported disappeared, and one million displaced (one-fifth of the population at the time), El Salvador's twelve-year civil war drew to a close.[16]

"The rifles of the guerrillas fired from happiness because the war had ended," Francisca recounts. "Father Jon came to celebrate a mass."

Tears traverse down Francisca's cheeks as she recalls Father Jon's gentle command. "Francisca, now we are going to begin. *You* are going to begin the investigation. She is your daughter, and you have to fight hard. You are going to fight hard."

Father Jon's words gave Francisca the resolve to search for Elsy and unite with other mothers who had lost children in the Guinda de Mayo. Despite the fear and mistrust still pervasive in the countryside, Francisca went to the Salvadoran police and to a judge in Chalatenango. The police asked for a birth certificate, but it had been lost in the home she'd fled under threat of death, over a decade earlier. The judge accused Francisca of abandoning her daughter. "I didn't abandon her. She was kidnapped," Francisca replied.

Francisca and the other mothers led demonstrations alongside Father Jon. In 1994, three days after a national television appearance to raise awareness about the disappeared children, a colleague of Father Jon's, Ralph Sprenkels of Save the Children, informed Francisca that a missing child named Andrea had been spotted in an orphanage near San Salvador, recognized by her missing limb. A young woman that fit Elsy's description was also seen.

Ten days later, on the second anniversary of the Peace Accords, Francisca reunited with her daughter. Elsy was nineteen years old, married, and seven-months pregnant. Mother and daughter tearfully embraced in the home of Elsy's in-laws. Elsy re-met her siblings.

Elsy didn't travel to the group reunion in the countryside because of her pregnancy, but Elsy's friend Andrea and three other disappeared children from the orphanage reunited with their families that same day in the soccer field in Chalatenango. Father Jon and other villagers observed and celebrated. Four of the five children were matched with their families based on shared memories and family resemblance. Maida re-met Juan Carlos, the baby that soldiers had ripped from her arms at gunpoint, now a boy of twelve years old. But, given Juan Carlos's young age at separation, the orphanage requested confirmation of their relationship—a problem soon solved with DNA.

The reunions brought hope to families in surrounding communities who wondered about the fate of missing children. Francisca tells me, "Father Jon paid for the first reunions with his own money so that others would begin searching, bringing cases and more cases. It got to the point that the majority of the people [in the resettlement communities] had cases of disappeared children."

The United Nations Truth Commission for El Salvador report, released in 1993, attempted to tally the devastation caused by the war.[17] The report attributed 5 percent of the wartime violence to the FMLN and 85 percent to the military and death squads, citing gross violations of human rights. Yet the missing children were not mentioned, an omission that motivated Father Jon to search.

Hundreds of families filed cases of missing children, but the government did not assist with the searches. So, led by Father Jon, the people mobilized. "Father Jon thought it was time to open an office, and he named the organization Pro-Búsqueda [Pro-Search]. That's how it started," Francisca explains. Founded in 1994 by Father Jon Cortina, Francisca, Maida, and forty-six other relatives of missing children, Pro-Búsqueda's mission is to search until every disappeared child separated from their family during the war is found.

. . . . . .

I thank Francisca for her testimony. We're seated on plastic chairs under the shade of a tree, about fifty feet away from her home so that her many grandchildren do not disturb the interview. Ripples of green mountains pour around us to the northwest, forming the valley of the Sumpul River. I can see Honduras from where I sit. I've traveled from California to Francisca's home in Los Ranchos, Chalatenango, to interview her for my master's thesis on the family separation and reunification of El Salvador's disappeared children. I'd started the interview by saying, "I'd like to hear about Elsy and a little bit of the history of Pro-Búsqueda." With that request, Francisca shared the account summarized above. It's January 2006, and today is my last day of interviews with disappeared children and their families. In two days I will return home to resume my coursework in the UC Berkeley–UCSF Joint Medical Program, where I study medicine and public health.

When I stand to leave, Francisca hugs me, her eyes full of expression. She kisses my cheek and says, "May things go well for you," with unusual fervor. Then she offers me a second hug and looks me in the eye, placing her hand on my arm. "When you go home, tell people what happened here. Let them know the reality of El Salvador—how the war was and how the children were lost so that young people in other countries can be in solidarity with us." With arms open and a wave of her hands, she gestures for the truth to be spread. Just before I head out for the next interview, Francisca's granddaughter climbs into Pro-Búsqueda's red Toyota pickup truck to show us the way to the home of a grandfather of a disappeared child. Francisca smiles and yells to us, "Go see Maida!"

I felt surprised to witness Francisca's tears during our interview, tears from a woman so strong that she survived years under military attack and then spawned the search for El Salvador's disappeared children. Francisca's courage and resiliency compel me to share her story and those of families like hers: stories of mothers, fathers, grandparents, sons, and daughters; of bones that can be mourned or of long-awaited reunions; and of new separations caused by slow violence in the aftermath of war. The stories of those who've survived and continue to survive the reality of El Salvador.

PART 1 **Pro-Búsqueda and the DNA Bank (Summer 2005)**

1 Arriving

It's close to midnight, late May 2005, when I arrive at the TACA airlines ticket counter at the San Francisco Airport. I'm a twenty-five-year-old UC Berkeley Summer Human Rights fellow headed to El Salvador for two months as part of my medical- and public health–school training. When I join the two-hundred-person line of Latinos, my eyes brighten as if I'm homeward bound. As a Cuban-American, there's a part of me that will always feel more at home in Latin America. On the flight, I meet a thirty-two-year-old Salvadoran single mother making her first trip home in seven years, a surprise visit to her ailing father. She invites me to sit beside her instead of leaving the seat between us empty. We sleep, and when the sun rises, we admire the verdant volcanoes, blue lakes and ocean, and red-brown farmland of El Salvador.

From shivering on the air-conditioned plane to sweltering, stagnant airport air—it's 8 a.m., I'm in San Salvador. I splash water on my face and cruise through customs with sixty-one-year-old Chilean geneticist Cristián Orrego. We are greeted by two employees from Pro-Búsqueda, the human rights organization that Cristián and I have come to volunteer with.

Pro-Búsqueda seeks "to offer disappeared children the opportunity to meet their biological families and to learn the truth of their history," according to Jesuit priest Jon Cortina, the NGO's director. In El Salvador's twelve-year civil war, soldiers took hundreds of children from their families and gave them to the Red Cross, which then handed them over for adoption or to orphanages, as occurred with Francisca Romero's daughter, Elsy. A smaller number of children became separated when FMLN leaders forced guerrilla fighters who were parents to place their children in the care of others. Many children also became lost in the chaos of *guindas* (flights from military operations), and others became separated when parents made the desperate decision to save their children by putting them up for adoption outside of El Salvador. Pro-Búsqueda refers to all these children as *desaparecidos* because, if not for the war, they would not be missing.

This summer of 2005, I will assist Pro-Búsqueda with creating a DNA bank—or database—to match disappeared children with their biological relatives. I will also begin research for my master's thesis on the disappeared children's experiences with family separation and reunification. These "children" are now young adults, roughly my age. I'm slightly nervous, as I've heard that El Salvador has the highest murder rate in the Western Hemisphere. The tiny country of six million is plagued by street gangs that have proliferated in the aftermath of war, and the economic divide has further widened. One in two Salvadorans live in poverty.[1] The right-wing Alianza Republicana Nacionalista (ARENA) party has held power since the war, and El Salvador has not experienced reconciliation—an amnesty law blocks prosecution of war criminals.[2] Political corruption feeds the security and economic crises, driving migration north. In 2005 one in seven people of Salvadoran descent live in the United States.[3]

Pro-Búsqueda is permitted to function but does so without government backing. Despite the amnesty law, the organization's staff receive occasional death threats, presumably from officials seeking to cover up involvement in child disappearances. Father Jon suspects that military and Salvadoran Red Cross leaders trafficked kidnapped children as international adoptees.[4] During the civil war approximately thirty thousand children were adopted. The United States alone issued 2,300 adoption visas to US citizens to bring Salvadoran-born children to the United States.[5]

On the ride from the airport, the two Pro-Búsqueda employees praise El Salvador's natural beauty and the deliciousness of *pupusas* (Salvadoran stuffed tortillas), and they gripe about the increasing culture of violence and the nation's dependence on remittances from relatives abroad.

After we drop Cristián off at his hotel, they reroute me—per Father Jon's instruction—from the guesthouse I had chosen to "the home of a friend, a social worker with Pro-Búsqueda." Ester's home sits among eleven others in a modest gated community protected by a security guard. Tired from the overnight flight, I shower before the water stops running at noon, then fall asleep on the mosquito-net–wrapped bed.

I awaken to the smell of heated tortillas, eat lunch, and then Pro-Búsqueda's driver brings me to the agency's one-story home-turned-office. Inside he introduces me to Lucio, a twenty-something-year-old investigator with a discerning gaze. Having read Lucio's testimony in Pro-Búsqueda's book *Historias para tener presente*, I'm aware that he is a *joven encontrado* (found youth), meaning that he was disappeared and Pro-Búsqueda found him.[6] I explain to Lucio—as I will to many others—that I've come to volunteer on the DNA project and conduct research for my thesis, so I'll be taking notes, if that's permissible. When I ask for guidance on how I can be most helpful to Pro-Búsqueda, it seems I earn a drop of his trust. Lucio will become my ambassador to the jóvenes encontrados in the weeks and years that follow.

Soon after, Cristián arrives at the office with the report he brought from California containing DNA results from the first batch of samples for Pro-Búsqueda's DNA bank. Cristián and seven geneticist colleagues from the California Department of Justice (DOJ) volunteered after-hours to process the samples in the DOJ lab, with permission from California's attorney general.

The collaboration began in 1994, when Father Jon asked a representative from the United Nations about DNA testing. Father Jon knew that Argentina's Grandmothers of the Plaza de Mayo had been using DNA since 1984 to find disappeared grandchildren. The UN representative phoned Boston to speak with Physicians for Human Rights director, Eric Stover, who had helped the Argentine grandmothers. Within weeks, Stover and Father Jon launched Pro-Búsqueda's first DNA-collection event, announced on the radio and held in a church in Chalatenango. The

Top: Father Jon Cortina presiding over a mass during a family reunion event, held in the home of a biological father who was reuniting with his daughter. Tecoluca, San Vicente, 1996. Courtesy of Pro-Búsqueda.

Bottom: Eric Stover (in background) and Bob Kirschner collecting one of the first DNA samples for locating the disappeared Salvadoran children. Photo was taken in a church in Chalatenango, 1995. Courtesy of Eric Stover.

first match confirmed by DNA was Maida with her son Juan Carlos, the desaparecido ripped from his mother's arms at gunpoint when he was an infant.[7]

By 2005, Stover expanded the DNA work to include the UC Berkeley Human Rights Center, where he serves as director and my research mentor. Pro-Búsqueda and its US affiliates now seek to construct a DNA bank to confirm suspected matches and potentially make cold-hit links between disappeared children and biological relatives in the database. Pro-Búsqueda collected the first batch of samples a few months prior to my arrival. Cristián's DOJ colleagues analyzed the hand-delivered samples in the California DNA lab—where I first met Father Jon—and Pro-Búsqueda eagerly awaits Cristián's results.

Seated at a round table in Father Jon's office with Pro-Búsqueda staff, Cristián shares the findings while teaching about DNA analyses. He goes through the DOJ report page by page, using the question-answer method to teach about DNA. Then a fascinating moment captivates all: it's plausible there's a match.

Cristián places before us printouts of the DNA profiles of a disappeared boy and two females who could be the boy's mother and sister. Using the profiles, a piece of paper, and a pen, Cristián conducts a back-of-the-envelope maternity analysis by hand. We first verify that the girl is the daughter of the woman stated to be her mother by confirming that each of the girl's twelve gene pairs tested include a gene in the purported mother's profile. The analyzed genes are rare enough that such a match has an infinitesimally small probability of occurring by chance alone. The staff members look over our shoulders in suspense as Cristián convinces the group of the power of DNA science and the importance of collecting DNA from multiple family members to have sufficient information for conclusive analyses. Locus by locus, we discover that the disappeared boy's DNA profile doesn't match the mother's, yet the enthusiasm in the room remains.

Pro-Búsqueda faces a monstrous task—in two months' time the organization must collect hundreds of DNA samples from missing children and searching family members, as well as from jóvenes encontrados and their biological relatives whose DNA can confirm existing matches made based on witness interviews and documentary evidence. Because of changes in

California law, the pro bono DOJ facilities and after-hours staff time will no longer be available after the summer.

At 5:30 p.m. Lucio's colleagues volunteer him to give me a ride back to Ester's house since it's on his route home. Lucio turns to me and says, "I have to run an errand. Do you want to come, or would you rather I do it and then come back to pick you up?"

"Whatever is most convenient for you," I say.

I slide into Lucio's 1987 Nissan sedan as he says that we're "going to the public hospital to pick up my nephew."

His nephew is a twenty-eight-year-old man who, while working as a security guard, was shot in the arm and across the forehead last week. I've been in the country for only ten hours, and I'm going to the hospital to check on a gunshot victim! Lucio's nephew is recovering well and healed enough for discharge but faces hours of paperwork, so we end up not taking him home.

In the car, Lucio orients me to the layout of San Salvador. He describes the neighborhood we're driving through as "very dangerous." But, he says, no one would seriously injure me "because those are different laws, the ones that apply to Americans."

"That's not right. Every life is worth the same," I reply.

"¿Qué [What]?" Lucio smiles and asks me to repeat myself. I sense he wants to hear an American repeat the words. (Earlier in the drive Lucio cited that Ronald Reagan sent $1 million a day for the civil war, testing my allegiances as he read my face for a response.)

He then asks if I've communicated with my mother since landing in San Salvador.

"Yes, I sent her an email," I reply. "She worries about me too much."

Lucio's eyes fix on the road. "My mother worried about me...." And then after a pause, "quizás [maybe]." His silence conveys that I should feel fortunate to have a worrying mother. Soldiers shot Lucio's mother in their home during the war. A military grenade killed his father.

When we reach Ester's, I thank Lucio for the ride. He's the first joven encontrado I've spoken with, and his presence stirred my thoughts about the Salvadoran Civil War. Having read his terrifying testimony, it inspires me to see him alive and well, working at Pro-Búsqueda, smiling and offering me a chocolate bar.

Lucio picks me up the next morning. At Pro-Búsqueda, elderly María Inés pauses from sweeping the hallway's tiled floor to introduce herself, leaning her chin on the broom as we speak. The deep wrinkles on her face widen her sweet smile; a scrunchie pulls back long, wavy gray hair. She's the mother of two disappeared boys found in Italy, but there hasn't been a reunion, she says. Her face puckers as if she just sucked on a lemon, then she resumes sweeping.

After lunch, Cristián leads a meeting to discuss obstacles to DNA sample collection. DNA is collected by scraping a plastic *palito* (little stick) against the inner cheek and, although most families do contribute samples, some older relatives say it might make their teeth fall out. Distrust and "political differences" also create barriers. Many people were stuck in the middle during the war, neither guerrillas nor soldiers, and some feel embittered and fearful of giving a DNA sample. Pro-Búsqueda employees work to diffuse this tension by giving explanations and wearing matching white T-shirts with the organization's logo: an image of a mother holding a young child.

After the meeting, I find Ester, whom I pay for room and board with my fellowship stipend. A former FMLN fighter, Ester teaches at a Spanish-language school and helps with gathering samples for Pro-Búsqueda's DNA bank. On our walk home, between buying tamales, oranges, and pineapples, Ester relates that her husband—her daughter's father—died during the war. As we step onto the sidewalk after a daring street crossing, Ester says that her daughter underwent a "crisis" upon starting kindergarten and realizing her classmates had fathers but she did not.

After dinner, Ester tells me about the war. In a voice slightly more audible than a whisper, she says, "I'm a survivor of the Sumpul River massacre." She describes the 1980 attack she endured as a youth in rural Chalatenango, during which six hundred refugees, including many women and children, drowned or were shot by Salvadoran soldiers while attempting to flee to Honduras.[8] "The conditions we survived were incredible. There were gunshots everywhere." After the gun battle, Ester's father, an unarmed civilian, searched for injured people who could be saved. He later received a plaque and cash award for his heroism. He used the money to create a memorial at the Sumpul River. "Unfortunately," Ester says, "nobody lives in the village anymore, and the memorial is deteriorating. Swimmers use it to hang their clothes on while bathing in the river."

Ester feels furious that, because of divisions within the leftist FMLN, conservatives tied to the military still dominate the country. The 1992 Peace Accords legalized the FMLN as a political party, but ARENA, founded by a retired army major and war criminal, has held power since 1989. Sensing Ester's fervor, I tell her that I believe in supporting social movements and that I want to keep myself alive to do so.

"Or maybe someday you will find a cause worth risking your life for," she replies. Her response jolts idealistic, comfortable me. She has risked her life over and over again.

A few moments later, when I remember that I don't have a house key, I ask how I'll get in each day. "Mélida will be home after 2:00 p.m.," Ester responds, referring to her teenage daughter.

"Doesn't she go out?"

"NO," Ester briskly replies. "Terrible, terrible things are done to girls on the streets. The death squads haven't ended," Ester says. Though the Peace Accords officially disbanded paramilitary groups, "it's easy to make a calculated death look like a result of gang violence."

I'm still feeling startled by her admonition when the phone rings, interrupting our conversation. It's my mother. "Everything's great, Mom. Good night."

The next morning, Pro-Búsqueda is buzzing about a press conference. When I see Father Jon, he gives me a good-morning kiss on the cheek. He's tall and slender, with gray hair, bushy dark eyebrows over warm brown eyes, and a tender yet mischievous smile. Today his mood is chipper and bright and he moves with grace in his step, free and loose like his cloud-white shirt.

"Are you ready for the press conference?" I ask.

"Yes. I'll just read a bit, and then I'll see how I can bite them," Father Jon replies, referring to the government for failing to comply with the recent Inter-American Court of Human Rights sentence in the case of the disappeared Serrano Cruz sisters. Pro-Búsqueda sponsored the case, and the victory signifies the first instance when a court held the Salvadoran government accountable for wartime child disappearances. Today marks the twenty-third anniversary of the disappearances of the sisters, last seen at ages three and seven. TV and newspaper reporters listen to Father Jon's account of the kidnapping, court stipulations, and the government's inaction. He remarks that El Salvador's president stalls by saying the administration is "studying the sentence."

As news crews pack up and people nibble on doughnuts, Pro-Búsqueda's lawyer explains to me that, based on extrapolations from the UN Truth Commission's report, an estimated ten thousand children were disappeared during the Salvadoran civil war. Pro-Búsqueda, even now in 2005, thirteen years after the peace treaty, receives three to five new cases of missing children per month.

After the press leaves, Cristián invites us all to lunch. Besides talk about whether the horchata is tastier than the blackberry drink, I overhear that Ceci, Pro-Búsqueda's petite, lovable accountant, is "a case." She sewed a button on my lime-green blouse earlier today when I realized it had popped off. Ceci tells me about her two brothers in Italy. "You're the daughter of María Inés?" I ask, recalling the sweet, elderly cleaning woman at Pro-Búsqueda, whom Ceci resembles.

"Yes," Ceci replies, with a sad nod. I mention that the taxi driver I met this morning said his mother was disappeared. No one at the table seems surprised.

Cristián and Father Jon have a 2:00 p.m. appointment with forensic geneticists at El Salvador's Supreme Court lab. At 2:15 p.m. Father Jon is still smoking a cigarette at Pro-Búsqueda. Driving to the lab, the Father darts through San Salvador traffic in his white Toyota Land Cruiser. Large government buildings create shadows on the street. When we park, the security guard greets Father Jon by name, though they haven't met before. I realize that Father Jon is a nationally known figure in El Salvador.

We tour the DNA lab, El Salvador's equivalent to the US DOJ genetics lab. Two Salvadoran women in white coats set up a DNA test. Cristián's vision is for all of Pro-Búsqueda's DNA testing to someday shift to El Salvador, so he's building relationships and exploring the trustworthiness of the government DNA lab.

Cristián Orrego (*fourth from left*), Ceci (*middle, with purse over her shoulder*), Father Jon Cortina (*beside Ceci*), myself (*with braid, beside Father Jon*), and others from the team at Pro-Búsqueda. San Salvador, 2005. Courtesy of Pro-Búsqueda.

When we return to Pro-Búsqueda, Father Jon invites me to accompany him and Cristián tomorrow to Guarjila, a community in the countryside. "So that Liz can get to know the real El Salvador," Father Jon says, decided and playful. He laughs because he knows I'm nervous about gangs. I accept the invitation.

I'm at Pro-Búsqueda until seven in the evening when I'm directed to the back seat of a car as I'm introduced to its driver, Amílcar. Sitting behind him, with her armless side closest to the door, is Amílcar's wife, Andrea, the first disappeared child found. Andrea's and Amílcar's testimonies comprise chapters 1 and 3 of Pro-Búsqueda's *Historias para tener presente*. On Andrea's lap sits Vladi, their dimpled three-year-old son. Andrea bubbles into laughter as she asks, "Did you read my story?" I nod and she wants to know, "Did you enjoy it?"

"Enjoy..." I respond after a pause, "doesn't seem like the right word. But I appreciated it and found it inspiring."

Andrea smiles. As Amílcar drives up the winding road to Los Planes, he describes his work as an airplane mechanic and shares his impressions from visiting Boston.

At Cristián's invitation, twenty of us, all connected through Pro-Búsqueda, gather at a mountaintop *pupusería* (pupusa eatery), with the glittering night lights of San Salvador below. Across from me sits Lucio's daughter, Michele, a chubby-cheeked three-year-old with braided, silky black hair. Beside her is Lucio's wife, Angélica, a joven encontrada raised in the same orphanage as Andrea, also disappeared in the 1982 Guinda de Mayo. Vladi scrambles on rocks, holding his father's hand. Amílcar's gentle smile, warm and full, contrasts with his history: he was raised on an air force base after soldiers assassinated his mother and brother. Vladi picks tiny red flowers and hands me three. Now Amílcar walks, holding Lucio's daughter's hand, attending to her as if she were his daughter.

After greasy, satisfying pupusas, we gather in a circle. The Pro-Búsqueda crew gives Cristián a plaque depicting Óscar Romero. "The first of many visits," Cristián remarks.

Lucio knows I won't be able to give directions to Ester's, so he draws Amílcar a map on a napkin. Then Amílcar, Andrea, Vladi, and I pile into their car for the ride home. In the car, we joke that my thesis will be the unwritten love story between Andrea and Amílcar. They met through Pro-Búsqueda's workshops, as did Lucio and Angélica. I comment that the jóvenes encontrados seem like a family network. Amílcar surprises me with the forcefulness of his response: "There's nothing like being with one's own family."

When I arrive at Ester's, two mothers are upset with me. Ester was slightly worried, and my mother very worried because when she telephoned, Ester guessed I'd gone out for Cristián's farewell dinner but wasn't certain. I'd felt so comfortable with the jóvenes encontrados that I'd forgotten about the everyday dangers of El Salvador. Lucio's watchfulness, Andrea's laughter, Amílcar's kindness, and the resilience of the community made me feel safe and at home.

2 Guarjila with Father Jon

I meet Father Jon and Cristián at Pro-Búsqueda at seven in the morning for our day trip to Guarjila, Chalatenango. Father Jon wants to show us the countryside where the movement to find the disappeared children began. He's kept a home in Guarjila since the latter years of the war, when he established a parish for repatriated Salvadorans. While the seventy-one-year-old priest pilots his Land Cruiser on the highway for our two-hour ride, I watch out the window as the volcano of San Salvador grows and then shrinks again. Cristián asks Father Jon, "How did Andrea lose her arm? Was it because of the war?"

"Yes," Father Jon replies. "Her hip was damaged too. She was one of the first jóvenes found. I care about her a lot, and about Elsy too. When Andrea was having her baby, Angélica—who was also found in the Aldeas SOS [orphanage] and was one of the first ones found—wanted to be near Andrea to help her. Angélica is Lucio's wife, and they were living in the countryside. So, Angélica and Lucio moved to San Salvador, and we gave Lucio a job at Pro-Búsqueda." Father Jon serves as a father figure for many of the jóvenes encontrados as they enter adulthood.

We accelerate up the steep cobblestone streets of Chalatenango's central municipality, traverse mountainous dirt roads replete with mango stands, and then roll into dusty Guarjila. We tour the community medical clinic that Father Jon, an engineer by training, helped construct during the war as a care center for the wounded. He shows us a procedure room where amputations and "all kinds of things" occurred. Then we wind through a narrow hallway, past sniffling, coughing patients; through the microbiology lab; and around back to the supply room, which we find nearly empty. "It used to be full," Father Jon says. During the war, he smuggled anesthetics and other medical supplies, along with powdered-milk cans stuffed with monetary donations for the clinic, hidden beneath the loose garb of a priest.

Next we meander down the town's main dirt road to Father Jon's one-story home. Guarjila's grateful villagers chose a breathtaking spot for his countryside residence. The home's tin roof, cement walls, and neatly swept dirt floor connect to a long patio complemented by a garden perched on the edge of a mountain. Ripples of mountains stretch all the way to Honduras to the northeast, with the Sumpul River tucked between. Powerful sunlight glazes the gardenias, orchids, pineapples, acacia shrubs, and banana trees in Father Jon's garden. His collection of endemic orchids adorns a hollowed tree trunk. A little boy arrives at the backyard garden and asks Father Jon, "May I take a few chili peppers?"

Father Jon nods and tells the boy he may "take a fistful."

As I sit on the porch and listen to the silent language of the countryside, I take in Father Jon's peaceful way of life on the weekends. It stands in sharp contrast to his hectic, chain-smoking pace at Pro-Búsqueda. Father Jon is clearly dedicated to his three vocations: professor, priest, and human rights activist. From Monday through Friday, he serves as an engineering professor at the Universidad Centroamericana José Simeón Cañas (UCA), the Jesuit university in San Salvador. He teaches in the mornings and works as the director of Pro-Búsqueda in the afternoons. And, every Friday afternoon since the 1980s, he makes the ninety-six-kilometer pilgrimage to his parish in Guarjila, where he attends to his parishioners and presides over Sunday mass.

Father Jon has survived two wars. Born in 1934 in the Basque region of northern Spain, he was two years old when Francisco Franco's troops attacked his native Guernica, and bombs from the Nazi and Fascist Italian air forces rained from above.[1] The bombing of Guernica left 1,600 civilians killed or wounded—one-third of the population—mostly women and children.[2] Father Jon's family escaped by fleeing over the Pyrenees Mountains to France. His family later returned to Spain, but his boyhood experience as a refugee led him toward a life of service.

In 1954, at age nineteen, he joined the Society of Jesus, a Roman Catholic order devoted to apostolic ministry, to fulfill his life's wish "to help poor people."[3] In 1955, as a novice Jesuit, he spent one year doing missionary work in El Salvador before resuming his studies. By 1973, Father Jon had completed his university studies in the United States, seminary training in Germany, and earned a doctorate in engineering in Spain.

After completing his education, Father Jon returned to El Salvador to teach seismic engineering at the UCA. As an engineering professor, he designed highways, bridges, and an aqueduct system. In the mid-1970s, he taught at the UCA and served as a priest in villages near San Salvador.

In 1977, government security forces assassinated Rutilio Grande, a Jesuit priest who advocated for Chalatenango's rural poor, making Grande the first martyred priest in the prelude to war. Religious leaders were no longer off-limits from the state-sponsored murders. The archbishop of El Salvador, Óscar Romero, sent Father Jon to the mountains to succeed their fallen colleague. Grande's murder prompted the previously apolitical archbishop to decry the state and promote the community activism that Grande had espoused as central to God's work.[4]

Despite intensifying violence, the Jesuit priests visited the countryside regularly, leading mass and lending support to rural Salvadorans—and risking their lives while doing so. On one drive to San Salvador with Archbishop Romero, Father Jon stopped at a coconut stand at the archbishop's request. Father Jon noticed a military post near the stand and suggested that they leave. The archbishop said to Father Jon, "We've done nothing wrong," and got out of the car and enjoyed his coconut water, all the while enduring the soldiers' glares.[5] On March 24, 1980, a sniper shot Archbishop Óscar Romero while he was giving mass in San Salvador. Moments before, Romero had remarked, "May we give our body and our blood to suffering and to pain—like Christ, not for self, but to impart notions of justice and peace to our people."[6]

As the ensuing armed conflict ravaged the country, Father Jon remained committed to teaching at the UCA and to fulfilling his role as a priest. He gave mass under gunfire, offered hungry soldiers tortillas ("but not too many"), and wielded "God's word" as his "machete." In 1986, as violence eased, Father Jon joined repatriation efforts in Chalatenango, helping families returning from exile, like Francisca Romero's, to rebuild. At the end of each week, after teaching at the UCA, he would drive past military checkpoints to reach Guarjila and other resettlement communities to practice what he called "liberation engineering." Father Jon helped finance and construct houses. When villagers suggested building ornate chapels, he would tell them, "You are the church," saying it was more important to build homes.[7]

From Father Jon's patio, I see a tidy kitchen through an open door. A recent poster of the Bilbao soccer team from his native Spain hangs on the wall. Father Jon shows Cristián and me the shrapnel decorating his porch, a "souvenir," he tells us, so that he "will never forget."

The United States had a strong hand in the atrocities of the armed conflict. The US School of the Americas, founded in 1968 and based in Panama, instructed Salvadoran soldiers on tactics of war and torture, many of which targeted civilians. The US-trained Atlacatl Battalion of the Salvadoran national army, which led the Guinda de Mayo attack on civilians that captured Elsy and Andrea, also tried to kill Father Jon.

In 1989, during what came to be known as the "Final Offensive" of the civil war, a fifty-two-year-old Father Jon led mass in the resettlement community, San José Las Flores, in Chalatenango. The next day he traveled five kilometers over nearly impassable terrain, avoiding gunfire between the military and FMLN rebels, to reach Guarjila. The Jesuits of the UCA had called for the military and FMLN to accept a negotiated peace agreement, and, in retribution, military death threats to the Jesuits poured across the radio waves. The military had threatened the Jesuits before for supporting the poor, promoting slogans such as "Be a patriot, kill a priest."[8]

Upon hearing the amplified threats, Father Jon wanted to return to San Salvador to stand in solidarity with his fellow Jesuits at the UCA. But, given the multiple military checkpoints along the route to San Salvador, the people of Guarjila insisted that he stay hidden among them. "I had to wait," Father Jon related, recalling pacing in circles as he listened to the radio while he hid in a mud home of dirt floors and a tin roof. "I felt afraid, but I thought they'd threatened us so many times before, that maybe that was all it was: a threat."[9]

In the predawn hours of November 16, 1989, in reprisal for the Jesuits' call for peace, twenty-six soldiers from the Atlacatl Battalion entered the UCA's dormitory where the Jesuit priests slept. The battalion executed six priests, along with their housekeeper and her teenage daughter, all still in pajamas, in the rose garden outside the dormitory. The soldiers disfigured the priests' faces and emptied their brains from their skulls.[10] With the Jesuits of El Salvador wiped out, the government had aimed to eliminate a beacon of hope and free thinking.

The next morning, the rebel radio station, Radio Venceremos, reported on the massacre. Father Jon listened to the broadcast from Guarjila. He later related, "The news was that they'd killed all the Jesuits in the UCA. They listed the names, and the third name was mine. I was tremendously impacted. I touched my body and said, 'I'm alive.' I didn't know what to do. I felt like I was a sleepwalker, like I was on automatic."[11]

Father Jon hid in Guarjila for one month—until the day a stray bullet shattered the femur of a child. He knew that without intervention the boy would bleed to death, so he set out to drive the boy to the hospital in San Salvador. He drove his Land Cruiser as gunshots blared—but a soldier at a military checkpoint told him he couldn't continue because the boy was a *guerrillero* (guerrilla fighter). Father Jon thought to himself, "How could he be a guerrillero, this poor little angel who was two-and-a-half years-old and barely knew how to walk?"

Father Jon would not be deterred. "The soldier put himself in front of my car so I couldn't advance. 'You will have to bear responsibility for this death,'" he told the soldier. "Then I shouted, 'If you don't get out of the way, I'm going to go forward, and I'll run over you, so *please* move!'... The soldier didn't move. I ended it by accelerating the car. I accelerated the motor and let the clutch slide. I pushed the soldier with the bumper, little by little. In the end, he moved and let me pass. But if I hadn't acted like a brute, he wouldn't have let me."[12]

Father Jon delivered the toddler to the archbishop of El Salvador for transport to the children's hospital. Then he went to the UCA to observe mass for the thirty-day anniversary of the slaughter of his assassinated friends, the six Jesuit priests. Being there, he "felt like a ghost," but hugs from friends and colleagues helped him get through it.[13]

Father Jon spent one night in San Salvador before returning to Chalatenango the next day. Meanwhile, photographs of the murdered Jesuit priests circulated among global leaders and activists. The gruesome photos of the priests' desecrated bodies elicited outcry from the international community, who called for an immediate end to the civil war, hastening the eventual signing of the 1992 peace agreement.

As the sole surviving priest of the massacre of Jesuits, Father Jon believed that "God had told me that I should spend more of my energy with these communities, dedicate more time to them. In the end, I was alive because I had been there [in Chalatenango]."[14] He wanted to channel the rage he felt at the loss of his friends into good deeds, and, in the people of Guarjila and the nearby resettlement communities, he saw a way. Women like Francisca who had lost children were asking him for help. Father Jon had heard rumors of soldiers abducting children to sell them to childless couples in the United States and Europe on the international adoption market, fetching up to $20,000 per child.

Months after the signing of the 1992 Peace Accords, Father Jon assisted families of the tortured, massacred, and disappeared to present their testimonies to El Salvador's Truth Commission. The Truth Commission, created through the peace agreement to achieve "public knowledge of the truth," had three commissioners—former heads of state of Colombia and Venezuela and the former president of the Inter-American Court of Human Rights—who reported to the UN secretary general. Though the UN-sanctioned commission heard two thousand witness testimonies and compiled twenty thousand witness statements, the Salvadoran government declared the findings "illegal."[15] Troublesome to Father Jon, the 1993 Truth Commission report, *From Madness to Hope*, listed the names of disappeared children as all deceased. Father Jon recognized several of the names and believed that many children recorded as deceased were alive and yet to be found.

Five days after the UN Truth Commission published its report, the Salvadoran government passed a blanket Amnesty Law granting immunity to the perpetrators of war crimes. Recognizing the gaps in the Truth Commission report and the failings of the government's reconciliation process, Father Jon helped families officially report the child disappearances. He held press conferences. He wrote letters to orphanages, he went on a hunger strike, and he marched with Francisca Romero and other mothers of disappeared children to bring attention to the cause of El Salvador's *niños*

March to the Presidential House, led by Pro-Búsqueda, to raise
awareness about the cause of El Salvador's disappeared children.
San Salvador, 2004. Courtesy of Pro-Búsqueda.

desaparecidos. By 1994, the list of names of disappeared children Father
Jon collected had grown to fifty-six and included children from multiple
regions of El Salvador. Father Jon and Francisca had started a national
movement.[16]

After founding Pro-Búsqueda in 1994, Father Jon took out a newspaper
ad with the names of the disappeared children. The ad included a phone
number to dial with knowledge of their whereabouts—a phone number
that a young Amílcar called, searching for his family.

In the early days of Pro-Búsqueda, Father Jon felt that the organization's mission should include punishment for those culpable for the child disappearances. But he soon realized that the families "just wanted to find their children, reunite with them, and have them in their arms." They wanted "the most human aspect of life."[17] Father Jon says that the families of the disappeared children taught him to forgive.

Sitting on Father Jon's porch in Guarjila, eleven years after Pro-Búsqueda's founding, I'm humbled by the impact this one man has had in helping to repatriate thousands of Salvadorans returning from exile. He searches tirelessly for missing children, in support of their right to identity and for justice. He smokes and swears—and has a brilliant mind and a gold heart. Father Jon is a man of action, a man of history, and a true leader—a man I feel privileged to know.

On our way out of Guarjila, Father Jon shows us his church of tin roof, dirt floor, and no walls, adorned by a wooden cross and portrait of his mentor, Archbishop Óscar Romero.

As a final stop, we visit the home of Suyapa, the older sister of the disappeared Serrano Cruz girls and the victor against the government at the Inter-American Court of Human Rights. She's appeared on television many times beside Father Jon, including at the press conference earlier this week. Suyapa twirls the corner of her T-shirt, ties it in a knot, then unties and reknots it again, as she speaks in a singsong voice of her kidnapped sisters and of her own baby boy who perished in the Guinda de Mayo. Suyapa heard when soldiers discovered her little sisters crouched behind bushes; one soldier said to another, "I've found children. Should we kill them?" The other said no, and the girls were never seen again.[18] Looking down, she notices the T-shirt knot and insists on changing her shirt and putting on sandals to cover her bare feet for the photograph Cristián requests. I admire how Father Jon has helped make Suyapa's truth heard. After a pose and hug goodbye, we're on our way to San Salvador.

It's 2:00 p.m. when we reach Pro-Búsqueda, only a few hours before Cristián's flight to California. The Pro-Búsqueda team races to complete the final paperwork and packing of the 139 DNA swabs collected over the past two months that Cristián will deliver to the DOJ lab in California. Each sample must be signed over from Pro-Búsqueda to Cristián to maintain a proper chain of custody. An hour later, Cristián departs carrying a suitcase loaded with DNA samples representing the hopes of families to find their missing children.

Moments after wishing Cristián farewell, Father Jon is back in his office. A flash drive dangles from a lanyard around his neck as he stands at his computer, leaning forward, palms pressed on the desk. To me the flash drive represents the Father's workweek. Rather than a decorative cross that would symbolize faith, he wears data close to his heart. Guided to serve, he sees God in truth. Father Jon has said that the government "couldn't kill the truth" the way they killed the people.[19] Tonight he will sleep as he does every weeknight, in the rectory at the UCA, the site of the 1989 massacre of Jesuits, each night's slumber an act of defiance, remembrance, and courage. But there's still time in the day at Pro-Búsqueda and *Padre* Jon, the man who fathered the movement to find the disappeared children, has work to do.

3 At the Nunnery

On my first Saturday in El Salvador, I attend a Pro-Búsqueda workshop at a mountaintop nunnery in Los Planes, overlooking San Salvador. The event aims to spread news of the Inter-American Court of Human Rights' verdict in the case of the disappeared Serrano Cruz sisters. Upon arriving, I meet a forty-five-year-old mother who is searching for two disappeared sons. She awoke at 3:15 a.m. to catch the bus from the eastern corner of El Salvador so that she could attend. The chapel where we gather has gray cement walls, rebar rafters, and a terracotta floor. The audience of about 150 university students, relatives of the disappeared, and others connected to Pro-Búsqueda sit on the wooden pews lining the chapel. Five Pro-Búsqueda poster boards displaying photographs of reunions lean against the wall, along with two posters diagramming the Guinda de Mayo. An ascetic dormitory with three tidy beds is across the hall.

After welcoming remarks from Milto, the Pro-Búsqueda staff member and event organizer, brown-robed Catholic nuns from the Hermanas Pobres Order kick off the workshop with a song. Then, after a moment of silent prayer, Father Jon rises to the podium. In a white polo shirt and khaki pants, he's dressed no differently than when at the office or his countryside home, but on the pulpit he brings a passion I haven't seen from him before. He describes the origin of Pro-Búsqueda: "In 1992, three mothers who lost children in the Guinda de Mayo united to find their children." Father Jon pauses, microphone in hand, and warmly addresses a young woman in the audience: "One of them was your mother, Elsy," referring to Francisca Romero.

Father Jon relates the story of finding the first disappeared children. "In 1993, a man from Chalatenango recognized a [missing] relative when passing by the Aldeas SOS [orphanage near San Salvador]. He obtained permission to work as a gardener at the orphanage to be closer to the child, and this marks how the first disappeared child, Andrea, was found." Father Jon's group identified other missing children at the orphanage, including Elsy, Juan Carlos, and Angélica. "The orphanage didn't allow the families to see the children, but they promised to take the children to Guarjila on January 26 [1994]. On the day of the reunion," Father Jon narrates, "the soccer field was full of people who wanted to see the children, curious and hopeful that the jóvenes encontrados would have information about their disappeared children.

"With this event hope was born, and requests for assistance with finding disappeared children began to pour in. From this hope, Pro-Búsqueda was formed. In October 1994, Pro-Búsqueda found three young adults, the brothers Amílcar and Mauricio, and one other. Amílcar and Mauricio had been living in the infirmary of an air force base of the Salvadoran army among the injured and the dead."

Father Jon reports that, to date (June 2005), "Pro-Búsqueda has facilitated 162 reunions. Reunions signify that the located youth re-met their biological family. Whether they decide to live with their families and the extent to which they cultivate relationships are not the focus of Pro-Búsqueda's work." Pro-Búsqueda, rather, seeks to give youth the opportunity for reunion and "to learn the truth" of their identity: their name, birth date, and family history. In addition, "In twenty-nine cases, Pro-Búsqueda determined that the missing child died, and, in ninety cases, Pro-Búsqueda obtained the contact information of a missing youth, but a reunion hasn't yet occurred."

"In 1993," Father Jon reminds us, "Pro-Búsqueda was comprised of three mothers." To illustrate the scope of the growing movement, he tallies the whereabouts of the 281 jóvenes encontrados at the time they

Jóvenes encontrados socializing at an event through newly formed Pro-Búsqueda.
Seated on the far right is Andrea, Angélica is seated beside her, and the young woman
seated with the child in her lap is Elsy. Above Andrea stands her future husband,
Amílcar, and Armando, the young man who disappeared in the massacre that
Philippe Bourgois was also caught in, stands beside him. San Salvador, 1994. Courtesy
of Pro-Búsqueda.

were found: El Salvador, 139; United States, 50; Italy, 28; Canada, 24;
France, 15; Honduras, 13; Netherlands, 5; Costa Rica, 2; Spain, 2; Belize,
1; Guatemala, 1; and Mexico, 1. He continues, "453 cases registered with
Pro-Búsqueda remain unresolved. The niños desaparecidos are children
of *campesinas* and *campesinos* [farmers]. This is unjust," he declares, his
voice rising into the microphone. He calls for the "indolent government"
to create a commission to search for the missing children, as decreed in
the Serrano Cruz case, asserting, "This situation is *absolutely* outside of
God, *absolutely* outside of a plan for democracy, and *absolutely* outside
of reconciliation. 453 young adults remain *stolen*."

Father Jon speaks more about the kidnapped Serrano Cruz girls and
the court ruling. The Organization of American States founded its judi-
cial arm, the Inter-American Court of Human Rights, in 1979, to moni-

tor human rights in the Americas. The ruling, issued three months ago (March 2005), signifies the first instance an international court has held the Salvadoran government accountable for child disappearances.[1] "The court stated that the government is using the amnesty law as an excuse to avoid complying with the sentence," Father Jon says. "Still, the sentence brings hope to the families of the disappeared."

Father Jon explains that the court determined that soldiers took the sisters by military helicopter and then handed them over to the Red Cross as part of a pattern of forced disappearances. Father Jon calls for the military and Salvadoran Red Cross to open their archives. Both entities transported children to orphanages and toward international adoptions, and both fail to provide records that can reveal the whereabouts of missing children. The Father's passion is still building as he says, "We have an individual and a collective right to truth." He pleads for justice and peace to prevail, pointing out that "in this era of pardon, nobody has apologized to me for *anything*. For example, no one has apologized for the murders of my friends, the Jesuits." Pacing between the podium and the audience, he says, "I give the human rights violators my moral pardon but *not* a legal pardon." The audience applauds Father Jon as he sits down.

"Hello to those listening by radio," Milto, the emcee, says into the microphone. He asks the audience if they have any questions.

A social worker takes the microphone. "Why would disappeared children [adopted abroad] want to return to El Salvador, a country full of violence and poverty?" she asks, then answers her own question: "We don't want to do what the [Argentine] Grandmothers of the Plaza de Mayo did. They were our inspiration, but Pro-Búsqueda's approach is different. The Grandmothers took the children away from the kidnappers—adoptive parents—but this could cause another trauma to children. So, Pro-Búsqueda's approach is to help children find their families, their roots, and, in some cases, their country. Then they can choose what follows."

Someone else asks about pressuring the FMLN to divulge information about missing children. In some instances, the FMLN coerced combatants, including under threat of death, to give up their children to the care of others. Once separated, many biological families lost track of their children in the chaos of war. Children of FMLN fighters were informally adopted in El Salvador or placed in FMLN security houses, where the facade of a family camouflaged clandestine activities, such as making bombs or storing weapons. When discovered by soldiers, security houses drew military gunfire and bombs. The audience vocalizes agreement with the suggestion to also pressure the FMLN, now a political party, to assist with the search for the disappeared children.

Milto thanks the audience and welcomes Suyapa's teenage daughter, who is in attendance. He then narrates the disappearance event of the Serrano Cruz sisters, emphasizing that Suyapa's sisters were "kidnapped, not abandoned." Then Milto invites thirty-year-old Elsy, daughter of Pro-Búsqueda cofounder Francisca Romero, to the stage.

"This is a testimony of war," Elsy begins. "I lived with my parents and my five siblings in a humble home. Because of the war, we had to leave our home. I was the second youngest of the children." Elsy was seven years old when they fled the military. "Because I was a child, I didn't understand why we had to leave. We walked by night. My mother was in charge of the older children and the baby. My father was in charge of me."

"We spent a few months in different places," Elsy says. "The intensity of the war increased. They began to burn farmland and kill our animals. We realized that we had to either leave or be killed. We walked by night and would occasionally rest and hide." Elsy then describes the Guinda de Mayo. "The five of us children and our parents were hiding." But the shrapnel penetrated their bamboo shelter, and they had to get out. "Nobody would have believed that would be the last moment we'd be together."

Elsy begins to cry. Father Jon quietly walks to the front of the room, pulls up a plastic chair, and sits beside her. Elsy continues. She describes the military siege: "All we had were tortillas and salt. The soldiers came and started killing people. My mom ran with my siblings and got away." She adds, "I was out getting food with my father and we got lost." Elsy and her father walked from two to five in the morning. When Elsy grew tired, she rode on her father's shoulders. He cut her a pineapple from an abandoned garden. Chickens roamed on patios where human inhabitants had fled.

Standing beside her father, Elsy realized, "There was nobody but us. There were only people who had been shot. Children who were dead, or sometimes the mother dead with the child beside—it was terrible," she says. "My dad and I reached a place where there were two paths and one lone house." Then soldiers found them. "They shot my father." Elsy is crying again. Father Jon puts his hand on her elbow. She takes a sip of water to allow herself a break. "Being a little girl, I couldn't understand what was happening," Elsy reflects aloud. "I shouted, 'Don't die, Daddy! You know I can't be alone.'"

Elsy's father took her by the hand and said, "Daughter, do everything they say."

Five minutes later, two soldiers came out. Soldiers desecrated the body of Elsy's dying father. "In my presence, they tortured my dad. They took off his shirt. They took a knife." Elsy puts her hand on her throat, motioning that soldiers cut his throat open. As the sky grew dark, she saw, visible through her father's cut open throat, the meat of his heart beating in his chest.

Soldiers took Elsy by helicopter out of the area, along with at least fifty-six other children. The soldiers made older children, like Elsy, wash their boots and look after the younger children. "There was a little girl named Marinita, who I took care of. When I woke up one day, she was gone. They told me her parents took her. They even took a fifteen-day-old girl," Elsy says.

After two weeks, soldiers delivered Elsy to the Salvadoran Red Cross, who then placed her in an orphanage, along with Andrea, Juan Carlos, and Angélica. As was common for rural children their age, the children didn't remember their last names or birth date, so the orphanage assigned them the last name of the orphanage director and gave each a new birthday.

Elsy continues, "I was never told that my family might still be alive." She felt too frightened to ask. When soldiers visited the orphanage, the children would hide under a bed. Elsy feared soldiers would cut her throat open, as they had her father's. No one told her not to worry. But, Elsy didn't want to forget her history. So, she gathered with the children of the orphanage in secret, remembering their families through their splintered memories.

Elsy describes life at the orphanage as difficult. "We were discriminated against in school for being orphans," Elsy tells the audience. "I was there for thirteen years. I spent my adolescence there. I wanted out. I didn't get the support or psychological help that I needed." Elsy felt alone and, in

1993, at age eighteen, she got married as a way out. Six months after Elsy's wedding and seven months into her pregnancy, "My mother found me."

Elsy describes the joy and pain of their reunion. "It was hard to be in contact with my family. There were a lot of people at my reunion. But, upon seeing my mom, I went right to her. I recognized my mom right away." Surrounded by family she no longer knew, Elsy's reunion brought an immediate sense of familiarity, relief, and elation—mixed with painful emotions that carried the trauma of the war, the years lost, and the awkwardness of reacquainting with close relatives. It also ushered the start of an adult relationship with her mother and siblings.

"The war marked our lives. It separated us from our families, from our own lives," Elsy says, as she lets out a big sigh. "Now I have three children. I live a peaceful life. I have a good relationship with my mom. I have two birthdays, but that doesn't matter. Now I have my family. Thank you." Elsy gives a brief and tight smile and retreats to her seat. Father Jon also returns to his seat in the back of the room. Reverberating from the power of Elsy's testimony, the audience remains silent. They have no questions.

Milto takes the microphone. "What we have heard is part of Elsy's story, but it's also part of all our stories. We are one people. We're a testament to history, and we're called so that this history doesn't repeat. So that this history was not lived in vain."

The program breaks for pupusas outside. As I wait in line for food, feeling awed by Elsy's strength, I comment to Pro-Búsqueda's lawyer that I cried during Elsy's testimony. "I cry every time I hear it," she replies. "So does Elsy."

The workshop continues with a documentary on the Serrano Cruz case, projected on a white sheet hung above a portrait of a wounded Jesus Christ and the Virgin Mary. At the end of the film, a statement reads, "In 2004, Victoria Serrano, the mother of the disappeared girls, died with the hope of finding her daughters. The hope remains that they will still be found." Victoria first filed unsuccessful court cases against the Atlacatl Battalion in 1993 in Chalatenango and in 1995 in El Salvador's Supreme Court. She died one year before the victory at the Inter-American Court of Human Rights, leaving a legacy of justice—and a reminder to hurry the search.

Pro-Búsqueda's lawyer speaks about the Inter-American Court case, relating that the government's defense was that the Serrano Cruz sisters never existed. Father Jon interjects, "I wouldn't mind if the jails became filled with all the criminals of the war." The Inter-American Court decreed that the government must apologize for the disappearances of the sisters, create a national search commission that includes a DNA database, and declare March 29 a national day of commemoration for disappeared children. Pro-Búsqueda carries out many of these functions, but the government remains inactive in the search for the disappeared children.

Milto thanks the crowd. Then, with the program about to wrap up, Juan Carlos, the son of Francisca Romero's friend Maida, goes to the podium. "I was six months old when I was taken," he begins. "As I grew, I had questions about my roots. [In the orphanage] I would ask for my family. It was as if I had a hole I couldn't fill because I didn't understand my history. Grain by grain, we make progress." The orphanage told him his mother had abandoned him. But, with the help of older children in the orphanage, like Elsy and Andrea, who had memories of the war, he began to understand the context of his disappearance. "The love, the roots that one comes from, nobody can invent," Juan Carlos tells the room. "Many nights in bed I would ask for my mom and dad. Thanks to God, I now know my mother." They reunited in Guarjila, when Juan Carlos was twelve years old. "We get along well. I consider her, gosh, my best friend. I think about other people who are waiting for that hole to get filled. If we don't know our roots, we are a people without history."

The workshop ends in true Salvadoran style, with a lunch of rice, chicken, tortillas, and soda, and then eleven of us pile into a jeep for a ride back to Pro-Búsqueda. I share the front seat with a forty-year-old woman in a red sweater who partially sits on my lap so the driver can maneuver the stick shift. From the back seat, Elsy says to her, "You were at my reunion. You asked me if I had information about your son?"

"Yes," the woman replies. She reunited with her twenty-seven-year-old son two years ago, after twenty-one years of separation.

"What was your son like when you reunited with him?" I ask.

"Tall," she replies. She invites Elsy to come over on Wednesday to meet her son because they "disappeared in the same guinda." They make plans, and I ask Elsy about her experience testifying before the Inter-American Court of Human Rights during the Serrano Cruz trial. She responds, giggling between sentences from her position in the back seat. When Father Jon asked her to testify, she didn't hesitate because when she met him, she felt like she'd found her father again. She loves him the way she loved her father, she says.

Once in Costa Rica to testify, Elsy felt nervous upon seeing the court-house with the judges' tall chairs. "'Daughter, stay calm,' Father Jon said to me and placed a miniature statue of the Virgencita, the patron saint of Cuba, in my hand," Elsy recalls with a smile. "He told me that holding the statue helps him when he feels nervous, and he said, 'Don't worry. You're going to do great.' I told him, 'I'm going to need tequila!' That's how I began to feel courage."

When Elsy testified, the head judge asked why she was hiding in caves during the war. Before she could answer, the judge accused her: "'Your parents were guerrillas!' I told him that I didn't know because I was little; what I remember is that my father was a farmer."

A judge from the Dominican Republic challenged, "Why have you never declared your testimony before a court?"

Elsy responded, "Because I've never had the opportunity."

When Elsy stepped down from the witness stand, her team members received her with "their arms open" to hug her. Father Jon testified too. After the trial, Father Jon gave Elsy the bottle of tequila she'd jokingly requested. Their group talked and danced until two in the morning.

As we near the foothill of Los Planes, Elsy talks about her life in the orphanage, where a male director and female supervisor served as "par-ents" to a small group of orphans. "He was the little one," Elsy says, point-ing to the trunk where Juan Carlos rides with three kids on his lap. "Juan Carlos and the others [from the orphanage] feel like brothers and sisters to me."

When we arrive at Pro-Búsqueda, Elsy gives me a generous hug and a kiss goodbye, still smiling over memories of the tequila and Father Jon's Virgencita figurine. I hold a steno notebook, rapidly filling with accounts of the disappeared children. At the nunnery, I witnessed a community working to heal itself—by speaking out, standing together, and demand-ing justice.

At the Inter-American Court, a judge had asked Elsy why she was tes-tifying in the trial. Elsy beamed in the jeep as she shared her response: "I was at the court as a symbol that the Serrano Cruz sisters are still alive. I told the court, 'I represent all of the jóvenes encontrados. I represent the hope of the families who lost children. The hope that they need. We should not let their hope die.'" When Elsy returned to El Salvador from Costa Rica, her friends asked if she felt frightened about having testified. "No," she responded, "I am a testament of what happened, and I'm not afraid because what I said was true."

4 Guerrilleras

When I return home from the nunnery, Ester talks with me about safety. She shares an account of when she was robbed and then mentions her approval that the guards at our living complex are not from a security agency. She explains, "The men who work for security agencies are ex-soldiers," whose method of security is "simply to kill." Later, over a typical Salvadoran egg dinner, Ester comments that *sopa de pata* (cow's feet soup) is good for bones, as it has lots of calcium. I mention that eggshells are rich in calcium too. Her response surprises me. "During the war," she says, drawing in a breath, "I was pregnant, so I'd consume teaspoons of ground eggshells for the nutrients. You have to grind them well, otherwise the graininess can irritate the intestines."

"What else did you eat during the war?" I ask.

"Tortillas and salt. There was very little food. Very little food."

"Were you ever hungry for a long time?"

"Yes, for example, there was a guinda that lasted one month. There was no way to buy food. One time, I was so hungry that I almost poisoned myself. We were walking at night, and you hold onto trees when walking in the dark. I grabbed leaves and they smelled like guava, so I ate them. Soon after chewing them, I almost fainted. Who knows if it was guava, or if the hunger made me sick? The biggest disadvantage women had during the war was menstruation," she says. "Can you imagine? There were no Kotex [menstrual hygiene products]. The worst was crossing rivers. Can you imagine how that would feel?" Then the conversation turns to a lament of the factionalism-induced decline of the FMLN. "That's why I stopped being an FMLN militant."

Ester bemoans the FMLN's lack of success in elections, stating that the right-wing ARENA party "bought" the recent election. She remarks, "The last campaign was the filthiest one yet. People sold their vote for a container of gas. ARENA uses the poverty they created to get people's votes. A poor person is given $20 dollars for his vote while another man is given $500." Then, looking at the dinner table, Ester remarks, "Who cut this rose?" The sole flower from the garden sits with her blossom closed in a glass, on the table.

"I did," Ester's teenage daughter, Mélida, replies.

"Why didn't you like it in the garden?" Ester grumbles. Mélida casts her eyes down and says little for the rest of dinner.

I see the memory of the war in Ester's mothering. She's protective of the daughter she almost lost when a bullet flew above the hammock where baby Mélida slept. After her husband's death, Ester chose to stay single for Mélida because "most of the rape in this country happens within families." The fourteen-year-old needs to blossom, and her mother holds on to her so tightly. Ester has nightmares about Mélida getting kidnapped, which she attributes to her wartime trauma. For Ester and Mélida, the normal struggles between mother and adolescent seem intensified by Ester's scars from the war.

Over dinner the next evening, Ester shares her views on US imperialism. As we bite forkfuls of homemade rice and beans and chomp on fresh tortillas, she discusses TV dinners as a symptom of eroding family values in a profit-oriented society. Ester says she enjoys having adults in the house to talk to. "We're a small family," she adds, looking at Mélida.

"Yes, but someday it might become bigger," Mélida responds.

"NO." A firm Ester adds, "This world is not one to bring children into."

"Do you have any hope that the situation in the world will improve?" I ask, calling back to Ester's comments on our dollar-driven society. "What can we do?"

Sounding defeated, Ester replies, "This capitalism thing is getting so huge." Then, as if struck by a bolt of clarity: "Our role is to make people conscious of it." Next, Ester reflects on the meaning of the war. "Do you know what makes me angry?" Her voice rises and quivers. "We lost all that we had, and now others are benefiting." She shakes her head in disgust. "Some people even lost children." Ester closes her eyes and shakes her head again. "We fought for twelve years in vain."

I think aloud, wanting to better grasp what she means about people benefiting from the child disappearances. "Before coming to El Salvador," I say, "I had the misconception that it was simpler, that all the disappearances involved the military taking the kids and—"

"NO," Ester interrupts. She gives the example of Ceci's mother. Deceived by a lawyer, María Inés placed two boys up for adoption, under duress and with the understanding that the boys would be returned in six months. "María Inés was so thin, all bones, from walking with five children." She continues, "I interviewed a woman last week. The same *cabrón* [asshole] lawyer sold two of her children in Italy. Took two little ones." Then Ester notes the FMLN's lack of cooperation with the search for disappeared children. "The FMLN could've done a much better job than Pro-Búsqueda, but too many of them are implicated." Though a former FMLN fighter, Ester's loyalty lies with the disappeared children, with the families who suffered the war.

"Do people know that you were a guerrillera?" I ask.

"No, not everyone. I tell some people. But, if people don't get it, I don't tell them."

"Do you have friends from the war you keep in touch with?"

"They killed all my best friends." Chewing on her bottom lip, Ester says, "My husband was killed. Mélida never knew her father." For Ester, fourteen years ago is today.

.   .   .

At Pro-Búsqueda the following morning, I translate the DNA View manual from English to Spanish. DNA View is the mathematical software that tests for matches between missing children and searching relatives based on DNA profiles, a more advanced version of the back-of-the-envelope computation that Cristián carried out.[1] A Pro-Búsqueda staff member enters the office to give me an avocado from her tree. Thirty seconds later, Pro-Búsqueda's psychologist walks in holding four lemons, a gift from the mother of a disappeared child.

At lunch, I sit with Ceci's office-mate at the small wooden table in Pro-Búsqueda's kitchen. As we gobble fresh avocado, corn tortillas, and cheese, I mention that Ceci showed me a photograph of Andrés, her brother adopted in Italy. Her colleague responds, "Wow, that's amazing. She never talks about him."

Margarita, the investigator who searches for disappeared children from her native Chalatenango, joins us in the kitchen and eats a homemade tortilla. She mentions that, because of rain that can cause dangerous mudslides, she has to leave work promptly at five to begin the long journey home to her "community."

"Her community?" I ask.

"Margarita lives in a community of people who were displaced in the war," Ceci's office-mate explains. During the late 1980s, displaced Salvadorans founded the resettlement community La Esperanza, on hills in the outskirts of San Salvador. But something's not making sense—I haven't heard Margarita mention anything about living in exile.

I turn to Margarita. "Where did you go when you were displaced?"

"I was in the *guerrilla*," she laughs and slaps my knee. Oh, that's the piece of Margarita's story I was missing! Margarita says she fought in the FMLN until she became pregnant. By 1987, she had two daughters, teenagers today. The first thing she mentions about being a guerrillera is the difficulty of menstruating, an echo of Ester's words from the night before. "There were no Kotex. There was nothing. You just had to keep walking with the stain." They were constantly hiding from bombs and shrapnel. "The planes that dropped the bombs were relentless. They'd go on for hours."

The mention of shrapnel prompts Margarita to recall a recent DNA-collection interview with a relative of a disappeared child. "This woman hadn't talked much about her experiences from the war." The woman spoke of a girl whose buttock was cut off by shrapnel. "The little girl was screaming, 'Put my *nalga* [buttock] back on! Put my *nalga* back on!' And a young boy who lost his leg cried, 'Put my leg back. Put my leg on!'" Margarita's warm coffee-brown eyes look to me and then appear distant. She speaks with an even clip, not giving a full account of her own experience but describing a pivotal moment during a massacre. "We were running at night, running over rocks and thorns. I was upset because I'd lost my shoes. There were so many thorns. That was when I lost my brothers." Four of Margarita's brothers were disappeared.

After the Peace Accords, Margarita married a man she'd known since they were children. A few people in her resettlement community were childhood neighbors in Chalatenango. They eat better, healthier, more naturally in her community, she says. They still grind their own corn by hand, hence the delicious tortilla she shared with me. We've finished our meal. "I have a lot more to tell," Margarita says, looking me in the eye. Despite having related horrific memories, she appears alleviated rather than depressed by our conversation, which contrasts with Ester's sense of disillusionment. Regardless, they share the same solution for moving forward: a commitment to find the disappeared children.

As a full-time investigator at Pro-Búsqueda, Margarita gathers accounts from relatives of the disappeared and other witnesses. She reads birth registries, adoption records, and orphanage logs and now helps build the DNA bank to confirm suspected matches and create new ones. She'll later tell me that her dream of finding her disappeared brothers motivates her work. Each time she sees a reunion, she thinks about her brothers. She has no leads on their whereabouts, but "even if I can't solve my own case, I know that others can. Each reunion keeps my hope alive." Margarita and Ester are warriors—guerrilleras—women who fight for their families, country, and communities, marching toward justice, even if success means bringing others what you may never have: the embrace of a lost loved one. They persevere in a battle for hope, serving the families still impacted by the long shadow of the war.

When I exit the kitchen, I encounter Pro-Búsqueda's secretary, Raúl, a joven encontrado with a ponytail and a big smile. He's wearing a black Metallica T-shirt and reading a socialist leaflet written by a gray-bearded Swiss guy who took up arms to fight alongside the FMLN back in the 1980s. "Do you like it?" I ask.

"Yah, he always writes great stuff," Raúl responds. "Are you socialist?"

I don't even have my own views on Cuba sorted out, the country of my heritage; I haven't reached clarity on which flaws to blame on Fidel Castro's communism versus the US trade embargo. But everyone at Pro-Búsqueda lost loved ones in a war fought for a socialist agenda, so I dodge the question by reflecting it back, asking if he considers himself a socialist.

"Yes," Raúl declares, "it's an inheritance from my grandmother and mother." Both guerrilleras, Raúl's mother and grandmother placed him and his brother, at ages four and two, in an orphanage, so the women could dedicate themselves to combat. Eighteen years later, Pro-Búsqueda reunited Raúl with his grandfather, but Raúl's mother and grandmother perished in the war. "When they fought, they were always together. And they died together too, in the same massacre." Holding the pamphlet, Raúl says, "They gave themselves to war. There was a cause to fight for. Now I have to do my best. Give it my all."

As I return to my desk, I consider that fallen guerrilleras leave a legacy of idealism but also orphaned children. The brothers yearned for their mother their entire childhoods—and still do. Raúl's younger brother prays to God just to have dreams in which their mother appears. I admire the brothers' adulation of their revolutionary mother, and I understand it serves as a coping mechanism. Some women risked and gave all. But the brothers yearn so deeply that I can't help but wonder, what war could have been worth that price?

At four o'clock Margarita and I use a spreadsheet to decide which relatives to prioritize for DNA-sample collection. Collecting DNA swabs often entails long drives into the countryside and an hour-long consent and interview process. So, we strategize to stretch limited resources.

"Margarita," a Pro-Búsqueda staff member announces upon entering the front office where we sit, "there's a mother of a desaparecido, and she wants to talk to someone."

Margarita speaks with the frail, four-foot-tall mother and, ten minutes later, returns. "It was the mother of a boy who was fifteen when he was disappeared," Margarita explains. "This isn't really a case for Pro-Búsqueda. At the beginning we took cases like that, but now, not really. A boy that age…"

"He was murdered," I cut in, the reality of her work sinking in for me.

"Yes. Her family's been living in the same area, and of course he would've come back by now if he were alive."

Later, when Margarita and I discuss consent for my research, she thanks me and says she started telling me about the atrocities committed by the military because she wants the information known. She saw grotesque violence. "Soldiers would cut open the bellies of pregnant women," she says. "They'd kill people and cut off the penises of men and insert them in vaginas. They killed civilians. The guerrillas wouldn't kill civilians. Of course, the guerrillas did things too—to the soldiers they captured—but not to civilians," Margarita says.

In the evening, I chat with Ester's daughter, Mélida. We even make a bet: if my mom calls *again* tonight, then I have to wash everyone's dishes after dinner. When I tell Mélida about my intentions for my thesis on the disappeared children, she responds that it's a *"fuerte* [strong] and important topic." She doesn't wince when I talk about war or child disappearances.

"Mélida, does your mom tell you stories about the war?" I ask.

"Yes, once in a while." The stories make Mélida feel "powerless and distressed," she says while touching her sternum, "for not being able to help and for the people who suffered." What amazing words to come out of the mouth of a fourteen-year-old!

I ask her, "Do you feel that San Salvador is dangerous?"

"Not really, but maybe that's because I don't go out much, so I don't get assaulted," the daughter of the former guerrillera responds.

On the table, the single, delicate red rose has blossomed. Its fragrance fills the room.

The next day at Pro-Búsqueda, I work on the DNA bank. We heard from Cristián that the samples he transported to the California DOJ lab have been analyzed and were all of good quality. While engaged in the tedium of searching for the interview number that matches the sample number, that matches the DNA profile, that matches the DOJ code, that matches the spreadsheet, that matches the file in the cabinet, that matches the

Pro-Búsqueda database, I reflect. I consider the context behind the mouth swabs. For example, Ester told me that, in many cases, we only have maternal DNA. For the children of guerrilleros, often the mother's side of the family doesn't even know the last name of the missing child's father because people met in the war. At the close of the work day, Ester and I walk home together. She says she wouldn't have met Félix's family except by chance. Today is the first day she says his name to me.

As we dodge traffic, past tamale vendors and pickup trucks packed with fruit, I mention to Ester my visit earlier today to the Museo de la Palabra y la Imagen, a history museum where I met the former director of the rebel radio station, Radio Venceremos. She responds by telling me about her own role during the war. She wasn't a combatant but carried a rifle. Her main role, though, was with Radio Venceremos, writing critical analyses of international politics to keep guerrilla motivation up. Ester is a penetrating political analyst, yet I haven't seen her pick up a newspaper. When I ask how she stays informed, she replies, "I read. I live. I analyze reality. It's free to just look and see what's happening around us." Ester says she was a guerrillera from 1978 to 1990, when Mélida was born. I comment on her innate leadership abilities. "I've been organizing communities since I was thirteen. People much older than me, they just listen to me."

Back home, after dinner, Ester, Mélida, and I sit around the table and joke about Spaniards' accents. Somehow we stumble onto discussing how names sound. . . . And this was this person's "war name," she tells me.

"Ester, what was yours?" I ask.

"She knows," Ester says, pointing to Mélida with a dip of her chin and her index finger.

We wait for shy Mélida to answer. "Custodia." Ester beams at the sound of her daughter saying her name from that era.

Ester survived a horrendous massacre at the Sumpul River, then fought as a guerrillera for twelve years. To protect her community, Ester felt obligated to take up arms. Yet, despite the agony of what she endured, I'm beginning to see the glory of the war for her. It was the time in her life when she was young, in love—at war, yet maybe in some ways freer than she'll ever be. It's important not to romanticize war. The Salvadoran Civil War was grotesque and unjust, but I can sense that Ester's war years were sacred for her. Ester loves Félix by loving his daughter—their daughter—

watching her grow, as one year she looks more like him and one year less. It's unfair that Ester cannot be with her husband, that Mélida never met her father. Ester loves Félix by loving Mélida, and she honors his memory by hating USA, not giving up the fight. I think we humans feel obligated that way when our heroes die.

5 Morazán

With a tamale in my hand, I speed out the door behind Ester to meet Pro-Búsqueda's driver, Don Jaime, for a DNA-collection trip to gather samples that can confirm suspected matches between disappeared children and biological relatives. We'll go to San Miguel and then Morazán, two of El Salvador's easternmost departments, both heavily impacted by the war. We plan to stay overnight to maximize our efforts in this hard-to-reach area. By nine in the morning, we're in Lolotique, San Miguel, where thick, yellow heat causes my sunbaked clothes to stick to my skin. Don Jaime winds through roads unmarked and unpaved, toward the families the organization has served for over a decade. Landmarks guide us—as do locals. The cousin of a disappeared child directs us toward a relative we seek and also suggests we ask the coconut vendor at the town entrance.

We soon arrive at the home of the putative family of a joven encontrada found five years ago living in France. Pro-Búsqueda located her by tracing available records and witness accounts. Though the family feels confident in the match, it hasn't been confirmed by DNA. Sweat drips from Don Jaime's forehead onto my leg as he leans over to put the DNA-sample barcode sticker on the envelope I'm holding. He scrapes the inside of his mouth with a ballpoint pen to demonstrate the DNA-collection procedure to the three presumed sisters of the joven encontrada.

On the patio, Ester gathers corroborating information by interviewing the sisters; the eldest was present during the disappearance. When Ester asks about physical characteristics, a younger sister goes inside to retrieve a pair of child-size sandals that approximate the sister's shoe size at the time of the separation. The shoes look to me like they would fit a four-year-old. The joven encontrada sent photos from France, but a reunion has not yet occurred. "Our mother only got to see her through a photo-graph," the eldest sister laments. Their mother has since passed away. The sisters show me the treasured photos sent from France as well as one of their mother, and I can see their mother's visage in her lost daughter's face.

I look up when the interview ends—and notice a dozen people crowd-ing along the patio of the one-room earth-floored home. Smoke from the cooking fire invades my nostrils, my arms are baked, and my feet avoid stepping on farm animals and their excrement as we cross the yard. I wonder what prevents the joven encontrada in France from meeting her biological sisters. And what would she feel if she met them?

After driving another hour on remote roads with the rebel radio station playing in the car, we reach the home of the likely biological parents of a joven encontrada who lives in Italy. During the interview, the elderly parents take turns sharing details. For example, when the mother doesn't remember which hand her daughter's mole is on, the father jumps to respond, "It's like mine. It's on the right hand." Like many relatives of the disappeared, he provides a thumbprint on the consent form because he doesn't know how to sign his name.

Next, we venture down a road rarely traveled by cars, searching for a joven encontrado believed to be living with adoptive parents. We seek DNA to confirm his kinship match. We pass "*Nicas*" (Nicaraguans) repair-ing roads and a Guatemalan man who walked through Honduras to sell hammocks and tablecloths. I gasp at this snake of a road, steep and curvy, which, for most of the way, requires four-wheel drive traversing over pure rock. Steep S-curves tilt so much that whole valleys drop before us as we wind down the bends and descend.

Eventually, we reach a barrier: a pile of lava rocks blocks the road. We park the jeep to look for the joven on foot, when out pop eight children from the nearby house. One of them scurries up a nearby mango tree so high that I'm below with arms outstretched to catch him because I'm sure the branches will break. The boy shakes the tree from among its limbs and rains sweet yellow mangoes on us.

Ester carries the DNA-collection kit as we walk fifty meters to a house on a mountain ridge, where a quiet, radiant seventy-year-old woman comes to the barbed-wire fence. Her remote country home is tidy. The backyard gives way to a valley; the front yard forms part of a mountain ridge. "Do you know a fellow named Héctor who was adopted?" Ester asks the woman. "He became separated from his parents during the war."

"Héctor left for the United States two weeks ago," the woman replies. She knows his adoptive parents, but they've moved, and his biological mother is in New York. She took care of him for three months during the war, but since her house was "overstuffed" with ten children of her own, she sent him to live with neighbors who were childless. "They did a good job [raising him]," she tells us. "Héctor is educated and humble." Her daughter plays us a CD from Héctor's band.

We've stirred her memories. "Here passed the soldiers," the elderly woman recounts. She points to the rock path that cuts through her property and climbs out of the valley onto the ridge. She recalls saying at the time that the soldiers carried "sticks," not knowing that they were guns. When the soldiers asked for food, she gave them what little she had. When the guerrillas came through, she fed them too. Having a "neutral kitchen" meant surviving, she says. She invites us in, but rain clouds loom and we have that perilous road to navigate, so we must go.

We traverse gorgeous green landscape populated by hens, wild horses, cows, and donkeys and, after a quick stop to pick guava, reach our third destination. I meet a ninety-five-year-old grandmother of a joven encontrado whose DNA sample can likely confirm kinship with her grandson. She's quick to understand the procedure for DNA collection. When Don Jaime compliments her adeptness, she replies, "One doesn't have gray hairs for nothing." Her grandson lives in Italy, and there hasn't yet been a reunion.

As we scramble down the hillside back to the jeep, Ester expresses frustration that we've spent the day collecting DNA for cases of young adults Pro-Búsqueda has already found. She'd rather focus on locating missing children. I respond that, in addition to using DNA to find missing children, scientific documentation of disappearances can confirm matches and serves a critical forensic value. Courts listen to the language of science, I say. The Salvadoran and US governments denied that soldiers had conducted a mass killing in nearby El Mozote, labeling the testimony of one of the sole survivors a "guerrilla trick." It wasn't until years later—after Argentine forensic anthropologists measured bones and pointed out that the majority of the remains were from the skeletons of children—that the governments admitted that a massacre at El Mozote had indeed occurred.[1]

When we reach the resettlement village, San José Las Flores, we stop for dinner. Upon meeting me, the restaurant owner mentions that his daughter just arrived in the United States, making the trip in what he describes as a speedy thirteen days. They paid a *coyote* $5,000 to smuggle her into the United States. He explains his daughter's motivation for departure: to work to send money home. Ester and Don Jaime tell me about El Salvador's recent dollarization, when, in 2001, the government adopted US currency instead of *colones*, a decision they feel further strained the poor. Billboards of Western Union ads for money-transfer services dot the countryside. I heard several radio commercials today advertising money-transfer services, along with a radio show to teach people how to read. The letter of the day is *D*.

By nightfall, we reach the jungle mountain village of Perquín, once an FMLN stronghold that the military "completely depopulated" during the war. "You wouldn't believe the bombs that fell here," Don Jaime says as we drive over rain-slicked cobblestone streets, around cows and horses, to the Noche de Sol, the town's modest hotel.

Alone in the hotel room, I think about the relatives of the disappeared we met today. As they scraped the *palito* (little stick) against their cheek eight times, their eyes drifted into a distant stare. What did they think about? I recall how Ester explains the DNA bank to families: "I tell them it's like a library"—one that can help lead to finding missing children, to recovered identities, and to justice. DNA unwinds uncertainty. The finality of genetic testing can force a government's apology and can heal wounds, accelerating grieving or mending trust among reunited kin. Elsy told me that in the months after her reunion with Francisca, she and her mother clashed over politics, causing Elsy to doubt whether Francisca really *was* her biological mother. But, as Elsy told me regarding genetic matches, "DNA doesn't lie."

Snug in bed, I ruminate on Ester's words from when we drove through the dark half of dusk: "I fought for twelve years without pay. When I demobilized, I had no clothes except for the olive-green uniform." She no longer wears a uniform or carries a rifle but wields the weapons of DNA science. Ester fights for mothers uncertain whether to hope or grieve and for mothers who wish to know their child as more than a photograph.

·   ·   ·

In ripe morning light, we drive to the eatery where we dined the night before. The cook heats tortillas by firewood over a mud stove, near a mango tree. A gray-haired campesino arrives, wearing a straw sombrero and a white shirt worn thin; a knife in an engraved leather satchel attaches to a belt that holds up his beige cotton pants. He orders breakfast while, on the far side of the outdoor restaurant, we arrange materials for today's DNA-collection gathering.

The Pro-Búsqueda board member representing Morazán notified locals of today's DNA-collection event, and the man has come to give DNA in search of two missing children, his daughter and son. He has trouble recalling the full names and birthdates of the desaparecidos, so his two high school-age children fill in details and also donate DNA samples. One of his sons was a soldier, two others joined the guerrilla force, and his two youngest at the time, a boy and a girl, were disappeared by the military. Soldiers murdered his wife and hung her mutilated cadaver by vines in a tree, presumably to instill terror in other farmers. He looks at me and says, "Do you see how sad this is?" His eyes, cloudy with cataracts, seem to want to cry, but he strains to hold himself together. After the interview, Ester reimburses him for his transportation and pays for his breakfast.

Later, we meet Jesusita, a thirty-four-year-old former guerrillera and putative mother of a joven encontrada. We seek DNA to confirm their match. During the war, the FMLN forced her to give up her forty-day-old baby, threatening then fifteen-year-old Jesusita that they'd kill them both if she didn't comply. So, Jesusita placed her daughter into another's care. Through Pro-Búsqueda, Jesusita and her daughter reunited a few

years ago. The daughter, now nineteen years old, still lives with her adoptive parents. Although the daughter invited Jesusita over for New Years,
Jesusita didn't go because she didn't feel welcome, she says. She smiles a
beautiful smile that is refreshing but also seems to cover up pain.

Next, I meet Noelia, a tiny woman who appears to be about sixty years
old. A single ponytail cinches her waist-long hair, brown with strands
of gray. She arrives breathless and thirsty, having ridden two buses and
walked one hour to meet us. "When did the children disappear?" Ester
asks. Noelia doesn't know exact dates, so Ester asks her to estimate
relative to the El Mozote massacre. Noelia's eyes water and she dabs a
handkerchief on her cheek. "We'll go little by little," Ester tells her. "We
don't want to ask anything that hurts. Have you eaten? Do you want
coffee?" Ester stands to massage Noelia's shoulders and stroke her back.
Slowly, Noelia speaks of her own two children who died during the war.
Noelia's pregnant sister was also killed, along with two of her children,
and Noelia searches for her sister's two children who she believes may be
alive. Ester patiently collects clues that may help locate Noelia's missing
nieces.

After several interviews, we stop at Radio Ecológica, a local radio station, to check on the status of Pro-Búsqueda's paid radio announcement
that will broadcast the date and location of the next DNA-collection gathering. Once back in scorching San Miguel, we enter La Linea (The Line),
a dangerous neighborhood built along an abandoned railroad track. A
naked, muddy three-year-old and his family stare at us as we climb out of
the parked jeep.

Ester feels nervous she'll get chastised for wearing shorts as we enter
the home of a "pious woman," a grandmother and aunt of three missing
children. Mud walls meet the dirt floor, and hanging sheets separate the
bedroom from the living room, which blends into the kitchen. I see a stove
but no food in the kitchen, except for a banana. I'm told that the bicycle
with large baskets that leans against an outside wall of the home indicates
that her son works selling coconuts. The home has a well, a latrine, and
no running water. I meet the eighty-year-old "evangelical" woman in the
blue-and-white-checkered dress, whose home we're in.

Ester's attempt to explain the purpose of DNA collection—to find the
missing children—degenerates. The grandmother, petrified by Ester's pro-

posal to donate a DNA sample, seems to relive the terror of the war before our eyes. Ester yells at the "stubborn" grandmother, and Don Jaime joins in. Then the grandmother remarks to Ester, "You look like the woman who took the children away!"

To build trust, Ester relates her experience as a survivor of the massacre of Sumpul and then bellows, "You say you believe in God, but you're not even willing to help with a sample."

I'm supposed to be present only as an observer, but I break my silence. "I can try to answer her questions about the DNA samples and explain what happens to them," I say. I pull up a plastic chair next to the woman's frightened body and reach for her stiff hand. I tell her that I'm from the United States and that I'll personally deliver the samples to California and make sure they get to the DNA lab. I explain the procedures for DNA collection and analysis. Eventually, tremulous Consuelo agrees to give a sample. Still holding my hand, she speaks of her daughter who lives in Los Angeles, has two children, and is struggling to make ends meet.

Consuelo asks if I want to see a photo of the disappeared children's mother. When I say yes, she wobbles over to the sheeted-off bedroom and comes back carrying a tattered, hand-sized Bible. Guarded in the pages of the Bible is a black-and-white photograph of her murdered sister. Ester and I look at the photo. "She was pregnant. They murdered her and cut open her abdomen like this and this," Consuelo says. Her hand traces her abdomen left to right, up to down.

I shiver. "It *is* chilling," Ester says, acknowledging my reaction. "The soldiers did barbaric things."

"What was your sister's name?" I ask. Consuelo's lips clench and purse. She shivers too and doesn't answer.

As we wrap up, we encourage her to join Pro-Búsqueda's local workshops. Then, DNA sample in hand, blessings and gratitude exchanged, we leave. In the car, Ester thanks me for intervening and expresses her amazement that we obtained the sample. "Her priest proclaims it a sin to donate a DNA sample," Ester says. Yet, once Consuelo understood how the sample could help find her missing loved ones, she agreed.

We stop by the home of the Pro-Búsqueda board member from San Miguel, an aunt of disappeared boys. Ester hands her some workshop flyers to distribute and asks her to please visit Doña Consuelo monthly. The board member knows Consuelo but says she's too frightened to go to La Linea, Consuelo's neighborhood, because there can be assaults of outsiders. A silent laugh escapes me, grateful that I've already made it out of that neighborhood. I'm an outsider in a land devoured by a civil war that my country funded.

On the ride back to San Salvador, we stop to put gas in the jeep. "Ester, doesn't she look like Mrs. Gonzales?" Don Jaime remarks, pointing to one of the gas-station attendants. They ask the girl her age, make small talk with her, and drive away, saying that based on the girl's green eyes and shape of her smile, they believe she may be the daughter of a mother searching for four missing girls. Ester scribbles the name, age, location, and appearance of the girl in her notebook.

After two long days in Morazán and less than two weeks in the country, returning to San Salvador feels like a homecoming. Upon arriving at Ester's home, I plop on the bed, exhausted. Ester sees me and bleats, "Get up. You contaminated everything!" When I apologize, she softens and connects her vigilance about cleanliness to what she lived in the war. A group of guerrilla fighters, she tells me, would all wash with the same bucket of water, conserving each drop. During the war, she had a big ulcer on her buttock due to a fungal infection. I should shower immediately when returning from the countryside, she insists, because I *can*.

I pour cool cupfuls of refreshing water over my shampooed hair. Ester, the former guerrillera, bathes and scrubs her home often. Through her service to the disappeared children and their relatives, Ester also fights to heal herself, while contributing to a larger mission. With each DNA sample collected, we provoke traumatic memories—and kindle hope for those still searching. The samples may lead to successful court cases and reunite families—or, at the very least, alleviate a mother's uncertainty after twenty years of not knowing what happened to her child. DNA brings hard evidence that the likeness of facial features cannot.

Determined to support the DNA bank and to document the powerful stories of family separation and reunion, I spend Saturday writing field notes. On Sunday evening, over a vegetable-soup dinner with Ester and Mélida, Ester asks about my friend from California, whom I went with today to a botanical garden. "Who does Allie live with?"

"With two gringos," I reply. "They used to be in the Peace Corps."

Ester scowls. "The Peace Corps is used by governments to infiltrate and to gather information about people."

Ester's scorn toward the United States is a rough reentry from my expat outing. Her rigid version of reality can be burdensome, but Salvadorans do have a right to be bitter. The acts of surviving, mothering, searching, fighting, and loving in the nights of bullets and stars command a bravery beyond any I've ever known. What if I had marched in the jungle as a guerrillera or a campesina running to survive? Would I be one of the women lucky enough to raise my own child?

6 Gunshots

2:17 a.m.
Gunshots shout in the dark of night.
This time I'm sure it's not a dream.
The twenty evenly spaced shots
Are a violation of another human being,
Which translates into a violation of me.
Feelings swirl around my umbilical cord,
I am safe in the bed where I lay.
Some blocks away, a man is dying.
I can see the wounds in his chest.
He is breathing his last breaths.
A car speeds away. Turns. Faster now.
I pay my respects to the life that was
And return to a semblance of sleep.
Yet the bullets have jolted my spirit,
And suddenly I realize:
Only through God could this *pueblo* endure
Barbarities of massacres and their aftermath.
It's the only way to remain intact in this chaos,
Resiliency through communion with a savior,
el Salvador.

·   ·   ·   ·   ·

It's 7:12 a.m. Ester did not hear the gunfire. Did I imagine it? I exit the gates of Residencial Santa Barbara. "Good morning," I say to the armed security guard, whose eyes are red with tiredness. Walking past him, and then pivoting on my feet, I turn and say, "Excuse me, sir. Did you hear gunshots last night?"

"Yes, it was on Antonio Abad Street." He points one block away.

"At about what time did it happen?"

"Around two in the morning."

"Do you know what happened?"

"No. But police cars passed by here on this street."

I thank him and then go to meet my friend from California, Allie, in front of Cuscatlán Bank, to walk to our respective workplaces together. She is sorry to hear that I had heard gunshots, and even sorrier to say that she's grown accustomed to them.

Thirty minutes later, I'm in the kitchen at Pro-Búsqueda. María Inés pulls up a chair beside me. "Tell me about your trip to Morazán." And she asks, "Did you rest this weekend?"

"Yes, but a gun battle at two in the morning woke me up. It's the first time I've heard one." She gives a sympathetic nod. An hour later, while I'm steeping myself in work, María Inés brings me a chamomile tea to soothe me.

Any news of the shooting? No, nobody has bought the *La Prensa* newspaper today. My coworkers at Pro-Búsqueda offer alternative explanations of what the sounds could have been: fireworks, military practice (I live near the military hospital), someone shooting into the sky. Others normalize it: "Oh, yah, you heard a *balacerito* [little gun battle]." They are entrenched in a culture of violence and trying to shelter me from it.

In the evening, at Ester's house, I catch the headlines on TV. Eight people murdered in San Salvador today. I learn that the San Antonio Abad gang, named for our neighborhood, descends from the notorious Calle 18, one of El Salvador's bloodiest gangs. The Salvadoran Civil War occurred on the streets where I walk and dwell, and a new war of gangs rages today. The civil war left behind guns and anguished hearts, leading to the proliferation of brutal gangs that extend beyond the US border—fueled by poverty, the unspoken pain of family separation, and decades of terror.

Faith brings solace among a people working to heal from the wounds of war in a country where bullets still reign: not capitalists versus communists, but gangs battling gangs, with the most vulnerable still under attack. In El Salvador's civil war, brothers fought brothers. Most of the frontline combatants were poor and lacking choice. So, too, in today's gang war—it's hard to tell where the innocence and brotherhood ends. It's not a question of blame, but, it seems to me, the victims are the fighters and the victims are everyone tangled in between.

7 Sonsonate with Ceci and Lucio

The next day, I head out with Lucio and Ceci, Pro-Búsqueda's reliable accountant, for a DNA-collection day trip to Sonsonate and Ahuachapán, the country's westernmost departments. They were the last to become battlegrounds in the civil war, and the 1932 *matanza* of indigenous people occurred in what is now Sonsonate.[1]

When we arrive at a house in Sonsonate, a protective neighbor demands an explanation for our visit. Lucio says we're with Pro-Búsqueda and that the woman we seek is the mother of two disappeared children. She sells fruit preserves in the open-air market and isn't home, the neighbor says. We search at the market, but to no avail. Forty minutes later, we return to her street and find that word of our arrival has already spread—a second neighbor tells us that the woman "sold her two children."

"That's not true," thirty-two-year-old Ceci says. Ceci may not know the details of the case, but she's heard the accusation before. Ceci's mother, María Inés, gave up Ceci's two brothers for adoption under extreme duress out of concern for the boys' safety.

My first week in El Salvador, I'd asked Ceci over lunch at Subway if she was the youngest in her family. Her pained reply surprised me: "The youngest... of the girls. I feel sorry that I was little and couldn't save my brothers. I know it's not right to feel that way, but I do." She told me about losing her brothers during the war. "We were desperately running from bombs, barely surviving. A lawyer came and told my mom that if she gave the youngest children—the two boys—to him, he would keep them safe. He said he'd bring them back while they were still young. I'm sorry to say, that was what my mother did. My two brothers were taken to Italy." Ceci's brother Andrés was a toddler when their mother last held him, Alvaro was a bit older, and Ceci was eleven at the time. "People think families got money for the children, but we didn't get anything. The lawyer got paid, and my brothers didn't come back. It was a lie."

Father Jon told me that lawyers in El Salvador made money orchestrating adoptions abroad, trafficking kidnapped children or children handed over by biological families under duress or coercion. Adoptive families in the United States and Europe saw themselves as rescuing orphans from war and poverty, unaware that many biological families, like Ceci's, had been deceived or even robbed of their children.

In 2003, twenty years after the boys' illicit adoptions, Pro-Búsqueda— by tracing adoption records and searching contact information online— found Ceci's brothers in Italy. An Italian deacon spoke with Andrés's adoptive parents two years ago. Andrés may not even have known at the time that he was adopted, Ceci told me. "According to the laws in Italy, those people are his parents." Ceci and her mother spoke with Andrés once by phone last year, but Andrés declined an in-person reunion. Ceci sent him a letter and hasn't heard from him since. She crossed her arms and sighed through fretted lips as she said, "Now isn't the right time. Things happen slowly. Andrés is having problems [with his adoptive parents] for having spoken with us. We don't want to cause problems for him. He's happy in his life there."

When Pro-Búsqueda reached out to Alvaro's adoptive father, an Italian police officer, the father threatened the organization, changed his phone number, and removed his family's contact information from the internet. Though Andrés now knows of his brother in Italy, no biological family members have spoken with Alvaro since his disappearance, and Pro-Búsqueda has lost contact with him.

After a few stops, we journey on to Ahuachapán. As we cruise down the highway in Pro-Búsqueda's red pickup truck, Ceci and Lucio belt out a guerrilla song calling for the *"Yanquis"* (Yankees) to get out. "Did you learn that song during the war?" I ask. Yes, we sang it as children, Ceci and Lucio say. "Was it dangerous to sing then?" Yes, they respond in chorus, smiling. Lucio points out an orphanage as we drive past, one of several that he lived in.

We visit a home deep in Ahuachapán, less than a day's walk from Guatemala. Rabbits, dogs, hens, and eight pigs populate the walk across the patio to the front door of the putative aunt of a joven encontrado. A large pig has a leg bandaged in a cloth wrap, stuck on with honey; the piglets have to be slapped away because they're licking the bandage. The presumed aunt donates a DNA sample, gives us soda and cookies, and waves goodbye until our truck is out of sight.

On our way home, we take a ten-minute detour to visit the ocean! I run to dip my feet. Then Lucio takes us to meet the parents of a friend from the orphanage, a former gang member sent away by his parents to escape violent peers. Greeting us at the door, the portly dad grins, chuckles, and welcomes Lucio into a warm hug. The family took Lucio in for four months when he first left the orphanage. Lucio reminds the father that, when they met, he looked at Lucio with angry eyes. The father explains, "My son was involved in gangs, so I assumed Lucio was too." Lucio says that although he's never been in gangs, many assume that he has because of his baggy clothes and parentless upbringing. We sit on the patio, bathed in yellow sunlight, thumbing through stacks of photos the father handed Lucio, reminders for Lucio of childhood friends now gone off to the United States. "Thank you for your kindness to Lucio," Ceci says to the father as we depart.

Joyful, we drive home along the coast through Sonsonate and La Libertad, with the sun dropping toward the green-blue sea. I savor every vista of the tangerine sunset. "We just passed some *tatus,*" Ceci says, referring to the camouflaged underground shelters families hid in during the war. "They were dug into the ground. I've been in two kinds. One kind you sit in. The other is shaped like an L; you put wood on top and cover it with dirt. That's the kind you can stand in. We heard soldiers' footsteps walking over our heads when we were in that kind."

"How did you know when it was safe to get out?" I ask.

"There were always people there to let us know." She refers to FMLN militants who kept watch over civilians and guided them to safety, when they could.

Lucio talks about hiding in a cave with his dad. "When we came out, we were covered with insect bites."

"Lucio, what year were you taken to the orphanage?" I ask. After soldiers killed Lucio's mother, he survived a few years in flight in the jungle with his father, before the detonation of a military grenade killed his dad too. Lucio says he entered orphanages in the mid-1980s.

"You weren't in the countryside anymore. Did you feel safe then?"

"No, the orphanage was across the street from a military headquarters," he answers.

"And you thought they might kill you?"

"Yes, that—and I wanted to poison their food. But," he adds, "it never happened," illustrating the self-restraint that kept him out of gangs and out of trouble.

Ceci also left the countryside in the mid-eighties, with her mother and four siblings. She doesn't wake up screaming anymore from memories of the war, but the nightmares persist, "depending on the experiences and the stress of that day," she says.

We shift to discussing friendship. "One good thing about being poor is that you always know who your true friends are," Lucio remarks.

Ceci furrows her brow. "I've never had a friend. I'd like to someday, but I've never achieved that." I'm sure Lucio sees her as a friend, and I do too. She exudes kindness, but what she lived through, and lost, seems to shape her experience of relationships, even today.

Graced by the sunset and gorgeous ocean views, we sing a Maná tune. "¿A dónde van los desaparecidos?...¿Y por qué es qué se desaparecen? Porque no todos somos iguales [Where do the disappeared go? And why do they disappear? Because we're not all equal]."

Lucio shows us a restaurant along the way that makes tasty paella. "If you come to visit me in California, I'll ask my mom to make you paella," I say. "She makes the best paella."

It feels as if a stone has shattered glass. "Liz...we'll never come to California," Lucio responds. "We'd never get permission to visit."

Then he talks about emigrating. "When people go, they know they are going to suffer—to suffer discrimination and exploitation."

"I would go to help my sister," Ceci chimes.

Lucio had two good opportunities to work in the United States, but his daughter, Michele, had recently been born, so he declined. "I was separated from my family once, and I won't let it happen again." Memory of losing his first family to the war binds his current family together. Similarly, Ceci feels she cannot leave her mother.

At seven o'clock, we deposit the DNA samples at Pro-Búsqueda and drop Ceci off at a bus stop. As Pro-Búsqueda's pickup truck nears my home, Lucio and I talk about his father. In a tone serious and sincere, he confirms what I already suspected. "If my father had survived the war, then I would've died." Lucio's father spent his last years in the jungle protecting Lucio from military attacks, from when Lucio was two to seven years old. Lucio's dad wouldn't have chosen to separate, but when his death made Lucio an orphan, farmers evacuated Lucio out of the combat zone to an orphanage. "He gave up his life for me. The shrapnel that cut off his leg..." It caused his father to bleed to death.

I interrupt. "He gave you life twice." We let silence talk. Then I say, "It must help you in life to know that he loved you so much. And it must hurt you—"

"To not be with him," he finishes.

. . . . .

The next day, I'm occupied with the DNA bank when a pregnant Pro-Búsqueda volunteer enters the psychology office, where I sit. She plops into a chair, letting out an impressive sigh. "That woman took tears out from my eyes," she says, explaining that a woman just spoke with her son in Italy for the first time since his disappearance. I step into the foyer.

Marco, Pro-Búsqueda's young psychologist, gathers around the phone on the receptionist's desk, beside an Italian woman who translated for the forty-year-old Salvadoran mother. The mother is beaming nearby; with an enormous smile, she appears as joy personified. "That was wonderful when he called me 'mamma,'" she sings. Lucio ushers her to the front room to donate a DNA sample, and the crowd of onlookers disperses.

I follow Marco into the psychology office. He asks me to sit in the psychologist's seat as he tells me the mother's first words to her son, Lazaro, after twenty years of separation: "Hello, son. I love you. I love you so much." The son replied, "Hello, *mamma*." Marco rolls the word *mamma* with an Italian accent. The son, a young man in the Italian navy, vowed to come visit and said he's studying Spanish. Pro-Búsqueda found him seven years ago, but mother and son didn't speak until today. "His [biological] sister also lives in Italy. She recently found out she was adopted, and she's in the process of discovering the truth," Marco tells me. The son suggested that maybe he could come to El Salvador with his sister. They've met and he'll let Pro-Búsqueda know when she's ready to receive a call.

"The mother offered to pay for their plane tickets," Marco says. When I ask if she can afford that, he explains, "She has a son in New York. I'm certain he'd pay. Her clothes are too nice for someone from Morazán. It shows she receives remittances." Marco continues, "When she told him that she hopes they can celebrate his birthday together on July 26, he replied, 'But July 26 isn't my birthday.' And she said, 'Yes, you were born on that day. I was there,'" Marco relates with a chuckle.

Back in the hallway, I see Lucio. He's just finished collecting the mother's DNA sample. "How's she doing?" I ask.

"Excited," Lucio replies. "Excited."

Then I see María Inés. "Did you see what happened? Did you hear about the phone call to Italy?" I ask. There's A BIG FAT FOOT IN MY MOUTH. I forgot about her boys in Italy.

"No, I removed myself," María Inés replies. "When you feel very emotional, it's good to be away from people." She accepts a hug and then sweeps by. Ceci, no doubt, heard the interaction with the Italian young man. I ask how she's doing. Her response: a scowl, scrunched nose, curled lip.

Back in the psychology office, I meet Fernanda, the biological mother of the jóvenes encontrados in Italy. She has huge smiles and SIGHS. With each SIGH, she deflates but then fills with emotion again. SIGH, SMILE, SMILE, SIGH, SMILE. We discuss the possibilities of travel to Italy, of her children coming here, of a telephone call with her daughter. Then she leaves the office to go home to cook dinner, still soaring with the elation of reunion.

At the end of the workday, Lucio invites me to dinner in his home, a one-bedroom apartment with concrete walls and floors. His wife, Angélica, offers to trim my hair, and I meet their boxer–pit bull, Roque, named

Michele and Vladi, both at age
three, the children of jóvenes
encontrados Lucio and Angélica
(Michele) and Andrea and Amílcar
(Vladi). San Salvador, 2005.
Courtesy of Mark Halpert.

for the revolutionary poet, Roque Dalton. Angélica combs and snips as
Andrea chats nearby, their children play, and Lucio places a sharp, metallic object in my hand. He smirks, waiting for me to realize that I hold
a bomb, an artifact from the war. "Guerrillas removed the gunpowder,"
Lucio explains. The bomb's shape resembles an arrowhead. "One like this
but bigger is what cut off Andrea's arm."

After my haircut, Lucio and Angélica's three-year-old daughter,
Michele, styles my hair, and Andrea and Amílcar's three-year-old son,
Vladi, hands me a toy piano. "*Para que le cante a su mujer* [So that you
can serenade your woman]," he says. I erupt in laughter. It feels so good to
laugh. Andrea and Angélica giggle together, "sisters" by virtue of growing
up in the same orphanage. Amílcar sits on the floor playing with Vladi.
For all the sad memories Lucio carries, he has such brightness in his life.

At nine o'clock, Lucio and crew pile into the car to drive me home.
Lucio concentrates on the empty road, barely stopping at stoplights. "Why
isn't anyone out on the street?" I ask.

"It's because they know it's better to be at home. People are in their
homes now."

The everyday violence in El Salvador rattles me. It dictates our daily routines. Lucio survived bullets and grenades, bounced between orphanages, and still calls on survival instincts to stay alive. I recall Ceci's words: "Our experiences in the war were not pretty, but what came after has been difficult also." She longs for her brothers, but her neighborhood in Apopa has one of the highest murder rates in El Salvador. The desaparecidos raised in Italy will probably never hear as many gunshots as Ceci and Lucio do. Lazaro's mother, Fernanda, shared a short phone call with her lost boy in Italy that began healing wounds. But she's also now separated from a son in New York, her family torn apart by immigration too—a result of El Salvador's violence and poverty ravaging in the aftermath of the war.

Despite the dangers and economic challenges in El Salvador, Lucio and Ceci have both foregone opportunities to go north. The yearning of forced family separation set their course. Lucio—a disappeared son, a husband, and a father—says that no amount of money would make it worthwhile to separate from his daughter, Michele. Ceci makes the same choice: to stay with her mother, who suffers the loss of three boys, one killed in the war and two who feel more distant than the ocean that separates Italy from El Salvador.

8 Fathers

On Friday afternoon, we celebrate Father's Day at Pro-Búsqueda. A handful of fathers of disappeared children have come into the office for the festivities. As we gather in the foyer, a joven encontrada invites Father Jon to make the first cut of the cake, deeming him "the father with the most children." The fathers of the disappeared slice their pieces after Father Jon, followed by dads who work in the office. Lucio and the other dads on staff each receive a small gift, delivered with a hug and congratulations from all. Then, we eat cake!

. . . . .

Early Monday, I hand Father Jon a pink floppy disc containing his letter I translated to English over the weekend. He composed it for the US Congress, to request monetary reparations to assist with the search for the disappeared Salvadoran children.

In the afternoon, we review the letter together. We pause at the paragraph describing the forced disappearances. "Father," I say, "as I was translating, I decided to make the language more powerful." I explain that, for example, I changed what previously read "children were disappeared" to "children were abducted."

Father Jon confesses, "Me too. I changed it this morning." He directs me to his edit where he added the detail that children were transported via helicopter, signifying that military commanders knew about the disappearances. He looks at me with innocent eyes and shrugs. "What can we do? It's the truth."

Under time pressure to get the letter to Washington, DC, Father Jon dictates in Spanish as I translate, rework, and type our ideas. Father Jon feels that since the United States financed the war that tore families apart, it has a moral obligation to assist El Salvador's disappeared children. Reparations from the US government would also signify something beyond money: an apology.

.   .   .   .   .

The next day, Margarita, Don Jaime, and I depart Pro-Búsqueda at dawn for Chalatenango. In a town plaza in the mountainous department, we pick up Enrique, a joven encontrado who notified families about today's DNA-collection gathering in the village Teocinte. Pro-Búsqueda reunited Enrique with his biological family two years ago.

On a dirt road, Margarita and Enrique climb out of the car to speak with relatives of the disappeared. Don Jaime and I stand in the shade. As we wait, a white cloud of pesticide spray descends on us. The cloud covers the front yard, where Margarita talks with a man about a missing child. Children breathe the white amorphous mass. "Mosquito control," I'm told. Don Jaime and I escape to the jeep, but white fumes waft in the rolled-down windows. The sweltering air tastes like turpentine. I see a man holding a metallic tank hanging by a strap over his shoulder and cradled by his two arms. I exit the car and the spray lands on me—on my hair and on my apple, which wasn't organic but, even if it had been, wouldn't be anymore. Don Jaime and I walk up the road. Delicate white flowers, fragrant like jasmine, distract us from the fumigation. Don Jaime places five stars of white flowers in my hair, decorating my pesticide-bathed ponytail.

At our next stop, we venture along an agave-lined walking path, across a bamboo bridge over a creek, and through a cornfield to collect a DNA sample from the mother of a disappeared child. The woman's plump, toothless sister-in-law tells me about cooking huge amounts of food for

the soldiers and guerrillas during the war. "We cooked out of fear," she says.

Driving into Teocinte, we see a crew repairing a paved road by lining it with rocks. The sole woman among the workers wears a bandana over long, brown hair. Margarita mentions the woman's name: Eulalia, and comments that Eulalia lent her bed for Ester's childbearing during the war. Holding two rocks in her hand, Eulalia walks over to our jeep and says her patio is ready for the DNA-collection gathering. The road follows a gorgeous creek through the jungle surrounding Teocinte. Gardens with banana trees and birds of paradise decorate homes of adobe, aluminum, and cement. We park. Margarita recognizes a man, a former guerrilla, from the war. "You're far from your land," she says, as we walk by. He nods with respectful salutation to his comrade.

At Eulalia's home, we unpack our supplies: clipboard, pens, ink pad for fingerprinting, consent and interview forms, gloves, and swabs. Presumptive relatives of our local guide, Enrique, have come to meet us. "What's this for?" Enrique's putative uncle, a slender, strong, dignified man of the countryside, questions upon seeing the DNA kit. Don Jaime gives a four-minute explanation and introduces me as a collaborator from the California DNA lab. Enrique's uncle directs his eyes to me. "I would like to hear from her," he says.

I explain the science and purpose of the DNA bank. It can reunite families and is critical for legal purposes, I say. "Especially in your case, where your nephew, Enrique, has been found."

The uncle rises from his chair. "Well, here. Take a seat. You have to work," he says to me. He puts on clunky glasses to read the consent document he just signed. When we finish, Don Jaime offers the family a ride up the steep road. Though the children accept, the uncle declines—he had come to Teocinte by horse.

Opposite top: Margarita gathering testimony from a relative of a disappeared child for Pro-Búsqueda. Tecoluca, San Vicente, 2017. Courtesy of Pro-Búsqueda.

Opposite bottom: Margarita collecting DNA from a paternal uncle of a disappeared child for Pro-Búsqueda's DNA bank. Suchitoto, Cuscatlán, 2012. Courtesy of Pro-Búsqueda.

Later, in a town with a rusted, broken swing set surrounded by trash, Margarita knocks on the door of a house that emanates loud singing. Two school-age girls open the door. "Yes, the man you're asking for is our grandfather, but he's drunk."

The girls approach their grandfather to inform him of our arrival. "*Hija de puta* [Daughter of a whore]!" he barks, then stumbles to the doorway. He confirms with a slur and a wagging finger that he's the father of a disappeared girl. As our team regroups in the jeep, a little boy appears and begs for money. Then the drunk father staggers toward us. "Don't put me in jail. I didn't do it. She sold my daughter!" he hollers, pointing at a neighbor's house. We end up not collecting a DNA sample because we determine him unable to provide informed consent.

Before we drive off, we see that another drunk man has obtained a can of sardines from the nearby shop and tries to pound the can open with a rock. He pierces the lid but, unable to remove it, drinks the juice of the canned sardines. As he teeters away, he tosses the can over a tall gate, into the front yard of a cement home. Don Jaime and Margarita look at each other and share a sad laugh. When the jeep engine rumbles, I notice the young mendicant who'd just asked for money hopping the fence to retrieve the can.

Back on the slick highway, we have sudden car trouble that sounds like firecrackers. Actually, the smaller explosions sound like a .28 and the louder ones like a .32 (revolver), Margarita says. Every other minute, the car emits a ruckus of bangs from the rear. Don Jaime says that the brakes feel funny, which is worrisome since we're winding down a steep mountain road in the rain. Besides the danger of driving with malfunctioning brakes, it would be unsafe, they insist, to drive into San Salvador with the jeep emitting explosive gunshot-like sounds: because you never know who's going to shoot back.

A 1970s taxi station wagon passes us as we creep down the highway. A few minutes later, the taxi reappears and the driver asks if we need assistance. He and Don Jaime spend one hour in the rain attempting to fix the jeep, interspersed with multiple tests at driving, with the taxi driver following behind to assess the repair. One little automotive part is missing, Don Jaime and the taxi driver deduce. At 5:30 p.m. Don Jaime and the cab driver leave in the taxi to purchase the needed part.

Margarita and I wait in the jeep, which hugs the shoulder of the hillside highway. She removes the keys from the ignition and hides them deep in the glove box to deter carjackers. But otherwise, she doesn't exhibit an ounce of fear at our predicament. "Liz, I very much believe in God," she remarks. During her childhood, her father was a fugitive who drank and got in fights, she says. He and her uncle almost killed someone in a fight. Her uncle was jailed. Though her father was found to be innocent, the authorities often came looking for him. Eventually, he stopped sleeping at home. Once, when Margarita was eleven, police were chasing her father, firing shots into the night. She ran after the police. "Why are you shooting at my dad?" she demanded. They responded by threatening, "We'll come to the house with tortillas if we have to," meaning they'd stay as long as necessary to capture him. Margarita says that her only next logical move was to join the guerrilla force.

In the parked jeep in the rain, Margarita speaks about her relationship with God. "In the war, I would always make a small cross out of sticks wherever I slept. That simple act helped me feel safer, so I had enough peace to sleep. But there were difficult moments when I doubted God and blamed him. The father of my oldest child was also a guerrillero. It was 1986. I took our child to him and, after seeing him, became pregnant with my second daughter. Then he was murdered. I was devastated. We'd shared so much together. We had so much in common. Both of our families had been murdered. I doubted a God that would make such pain.... Now I know that I will never understand the mind of God. He does things for reasons we cannot understand."

At seven o'clock, the taxi returns with Don Jaime, then leads us four miles to a Texaco. Don Jaime proceeds slowly because the brakes barely work, and we're traversing down a wet slope.

"The children of God are always taken care of," the taxi driver says.

At nine, I'm home. I reflect on a day of fathers driven to drunkenness by the sorrow of war and forced separation, and of the heroic fathers who rescued us from the highway in the rain. I think of Margarita's faith in the ultimate Father and of Father Jon, who created the movement to reunite the lost children with their fathers, uncles, and granddads who love them.

9 Sonia's Reunion

The next morning, the running water is out at Ester's and there's barely enough in the barrel for a rinse, so my pesticide hairdo will have to stay. When I walk into Pro-Búsqueda, Marco informs me that there will be a *reencuentro* (reunion) today, planned yesterday while I was in Chalatenango. He asks if I'd be willing to translate, as the US adoptee doesn't speak Spanish.

Three minutes later, radiant Sonia, a fourteen-year-old raised in Connecticut, arrives with her adoptive parents, both dentists. We share introductions, then Father Jon calls the adoptive parents out of the room, allowing Sonia privacy for the first moments of reunion. I hand slender Sonia tissues as she sheds tears. She fears that her "birth mother" won't want to meet her, she says. Last night, she "cried lots" after seeing a photo of her biological mother for the first time.

Moments later, Jacinta arrives, a middle-aged woman in loose pants and a blouse, with long, dark hair and expressive brown eyes. When Jacinta enters the yellow room, she and Sonia cry as their outstretched arms draw each other in. They stand with waists far apart but embrace chest to chest, cheek to cheek, kissing and crying into each other's hair and shoulders. "*Mi niña, mi niña bonita* [My girl, my pretty girl]," Jacinta coos as they hug. They walk over to the plastic chairs set up for the reunion in Pro-Búsqueda's front room. Still in a half embrace, mother and daughter sit down.

Sonia's hand rests on her biological mother's shoulder as they speak to each other for the first time, through translators, Marco and me. Tears flood out of Sonia as her words squeak above sobs. "I understand why you gave me up for adoption," Sonia says. "I know it was very difficult to do. And I love you for it because I am happy. I'm happy where I am."

Jacinta turns to me to translate her response: "Every Christmas, I would think of you. My little boy—you have a brother. He's eight years old—he would ask me, 'Mommy, why are you sad?' and I would say, 'I'm thinking of someone I love.'"

Sonia responds, "Every night, before I went to sleep, I would think of you. I'd try to imagine what you look like."

"Every morning," echoes Jacinta, "I'm alone cleaning, and I think of you. I ask God to please keep you safe, to make you a person with a good heart and an educated person." Then Jacinta says, "I'm sorry. I didn't have the resources to take care of you. If I had the resources then that I have now, I never would have made that decision." She placed Sonia up for adoption during the war. Her eyes look to her daughter's. "Please forgive me," she says twice.

"I understand. I forgive you."

Jacinta apologizes again, and Sonia repeats that she feels grateful to her biological mother because she is happy in her life in Connecticut.

Jacinta's husband and three-year-old daughter, Celina, enter the room. Celina climbs into Jacinta's lap. "Celina, she is your sister," Jacinta says. Celina's big eyes stare up at Sonia. Sonia reaches her arms out to hug her sister.

Now it's time for the two families to meet. Pro-Búsqueda staff lead Sonia's white adoptive parents into the room. Even in casual traveler's clothes, their garments reveal an air of professionalism. The two mothers hug. Both say to me at different points, "Tell her that I am so grateful. I don't have words to express how grateful I am." After several minutes, Sonia's adoptive parents return to their hotel to allow Sonia more private moments with Jacinta.

The big emotional balloon has released some air. Sonia tells her mother about her life at home. "I wake up at seven, school starts at eight, and I get home at three. I play soccer and lacrosse." Jacinta seems thrilled to hear about Sonia's education.

Jacinta's husband reminds her they have to leave soon because their eight-year-old will be returning home from school. So, we (Marco, Sonia, Jacinta's crew, a Pro-Búsqueda investigator, and I) pile into Father Jon's jeep to take Sonia to Hotel El Presidente. Then we'll take Jacinta home. I sit in the back seat with Jacinta and Sonia. Jacinta tells Sonia how she chose her name. "At least I was able to give her that," Jacinta says.

"But that's not my name," replies Sonia, who goes by Teresa in the United States. I can't bring myself to translate the remark to Jacinta.

Sonia tells me about the beach house where she spends weekends during the summer. I translate. With a raise of her eyebrows, wide eyes, and a smile, Jacinta indicates to Sonia that she's impressed. From the corner of her mouth, Jacinta mumbles to me, "I never would have been able to give her that. We live in a neighborhood where there are murders at night."

We wait uncomfortably in the hotel's extravagant lobby while Sonia goes to get her adoptive parents and siblings. Sonia has an older brother and sister, both adopted and Salvadoran by birth, who also hope to meet their birth mothers someday. Their adoptive parents registered the three siblings' cases with Pro-Búsqueda at the start of their family trip to El Salvador. Within three days, the small human rights agency located Sonia's mother by tracing adoption records. The siblings' cases remain unresolved. Sonia's adoptive brother and sister didn't attend her reencuentro because "they were sleeping at the hotel." Sonia's adoptive mom privately tells me they didn't attend because "they were jealous."

Sonia seems elated to introduce her biological mother to her brother and sister. Her sister fights against tight lips, forcing a passably polite smile as she extends her hand to meet Jacinta's. The Pro-Búsqueda investigator later comments to me, "The siblings look like they are from Usulután." We pose for photographs in the hotel lobby. They invite us for lunch, but we can't stay because Jacinta has to get home to her son.

Sonia will depart El Salvador early tomorrow morning but wants to meet her biological brother. I navigate logistics, language, and cultural barriers before an audience of twelve invested listeners. Finally, a plan: Sonia's adoptive parents will pay for a taxi to bring Jacinta and her son to the hotel in the afternoon, and the two of them will return home before dark—because of the dangers in Jacinta's neighborhood.

As we near Jacinta's home to drop her off, I ask, "Jacinta, have you thought about what you're going to tell your son?" He doesn't know about Sonia. Jacinta's husband found out about Sonia's existence only two days ago, when Lucio, on behalf of Pro-Búsqueda, phoned Jacinta. At first, Jacinta denied being the mother, but Lucio perceived a cover-up, so he went the next day to visit her. She confessed to having given a baby up for adoption during the war and reluctantly agreed to meet Sonia. She told Lucio she feared rejection, just as Sonia had expressed in the moments before reunion.

Until two days ago, Jacinta's sister was the only person she'd told about the adoption. Jacinta was away from her family when she became pregnant and, promised that Sonia would go to good hands, she had kept her pregnancy a secret. She's not sure if she's going to tell her son about Sonia because "little boys talk." She adds, "Maybe I can bring him [my son] to the hotel and tell him that Sonia is a cousin."

As Jacinta climbs out of the jeep, Marco, the psychologist, advises, "You have to tell your son the truth. You can tell him the truth at your own pace. Little by little, with the years, he will come to understand it better. But if he comes to the hotel today, he has to know the truth."

After a lunch break, I sit in Pro-Búsqueda's psychology office when the secretary comes in. "Marco, the lady Sochil is here to see you."

Marco sighs, then turns to me and says, "Now you'll hear a Spanish that is difficult to understand." He explains that this woman—mother of a twenty-something-year-old joven encontrado—speaks differently, perhaps because of dentures and a hearing deficit. Tiny, fragile Sochil enters the office. I've noticed her at Pro-Búsqueda before, and, to be honest, I thought she was a beggar off the street. Marco shouts so she can hear him. Sochil from Apopa wears a soiled, cotton flower dress and a flowered apron. Her hair is shaved short on the top of her head and long and frail on the bottom. I find myself wondering if her mental facilities are intact.

"Liz, would you be willing to call Charles, Sochil's son?" Marco asks. Charles is a joven encontrado. Marco continues, "He lives in Michigan. They [the adoptive family] send money to support his [biological] mother, but the money has dried up." Marco outlines the phone call's three objectives: to ask about Sochil's *cuota* (allowance), to allow Sochil an opportunity to hear Charles's (Carlos's) voice, and to find out how Charles is doing since Sochil hasn't heard from him lately.

From the secretary's desk in the foyer, I phone Charles Eden in Michigan. A woman with a midwestern-US accent answers. I ask for Charles. She seems guarded. "Is this Nancy?" I say, stating the name of Charles's adoptive mom.

"Y-e-e-s-s-s-s," she draws out in more of a question than a response.

"Hi, my name is Liz, and I'm calling from Pro-Búsqueda in San Salvador."

"Oh, hello," Nancy sings. "Yes, yes. I'm so glad you called. How is Sochil? I was just thinking of her today. I haven't sent her money in a while. How's she doing with that? I sent her $200 at Christmas."

That was easy. Nancy Eden will send a check for Sochil on Monday.

"Yes, we helped her with some other things. Fixed her teeth. Got her a bed," Nancy says. "Charles will be so sorry that he missed her call. He would have loved to have spoken with her. Now, don't get Sochil's hopes up," Nancy trills, "but Charles is hoping to come to El Salvador next year. A delegation from our church goes every year."

"How is Charles doing? Sochil wanted to know."

From what Nancy says, Charles seems to have a full life with fatherhood, graduate school, sports, and teaching. "This was a stressful year for him. He became very sick at winter. But don't tell her that because it will make her worry. Just tell her that he's fine."

As the phone call draws to a close, Nancy expresses gratitude for the call, appreciative that we could communicate in English. "Tell Sochil that we love her. Give her a big hug. Tell her hello and that we think of her often. She is always in our prayers." After the call, I walk back into the psychology office where I tell Marco the update Nancy Eden had given me. He relays it through shouts to a grateful Sochil.

At 5:15 p.m. Lucio and I drive over to Sonia's hotel to deliver photographs from this morning's reencuentro. I promised the adoptive mother we'd bring them over when she told me Sonia wouldn't let her take pictures of the reunion. In the hotel lobby, we bump into Sonia's adoptive siblings. They direct us to their father, who sits at a poolside table. Lipstick marks the glass of juice the adoptive mother has been sipping from.

I hand Sonia's adoptive father a CD with digital photos of the reunion. As we say goodbye, I ask him, "How was your afternoon?"

"It was nice. Jacinta came with her son, and he swam in the pool." I feel delighted to hear that Sonia met her biological half-brother.

As Lucio and I walk toward the lobby, Sonia's adoptive mother intercepts us. "Hello, Sonia knows you're here but she's in the room crying. She wants to be alone." We say our goodbyes to her mother and express mutual gratitude.

Lucio and I drive off, closing out an exhausting workweek. "I have to buy a wedding present," he says. "The wedding starts at six [in the evening]." I soon find myself in a department store, perusing towels as a potential matrimonial gift for Lucio's friend. Lucio laughs at my suggestion of a picture frame. "We poor people only give gifts that are useful." He settles on a set of glasses with a matching pitcher. "You're coming to the wedding," he insists. "I already told Angélica." Lucio has to tell me ten times that crashing a wedding would be socially acceptable.

When I arrive at Lucio's, his daughter, Michele, puts confetti in my hand and sprinkles some in my hair. We walk next door to get Andrea, and she offers me clothes to change into. At the wedding celebration, thirty people cram into a one-bedroom apartment, sitting around a big table eating *panes con pavo* (Salvadoran turkey sandwiches). Streamers and balloons are taped to a bright-green wall. The bride and groom welcome me. The bride still wears her makeup but is now in a T-shirt, which facilitates breastfeeding. The wedding's unpretentious setting and lack of pomp remind me of Sonia's almost-impromptu reunion at Pro-Búsqueda. At both events, it was the love shared that mattered most.

Five days later at Pro-Búsqueda, Lucio asks me to translate to Spanish an email Sonia sent from Connecticut for her biological mother, Jacinta. In Sonia's message, she wrote about wondering every night what her mother looked like and tells Jacinta that meeting her was incredible—that she cried when she learned that Jacinta had agreed to a reunion because she knew that, after meeting, she would feel complete. She reassured Jacinta that she understands why she was put up for adoption and that she loves Jacinta for making that decision. It is because of Jacinta that she is happy, she concludes, noting that saying goodbye was the hardest thing she's ever had to do.

When I finish translating Sonia's letter, I stroll a few blocks to buy a chocolate-covered banana and encounter Jacinta! She bundles Sonia's half-sister in her arms. I tell Jacinta about the letter. She's headed to Pro-Búsqueda to receive photos. Her huge smile cannot outshine the sadness in her eyes. "I've been desperate to hear about Sonia," Jacinta says. She misses Sonia and worries that Sonia may be feeling sad too. She doesn't want to interfere with Sonia's happiness or her studies, she says.

When I return to my spot in the psychology office, I find Marco attending to Jacinta. Before exiting the room, I place a kiss on Jacinta's cheek to say goodbye. After she leaves, I translate to English the message she dictated to Marco. I paste into email her paragraph expressing maternal love, yearning, joy, gratitude—and send it to Sonia.

Though I don't ever speak with Sonia or Jacinta again, I wonder how their paths have changed for having found each other. I think about Sonia's eight-year-old brother, who lives in a dangerous neighborhood in San Salvador, swimming in the pool at Hotel El Presidente with a sister he didn't know he had. I recall the question he would ask his mom at Christmas: Why was she sad? Now he can understand that her sadness came from missing Sonia and worrying about her. Will Jacinta feel sad this Christmas, thinking of Sonia far away but thriving? Perhaps she will, but likely less so, thanks to the courage of a daughter who was thinking of her too and an adoptive family who supports their daughter's search for her biological roots and family origin.

10 Carmen's Reunion

Today Marco drives the jeep over a bumpy countryside lane, and Milto and I join for a three-hour journey to Morazán to prepare a mother for her upcoming reunion with her daughter. After choosing the wrong fork on a muddy road, we backtrack through a farming town to arrive at the home of Filomena Ramírez. In three days, Filomena will reunite with her twenty-seven-year-old daughter, Carmen, a young woman now herself a mother to a seven-year-old boy. When Filomena last saw her daughter, Carmen went by a different name and was two years old. Following her disappearance, Carmen was informally adopted and raised in El Salvador.

Corn husks protect the outside of Filomena's adobe home, and bamboo provides structural support. Filomena sits on a bed, a wooden plank surrounded by burlap sacks that serve as mosquito nets. The bed is one meter from the kitchen. A mud stove rises out of the floor of moist earth of uneven grade. Without electricity or windows, not much light enters the home, so we leave the front door open to see. Milto and Marco occupy the two chairs. I sit on a wooden board. Filomena, wearing a light-blue dress and white apron, perches on the edge of the bed, with her ankles crossed. She appears nervous. "I have fever," she says. The bandana on her head holds a large leaf in place, to relieve her pains, she tells us.

Milto and I leave to wander the village while Marco speaks with Filomena. As we stand on a lush soccer field on a plateau overlooking a valley nestled in the mountains of Morazán, Milto tells me about Carmen's
disappearance. "This zone was heavily impacted by the war," Milto narrates. "Filomena went into hiding in Ciudad Barrios. Fleeing for safety,
she could carry only one of her two children with her, so she left Carmen
behind in her uncle's care. When a grenade explosion injured Carmen's
left ear, her uncle took her to an FMLN clinic hidden in the jungle." I look
into the green valley at the treetops that ensconced the clinic twenty-three
years before. "When Carmen was at the clinic, her uncle lost track of her.
A woman affiliated with the FMLN adopted Carmen, and her biological
family lost contact with her. Carmen was treated horribly there and, at age
seven, ran away. When she was running away, a Salvadoran woman on a
bus took pity on her and brought Carmen home. That's the woman who
raised Carmen, but she has since passed away."

Milto's account elucidates reasons behind the simmering tension.
Marco warned us on the ride to Morazán that conflicts might arise during the reunion. Filomena blames her brother for Carmen's disappearance
since he was the last family member to have contact with her. Carmen is
also angry. When Marco contacted her about a reunion, she responded,
"Why do they look for me after all these years when I've suffered so much?
Why now?" Marco whistles to call us back to the house. When Milto and I
return to Filomena's, Marco tells me that when we first arrived Filomena
felt "so happy" because she thought I was Carmen. I bear no resemblance
to her family. Imagine how it would feel to have no conception of what
one's own daughter looks like.

Milto, sitting in a chair beside Filomena, asks whether she'll invite her
brother, Don Orlando—the man she blames for her daughter's disappearance—to the reunion. Filomena says he can't attend because he's a "drunk"
whose presence will ruin the event. Don Orlando is central to the reunion
and should be invited, Milto responds. Don Orlando brought Carmen's
case to Pro-Búsqueda, giving information that enabled Milto to find Carmen. Filomena repeats, "A drunk."

A four-year-old niece who has overheard chimes, "My uncle doesn't
drink anymore."

Milto and Marco then help Filomena plan for the "party." They count together that Filomena expects about twenty guests and suggest that she cook chicken and rice because "it feeds a lot of people." Milto encourages her to decorate the house for the reunion. "The important thing is that the family can sit together at the table," Marco advises. He gives her $50 from Pro-Búsqueda to "spend as you see fit" for the reunion.

Filomena's eighteen-year-old son, Samy, arrives, having just returned from working on a coffee plantation. The youngest sibling, he has a bright smile and honest, innocent eyes. "Forgive me, but I'm poisoned," he says, refusing to shake my extended hand. His clothes appear wet, not sweaty but oily.

As Marco, Milto, and I tramp through bamboo back to the jeep, I ask, "What was Samy poisoned with?" They confirm that he works with pesticides. Filomena cannot sustain the home on the meager amount she earns selling bread to dip into coffee. In the muggy jeep ride back to San Salvador, I think about Carmen. How will she react when she arrives to the earthen home in Morazán, to a mother seemingly afraid to greet her? Will the joy of reunion—the power of seeing herself reflected in her mother's eyes—soothe traumas from the grenade explosion and years of feeling abandoned? Many unknowns, but the next step is clear: for mother and child to re-meet.

. . . . .

Three days later, Marco, Milto, and I head out to Morazán for the reunion. "Carmen will ask the hard questions," Marco tells me in the car. "It will be the opposite of Sonia and Jacinta's reencuentro," one filled with love, forgiveness, and embracing. In Soyapango, we pick up Carmen and her son, both of whom I meet for the first time. Carmen refuses to eat breakfast. Before the long highway ride, we also stop to load in Carmen's best friend, Fidelia, and drop off Carmen's seven-year-old son with Fidelia's family, where he will stay for the day.

Traversing rocky, bumpy roads, we reach Filomena's home. Little girls wearing dresses, young boys, and eager adults wait on the dirt road, frozen in place. Their eyes study us as we pull up. Carmen steps out of the jeep, and Marco places his hands on Filomena's shoulders. He guides Filomena to where Carmen stands on the road. "Carmen," Marco says, "I'd like to introduce you to your mother, Filomena." The two women—mother and daughter—look at each other. Carmen cries first. They stand still in a face-off. Tall Milto puts one long arm around each, drawing them into a three-person hug. Then he backs away as the two women embrace. Their hug appears natural and forced at the same time.

Carmen lets go of her mother and paces toward the jeep to take refuge. "I want to go now. I want to go away from here," she whimpers to her friend Fidelia.

"Just drink water. Take a break," Fidelia says. "Everything will be okay."

Carmen crosses through the thick patch of bamboo leading to Filomena's house. I'm glad to see that Samy got the day off from work. One day without exposure to pesticides—and he can welcome his sister. The air is hot, the ground wet. There are flies and nowhere to sit. A woman introduces herself to me as Carmen's aunt. "I was with Carmen grinding corn when the grenade injured her ear." I noticed Carmen's jagged scar on the ride over. It looks like the bottom of her earlobe was sewn back on. The scar extends from her earlobe to the skin overlying her jaw.

Mother and daughter don't know how to interact. Marco admits in my ear, "I don't know what to do." He follows my suggestion to lead them on a walk. Marco later tells me that during the walk, Filomena repeated over and over, "Daughter, forgive me. Forgive me."

Filomena's brother, Don Orlando, the "drunk uncle," is here after all and seems clear of mind. After we visited Filomena to prepare her for the reunion, she apologized to her brother for blaming him for Carmen's disappearance and invited him to the reunion.

Relatives tell me that Carmen bears a strong physical resemblance to her sister. Her sister is a few years older and was with Carmen when Carmen became separated from their mother. Ill today, the sister is unable to trek the one hour to the reencuentro. While Marco leads the awkward mother-daughter walk, Milto and Don Orlando volunteer to pick up the sister. But minutes after their departure, she strolls in, wearing a lavender shirt, ponytail, and bright smile. She and Carmen do look so much alike!

Tough Filomena has transformed from the timid woman with the analgesic leaf on her head whom I met three days ago when Marco prepared her for the reunion. This woman wears a bright orange T-shirt, a trendy flower skirt, her hair gelled back in a tight ponytail, and a gold chain around her neck. She stands next to me along the side of the house while her daughter Carmen meets her sister. I put a hand on Filomena's back. "Do you want to hug your two daughters?" I say. In tears, she nods and reaches for the two girls. I encourage the aunt, who has told me of some of her sorrows, to join the group.

I leave them and stroll past the cornstalk-decorated entrance to the home. Inside, a string of balloons and poinsettia-patterned foil brighten the walls. The home is dimly lit by the morning sunlight that creeps in through the open door. A table covered by a tablecloth has been placed in the corner where Samy's bed had been on Wednesday. Don Orlando, Carmen's uncle, tells me that today is a happy day but also sad. Two of his own daughters were disappeared. Will he ever have a reencuentro with them?

A short walk past mango trees and chickens leads me to Milto, whom I find in the home of Filomena's niece. Carmen and Filomena recount the story of Carmen's disappearance. Samy and Fidelia stand outside, listening. I encourage Samy to enter. Just as Samy walks in, I hear Milto ask Filomena, "And you were pregnant when you lost Carmen?" Carmen wears a pained smile.

Outside, Carmen's confidante Fidelia fidgets with a water bottle as she leans in to me and Carmen's aunt. "Carmen has told some of her story to Pro-Búsqueda, but that's just the beginning. She has so much more to tell. She has suffered so much."

When our hosts call us to lunch, I linger outside with Marco as the honored family and friends file into Filomena's home first. By the time I walk in, all the guests have plates with rice and chicken, and two tortillas in hand, but no one is eating. They aren't talking either. Milto communicates "uncomfortable" to Marco with his eyes, and Marco shrugs. Then I see Milto's eyes change—he has an idea. "Filomena, this is your home," he says. "Maybe you want to lead us in a prayer. You're the head of the house."

Filomena nods.

"Maybe you want us to stand or get on our knees. However you like," Milto prompts.

"On our knees," Filomena replies. She then speaks for fifteen minutes, a mystical incantation of joy while forty knees rest on the damp, mud floor. Her lyrical voice lifts a prayer. "I thank you, God, for bringing her back to me. I thank you for my family.... May your blessings enter my brother....

I thank you, Father. Your love is great." She concludes, "Thank you, Jesus, for entering my body." Then the family sips a bountiful chicken soup, but uncertain silence still fills the room. Guests, some seated in plastic chairs in the room and others on foot in the doorway or outside, nibble at rice and tortillas served on disposable plates.

Despite Filomena's prayer, the atmosphere still feels dark and stagnant. Carmen shares a photo of her son, and Milto lends a flashlight as the photo is passed around. Marco suggests that the family introduce the guests to Carmen, but unsettling silence persists. After five more minutes of quiet and then more gentle prodding by Pro-Búsqueda, a round of introductions begin. Many are immediate family members, and a number of guests identify as Filomena's "Sisters in Christ." The tense silence resumes. Milto suggests singing. People smile shyly. At Milto's request, he and I belt out the chorus of a Cuban song. Then, Carmen's aunt says to Filomena, "Sing, my sister." Filomena warbles a hymn with a wiry, enchanting, sometimes piercing voice, rugged and natural like the hills of Morazán.

When Filomena announces that she'll sing another song, Carmen quietly asks Fidelia to leave with her. The two friends confer outside in the warm afternoon sun. "I want to go," Carmen says aloud. "Now." Carmen satisfied her commitment and doesn't want to stay a moment longer. We arrived at ten, and it's two in the afternoon, exactly the time we'd planned to leave. They tell Milto.

"Okay," Milto replies, "but you have to say goodbye."

Carmen shrinks and then agrees. "Okay, I'll stay for a bit more then."

When I reenter the cool, cave-like house, I see Fidelia standing at Carmen's side. Carmen addresses her family. "If you want to contact me, you can do so through Pro-Búsqueda."

"But do you have a telephone number that we can call?" Don Orlando asks, perplexed.

"Through Pro-Búsqueda," Carmen repeats, staring into the ground. Her aunt asks again for a phone number. Carmen gives the same answer.

The aunt, uncle, and mother seem surprised and protest together. "Can't we have a phone number? Isn't there a number where we can reach you?" Their longing and Carmen's hesitancy is heartbreaking to witness.

"Thank you for everything," Carmen responds, poised by the door for her exit.

Don Orlando stands for the goodbye. Filomena stands as well. Filomena's farewell remarks, slightly warmer than polite, express gratitude but feel reserved. Carmen is visibly relieved when we climb into the jeep to drive away.

After we drop Carmen off, Milto, Marco, and I talk about Carmen's refusal to give her family her phone number. Optimistic, Milto says, "I'm sure that when the corn is ripe in the cornfields, they will invite Carmen to eat tamales, tortilla, and *atol* [sweet corn drink]. I'm sure they'll be calling Pro-Búsqueda to invite her."

As we near the end of the long drive back to San Salvador, Milto reveals a final piece of Carmen's story. "It's because of Carmen's older sister that Carmen was lost. The sister was clinging to Filomena, saying, 'Mommy, don't leave me. Mommy, don't leave me,' and Filomena could carry only one of the two children, so she left Carmen."

"Do you think that the sister feels ashamed?" I ask.

"Yes," replies Milto, commenting that he observed signs of remorse in the sister. Though I can understand the family's pain, Carmen's sister shouldn't have to carry a lifelong repentance for clinging to her mother as a young child during a war, and neither should her mother. Filomena faced an impossible choice, thrust on her by the oppressive violence of the war.

At dinner, I describe the reunion to Ester, explaining that Carmen became lost after a grenade explosion severed her ear. "Reunions of children forcibly separated from their families are the most moving," Ester says. Families such as Carmen's faced the agony of not even knowing if their missing child had lived or died. Children didn't know they had a family.

How will the reencuentro alter Carmen's life? Her wounds cut deeper than the scar zigzagging across her ear. Carmen made it through the awkward reunion, where her closest biological kin felt like strangers. Pro-Búsqueda facilitated the reunion and will be available for support in the months that follow, but Carmen and Filomena will have to do most of the work of developing a successful relationship on their own. I pray that the corn harvest will bring the reconciliation that mother and daughter need to move forward after so many years apart.

.   .   .   .   .

The August Fiesta de Maíz (Corn Festival) comes and goes in Morazán, and, as the season turns, new seeds are planted. I don't ever see Carmen or Filomena again, but eleven months after their reunion, I'm home in California, and I telephone Marco at Pro-Búsqueda. He jokes that I'm calling from "the other side of the [border] wall." Marco tells me that Carmen came to his office recently. Carmen wants to have a telephone line installed in Filomena's home so that they can talk even more often than they already do.

11   Suchitoto with María Inés

On Sunday, the day after Carmen's reunion, I accompany Margarita and Lucio on a DNA-collection trip to Suchitoto in Cuscatlán, El Salvador's central and smallest department, located adjacent to San Salvador. María Inés, Ceci's mother, who does the cleaning at Pro-Búsqueda, has joined us to visit her native land. When a familiar tune comes on the car radio, I mention that I love the song. Margarita turns up the volume, and her face pales as she says, "Oh . . . this brings back memories. We were burying a compañera. We had just lifted her up by her arms. Somebody had a radio, and this song was playing."

> *Levántate y mírate las manos*
> *Para crecer, estréchala a tu hermano.*
> *Juntos iremos unidos en la sangre*
> *Hoy es el tiempo que puede ser mañana.*
>
> [Arise and look at your hands
> To grow, extend them to your brother.
> Together we go united in blood
> Today is the time that can be tomorrow.]
>
> —*"Plegaria a un Labrador"* (Prayer to a Farmer), Víctor Jara

We turn off the highway and cross a steel bridge, signifying our arrival to the farmland surrounding Suchitoto. At the first house we visit, María Inés and I sit with the eighty-year-old grandmother of a disappeared boy. Margarita asks, "How tall was your grandson when he disappeared?" The grandmother recalls that his head reached just below her waist. She stands and Margarita measures and records ninety-six centimeters, the average height of a three-year-old. The grandmother tells of running from bombs and surviving massacres. She's blind and cannot see the flies landing on her tropical mamey fruit, so Margarita and Lucio swat them away.

Margarita and Lucio collect DNA samples from the family while María Inés speaks with the grandmother about mutual acquaintances, asking each other who survived the war. I lay in the patio's hammock, admiring the garden and butterflies when for the first time I hear María Inés speak aloud about her sentiments on the war. María Inés tells the grandmother, "The armed conflict was very difficult. And who suffered the most? We did. The others are still in power. But what's most important is that we have a clean conscience." María Inés recounts hiding with her children in *tatus*, the underground shelters that Ceci had described to me. She tells of someone handing her candy, one piece for each child, and of feeding the *cipotes* (little children) sugar water so they would survive. The children would "walk all night, sleep on the path standing up, each with their backpacks on."

In our one-on-one interview at Pro-Búsqueda six months later, María Inés tells me more about her family's experiences in the war. "The death squad would come wearing civilian clothes to catch people at night and in the day. So many dead bodies filled the streets, people I knew, people who were hard workers, [killed] simply because maybe they had interacted with the guerrilla force." They lived in "horrible fear," caught in the middle of the war. "We all stayed quiet. If the soldiers came and asked us, 'Have you seen the guerrilla force?' 'No, we haven't seen anything.'" Then "when the guerrillas came by, they'd ask, 'Have you seen the army?' 'Nothing,' we'd say." As the danger increased, she faced the choice of staying with the guerrillas or being killed by soldiers. So, forty-year-old María Inés fled with six of her seven children, under the protection of the FMLN. Her oldest son, Arnulfo, age eleven, had joined the FMLN with his father.

I ask María Inés about Arnulfo. "Did you send him into the guerrilla force, or did he choose to go?"

"No, Liz. At the time, we didn't have a choice. They took him." I knew the military had drafted—kidnapped—child soldiers. Her words imply that the FMLN may have forcibly recruited Arnulfo, as is said to have occurred in some locations during the war.

María Inés spent three years in flight with her six young children. "We were like pilgrims. There were times we packed suitcases of clothes, and we had to toss them along the way." In her arms, she carried her two youngest sons, an infant and a toddler. Her son Arnulfo, the child guerrillero, would sneak off to find his mother. "When I was in the mountains in flight, we were hungry, and he would gather fruit—guavas, little green bananas—and bring them to me. Even though he wasn't with me, he'd find me." Soon after, Arnulfo was shot in the leg, an injury he never fully recovered from.

After the guinda, she returned home. "They [soldiers] had burned the house. Everything I found was completely burned." María Inés's constant flight resumed. One night, she went to a stream to wash clothes while holding her baby and tripped and broke her arm. Despite excruciating pain, she had to continue, carrying children through the night. Her elbow still bears the deformity.

Three years later, when Arnulfo was fourteen, he came to her and told her to get out. "'Look, there's going to be a land invasion and one by air without stopping for one week,' he said. 'Take Ceci, Andrés, [and] the [youngest] children and leave me the big ones [Rebecca and Carlos]. Rebecca started to cry, but I couldn't lose time. I had to come [to San Salvador], but they [Rebecca and Carlos] stayed." Her son Carlos was about nine, and her daughter Rebecca was thirteen. "They stayed and I came with that huge pain." She ached for Rebecca and Carlos, and especially for Arnulfo, who still struggled from the gunshot injury. "I remember all the love I wanted to give him, I couldn't." But she focused on "freeing the [younger] children so they wouldn't get killed." It was their best chance to survive.

María Inés fled to San Salvador with Ceci (age eleven), Alvaro (age seven), Andrés (a toddler), and her baby, Cristián. "My boy Arnulfo got me out. God gave me strength. But the people here treated me like a leper.

When you came from the war, they looked at you with contempt. My own relatives didn't take us in." María Inés had profound anemia and felt too weak to run. She had no money. Her baby had a belly bloated from malnutrition, and the two boys had measles and were vomiting, María Inés says, with reddened, watery eyes. "But God is great, and He gave me strength to survive."

In San Salvador, "my children would go out and beg." They would come back with tortillas—and the influences of the street. Once, her son Alvaro, at seven years old, came home drunk. "I said, 'What's going on son?' and he said to me, 'A man gave me a soda and since I was hungry, I drank it.'" An old lady from the market warned that the children would become lazy alcoholics. When María Inés's husband returned from the battlefield, he rejected the family. He was disgusted that the children were begging and angry that María Inés had left Rebecca and Carlos in Suchitoto with Arnulfo.

He said, "I don't forgive you, but I'll pay the rent." Still, it wasn't enough to sustain them. He pressured María Inés to put two of the boys up for adoption. They had heard of a lawyer who put children in places where they could be educated. Her husband said to her, "I prefer to see them with other people, that my children are eating and not drunk on the streets." When María Inés handed over her boys, Andrés and Alvaro, to be sent for care in Italy, she was told they'd be back within six months. But they were not returned, and she had no way to reach them. She had been deceived into placing them in permanent adoption.

After the war, she saw Pro-Búsqueda on television and put forward a case to find Andrés and Alvaro. "I didn't even ask [the lawyer] for five dollars for Andrés. They said they would help us with the children's studies. It was a lie. That lawyer got rich. He took the children far away from here. But we'll take him to justice. Father Jon said they gave him $20,000 per child."

Ceci and little Cristián remained with her all along, and Carlos and Rebecca eventually joined them in San Salvador. Arnulfo died in the war, a sorrow María Inés still holds present, and she yearns for her boys in Italy. Father Jon encourages her to accept herself. She shares with me Father Jon's words to her: "Nobody should shout at you, not even scold you." She feels better at Pro-Búsqueda than in her own house, where sometimes only music can distract her from her sadness.

Pro-Búsqueda located Andrés two years ago. "I was so emotional, I couldn't speak," she says about their reunion phone call. "Father Jon was with me, and I felt he gave me peace and strength."

She relates her first exchange with Andrés: "I said, 'Hello, son.' He said, 'Hello' in a different language. I said, 'It's been so many years since I've heard your voice, and today's the day I hear your voice. Thank you, son.' And 'How are you?' He said to me, 'Good, very good.' I said, 'Do you remember me?' 'Over there, in dreams,' he said. I couldn't speak, and he said, 'But you—are you well?' 'Yes,' I said, so excited. He couldn't speak either." María Inés then gave the phone to the Italian translator who passed on the message that Andrés felt "very happy and surprised."

Ceci spoke to Andrés too. "She said she was so happy, and she told him that he has lots of siblings here [in El Salvador], that we love him, that she dreams about him, and that she's missed him for so many years."

María Inés sent Andrés a letter because he was asking about his family's experience in the war. "I wrote him to tell him a little about the suffering in the war and said there was a lot I couldn't explain in a letter." She mentioned the adoption. "I told him that they [the lawyers] tricked me. I thought they [her two sons] would be together. Alvaro, the one who is studying to be a lawyer, is far [from Andrés]. I felt bad for so many years after [the reunion]." Her pain remains unresolved. "It's been a terrible shame that, despite the children I have at home, I can't overcome the emptiness I have in my heart. I still dream—I still talk with them." Therapy sessions at Pro-Búsqueda have helped but can't heal her irresolvable wound. "His [Andrés's] parents say that they don't want me to see him, and they don't want him to come. This situation is making me sick," she says, abruptly ending our one-hour interview at Pro-Búsqueda's office.

In Suchitoto, on the warm day in July on our data-collection excursion, María Inés tells the blind grandmother holding the mamey that her oldest son died as a guerrillero protecting the *masa* (civilian masses) during a guinda. She explains to the grandmother, "Two children were disappeared. They're in Italy now. I've had contact with one of them, Andrés. I don't know where the other is. I spoke with Andrés on the telephone last year." María Inés describes the strained relationship with Andrés.

"Don't you write him letters?" The grandmother's niece, who's joined us on the patio, asks.

"I can't. It creates problems for him with his [adoptive] family."

The niece's questions persist. "Can't you mail the letters to a different address?"

María Inés doesn't want a clandestine relationship. With wistful eyes, she says, "We have to wait. I hope to see him once before I die." She prays to God to give her life so she can hug and see them again.

As we drive along the open fields of Suchitoto, I observe something María Inés mentioned earlier: There is no place to hide. In the flat, dry plains, trees and shrubs are sparse. I mention the observation aloud as we drive past patches of chest-high cornfields. María Inés nods and responds, "Sometimes people would hide in the cornfields. The soldiers would burn the fields to get the people out." Across the open fields, distant mountains surround us, where Margarita fought as a guerrillera and sometimes descended to protect the people of Suchitoto.

At our next stop, Margarita interviews a man wearing a sombrero, the uncle of a disappeared child. María Inés takes my hand, leading me through his garden, showing me medicinal plants and vegetation we can eat. She tells me to take a bite of a chili pepper. It burns! She shows me a fruit whose dried rind is used as a spoon to serve beans. I ask how she learned so much about plants. "Liz, when one is poor, she cures herself with plants. And I observed how they treated the wounded during the war." She tells me of treating her son's gunshot wound with a salve, before sending him back into the hills. María Inés has a habit of picking plants and then requesting permission. Perfumed *paraíso* flowers are abundant in our hands when she asks the man if we can take them. He responds that of course we can and offers María Inés one of the dried rinds for scooping beans.

In the garden, she tells me about the romances of her life. During the war, "I wanted an illusion of safety, so I found someone else," she says. But FMLN factionalism kept them apart. "I was with the ERP [FMLN faction] and he wasn't, so we couldn't talk to each other. Sometimes we'd pass each other in the night, and I knew he was there, but we couldn't talk to each other. Since then, I've had no more."

Her longing, for her boys and for love lost, permeates a life she decorates with fragrant flowers. She survived the war, navigating six young children to safety. Two of her boys have yet to return to their mother's arms, but María Inés finds comfort in knowing they survived Suchitoto, where there was nowhere to hide. She prays for their well-being, even though she may never see them again. María Inés aches, and I imagine her boys in Italy do too, even if they fare well there. Love can stamp out the fire of war, but when it is impeded the innocent child survivors continue to suffer, even years after the cornfields have regrown.

·   ·   ·   ·   ·

We drop off María Inés near her home in Apopa. On our way back to the capital, Lucio announces, "Liz, you're going to get to see downtown San Salvador." The first historic site he and Margarita point out is the location of a massacre. Then Lucio draws my attention to workers on a hunger strike. A row of cots and tents line the entrance to San Salvador's Metropolitan Cathedral.

We drop Margarita off at the bus station, and, as Lucio navigates chaotic traffic past the multitude of street vendors, child beggars, and litter, he says, sounding ashamed, "There's a lot of disorder." He seems to know some of the street kids; at the very least, he knows the scene. He explains that they have a ringleader who sends the kids to beg. At the end of each day, they convene, divide the money, the leader takes a big cut, and they buy drugs.

Lucio offers to show me Cuscatlán Park. "There's a memorial here, a wall with the names of people who died during the war." Parking the car, Lucio says, "I suppose you don't want to get out because it's raining."

My seatbelt is already half off. "I do."

The wall lists, by year, the names of civilians assassinated during the war. The military created a separate memorial for soldiers. Also listed by year are the names of the disappeared. Lucio helped collect names for the wall, he tells me. I walk the eighty-five-meter length of the wall and then plant my feet to start reading names. Surprised, I notice that the first portion of the long wall is dedicated to the jóvenes encontrados. My eyes jump to Lucio's name. This is the first time he is seeing his name on the wall. I find the name of his wife, Angélica. And Amílcar's and Andrea's. I mention to Lucio that his is one of the few names on the wall of someone who is alive.

In the panel titled "1985," I look for the name of Lucio's father. Lucio discourages me. "It will take too long." I can tell he doesn't want to find the name today.

Marco, Margarita, and I go to La Libertad, the coastal department west of San Salvador, to prepare the family of US adoptees Isabel and Gloria for their reunion. At a fork in a dirt road, we pick up Ysidro, their oldest brother, a short, chubby man in his late thirties. He shows us the home he'll borrow for the event, with a generous patio, cement walls, and flushing toilet. Ysidro and his two siblings in El Salvador are convinced that their aunt sold Isabel and Gloria. "Ysidro, whatever conflict you have with your aunt can be discussed later," Marco advises. "But the last thing we want here is a fight. This is a wonderful opportunity to reunite with Isabel. And possibly for reconciliation." Ysidro nods and agrees to visit his sister to prepare her.

Thirty-one-year-old Isabel and twenty-six-year-old Gloria, raised in New York, will reunite with their siblings who remained in El Salvador, a sister and two brothers. Ysidro served in the Salvadoran military, as did their brother Chuy. Another brother died fighting for the FMLN. When we drop Ysidro off, Margarita comments, "I didn't like what he said about wanting to have two soldiers at the reencuentro."

Marco nods. "The last thing I want is to see rifles in the house." Then they talk about how *"re-loco"* (super crazy) Isabel and Gloria's brother Chuy is, a former soldier with a head "full of drugs and murder training."

Pro-Búsqueda feels busy for a Saturday morning. Marco's been preparing Isabel and Gloria for their reencuentro today. I see him in the kitchen, where he grabs glasses of water for the sisters. His worried eyes look from behind black-rimmed glasses. He sighs, "Margarita didn't tell them that their brother was in the military. Isabel just found out and is very upset. She's been in El Salvador doing human rights work."

When I emerge from the kitchen, Marco introduces me to Isabel, a young woman with black hair, wide brown eyes, and straight, white teeth. I extend my hand, and Isabel shakes it as she tells me, in English, that she spent the last month in El Salvador volunteering at an orphanage, where she's helping to build a greenhouse. She shows me a photograph of two girls in front of a bush with burgundy flowers. "This is my sister and me." In the photo, Isabel appears elementary-school-age and Gloria a toddler. When I ask how she got the photo, Isabel crisply replies, "My aunt gave it to me when she dropped us off at the airport. I was seven years old."

"You must remember a lot," I say.

"Oh, yah, I remember everything," Isabel responds, then rushes off.

I climb into Lucio's car. Marco drives Isabel and Gloria in Pro-Búsqueda's jeep, along with two US newspaper reporters. The US-raised sisters and siblings in El Salvador both agreed to the media coverage—to raise awareness about Pro-Búsqueda and the child disappearances.

We reach the godmother's home in La Libertad. Isabel and Gloria step out of the car. They stand hand in hand outside a tall gate, awaiting the moment they will set eyes on their family. The sisters cross through the gate onto the patio.

The family swarms together in one huge hug. Isabel and Gloria hug their two brothers and Pilar, their older sister. Pilar has thick, dark hair, like her sisters. The three sisters are crying. Isabel and Gloria place smoochy kisses on their brothers' and sister's cheeks.

Fifteen minutes pass. Few words have been exchanged. The US

reporter's barely legible notes read, "Still hugging and crying." The loudest sounds are the kisses delivered by Isabel and Gloria. Their tears pour onto Ysidro's shoulders as they stand in an embrace. The sisters move to the side of the house, squatting by the dirt, breathing and resting. Young relatives run over to meet the sisters. More kisses. I approach Gloria and touch her warm arm. "Gloria, whenever you're ready for English translation, I'm here." She responds with a nod. But the family is still filled by physical expressions of emotion. No words are needed.

The giant hug has moved to the shaded patio in front of the house. A *tía* (aunt)—not the aunt Gloria remembers who put the girls up for adoption—introduces herself to the girls. Marco and I translate. "I took care of you when you were *tiernita* [young]," the aunt says. Gloria melts with the aunt's words. The aunt, a *señora* (lady) advanced in age, beams as she extends her arms to embrace her niece.

Chuy, the *"loco"* second brother, introduces himself to Isabel and Gloria. He wears a red McDonald's T-shirt and black jeans. Two metal crutches brace against his forearm to support his weight. He leans forward on the crutches as his legs and feet curve limply backward to meet the ground. I translate an exchange between Chuy and Gloria. "Our parents were killed at 11:30 p.m. on the last day in August in the year 1980," Chuy relates. He tells Gloria, "You were one-year-old at the time. You were taken to a relative's home."

"Isabel, did you hear that?" Gloria shouts in shock. "He says our parents died at—"

Isabel interrupts, looks at me to translate, and commands, "Ask him how we came to be put up for adoption." When I translate Isabel's question for Chuy, he replies in Spanish that the older siblings were taking care of the girls, but then the aunt found the girls and sold them.

I pause a bit too long, thinking about how to translate his words in a sensitive way. "What did he say?" Isabel implores. I call Marco over by shouting his name.

Marco rushes to where I stand. I tell him quickly in Spanish, "He's talking about the aunt and that she profited from selling the sisters." The aunt, whom the older siblings in El Salvador view as "evil," declined an invitation to the reunion.

Marco addresses Isabel and Gloria with a veneer of calm. "He's just saying what he said before about your family." The sisters seem ready to move on, but a Salvadoran journalist translates Chuy's words into English. "He says that your aunt trafficked you to the United States. She made money from selling you." The US reporter scribbles hastily on her notepad, a jarred look on her face. Isabel, with eyes and mouth agape, lips twisted, and head tilted for a better angle, looks confused but keeps on listening.

Marco interrupts in English. "Hey, just know that's not the whole truth. There are two sides to every story."

I walk across the patio to the free-standing kitchen to get Ysidro, who has been busy preparing the meal. He motions to me with his hands that Chuy is crazy and then joins Isabel and Gloria on the patio.

I stand against the wall, where the US journalist is scribbling and ask her, "Were Isabel and Gloria adopted into the same home?"

"No, they went to separate families. Isabel fared much better than Gloria. Isabel went to a home where the family cared for her."

"And Gloria?"

"She was adopted by a family that didn't treat her well. By age twelve, she was bouncing around between foster homes. She's basically raised herself since she was twelve."

Ysidro approaches Isabel and places a sleeping baby in her arms. Without stirring, the chubby, slumbering infant naps with his head resting over Isabel's left shoulder, his small body supported by her chest. I watch five minutes of Isabel rocking her sleeping nephew and talking to other family members while still meeting cousins, nieces, and nephews for the first time.

The family serves an early lunch. Isabel hears that she has cousins in Dallas, Los Angeles, Arkansas, and New Jersey. "I'll have to take a road trip around the entire country!" she says. I struggle to swallow my tortilla because now I hear Isabel asking hard questions at the next table. "Was I in the room when my parents were killed?" Marco seems to grow more nervous with each question. Isabel has just learned she had two older sisters, nineteen and seventeen years old, both killed on the same day as their parents, and that their mother was pregnant when slaughtered.

A few minutes later, I pull Marco aside to tell him that I heard that the parents' graves are nearby. Then I ask him in private, "Do you believe that the aunt really sold them for money?"

He responds, "She put them up for adoption, and sometimes there is money involved. But we will never know if she received money. I think that she was doing what she believed was the right thing. And time has proved her right—Isabel and Gloria are both well."

Isabel and Gloria do seem *well*. Despite the hot sun and overwhelming emotions, they embraced tough questions. They're alive, educated, and making their way through early adulthood in the United States. Respectful of their relatives and the memory of their murdered parents, the sisters have started a new chapter: of belonging and reconciling the violent past of their early years with the promise ahead.

•   •   •

After lunch, Marco drives Isabel, Gloria, Ysidro, and the US reporters two kilometers east along the dirt road to Ysidro's adobe home. I wander to a neighborhood shop with Margarita and the Salvadoran journalist. He tells us, "Ysidro joined the military because he wanted to figure out who killed his parents and seek revenge. Chuy was drafted and was in the Atlacatl Battalion. He had no choice but to join. He stayed because of his family's poverty. He was earning a wage in the military. Who knows what he did to get himself up to the Atlacatl Battalion." The journalist takes a bite of Chiky cookies and gulps a cola.

I walk back over to Lucio, who hovers near the trunk of his car. I ask him about the Atlacatl Battalion. "Not now," Lucio says, because Chuy is only a few paces away. Lucio and I move to the front of the car. Leaning on the hood, he tells me, "The Atlacatl Battalion was one of the worst, most barbaric of all." I have trouble getting the syllables in the correct order, so Lucio grabs a stick and writes the battalion name in the sandy road. He scratches it out as soon as I've read it. "Atlacatl. The US trained them. They were notoriously violent with civilians. They'd cut open the wombs of pregnant women, cut people's heads off. I spoke to a survivor once. They shot him, but he didn't die. He played dead. They cut at his hand to remove his rings. He was still playing dead."

I'm reminded of Chuy's limp. Looking at Chuy to be sure he's not listening, I ask Lucio, "Do you know how Chuy was injured? Did it happen in the war?"

"Yes, I know about it," Lucio says, squinting, his gaze looking to me and the faint reflection of sun on the beige rocks of the dusty road. "I worked on this case for a while. A couple of years ago, Chuy told me. A grenade exploded on him during a military operation." Lucio's eyes widen. His forehead tightens and eyebrows raise, his tone somber, respectful, pitying.

Lucio, a joven encontrado, has seen a lot. "What was your reencuentro like?" I ask him.

"There were two," he says. "The first was in 1995 and the second in 2001. In 1995, I reunited with my two sisters. There was a third sister, though, and I knew that she was alive. No one believed me until we found her. In 2001, the rest of us reunited with her. I didn't cry, but she fainted when she saw us." Lucio continues talking under the searing sun. "My mother was murdered on November 9, 1980." The same year Isabel and Gloria's parents were killed.

"Do you know why they killed your mother?"

"They said that she cooked for the guerrilla force," Lucio says, even and calm.

"Is that true?"

"Probably. The soldiers came to the home and asked for my father. My mother told them he wasn't in the house. They took her. She told me that she'd be back, but she didn't come back. My sister was with me. By night-fall, I was crying. My father found her [corpse], and we buried her. They say that I saw her body, but I don't remember. I must have blocked it out. Her breasts were cut out. She was pregnant. Her belly was cut open."

Lucio prides himself on remembering precise details from the war, but this marks the first time I hear him admit that some aspects were unrememberable. Like Gloria, he was two years old when soldiers killed his mother. "We were eight boys. Only the youngest survived—me. The other seven died. My three sisters are alive. I remember when my first one [brother] died." His brother, a guerrilla, died in an ambush.

Then, as we stand near the car, Lucio tells me about his father's death. "My father had a dream before he died. He dreamed that he cut his leg while planting seeds, and blood sprang onto the earth. Then shrapnel cut off his leg, just the way it had in his dream. Lots of blood spilled on the earth. There was a hole in his head too, where his nose had been. The day it [the fatal grenade blast] happened, I'd gone out from the camp to get fruit because I was hungry. My dad found me and hid me. He told me to stay at the camp. He left. I climbed a tree to see where he went. I heard an explosion. I was filled with a horrible feeling. I knew it was him when they came back to the camp carrying someone in a hammock. I attended to him. There was so much blood. 'I want to go poo-poo,' he said. 'It's okay. Just do it right here,' the lady told him. I cleaned him after he went to the bathroom. It was two in the afternoon, this time of day. The sun was like it is now."

"Do you remember what his last words to you were?" I ask.

"No, I don't remember exactly. 'Te quiero [I love you],' maybe. I was seven years old. I was in shock. The ladies there told me to go to sleep. I don't know where we buried him. And I didn't even know which way to tell them to put the cross, because here the cross goes at the head if it's an adult and at the feet if it's a child. I didn't know where his head was, and I would never be able to find where he's buried."

I feel myself turning pale just as the Pro-Búsqueda jeep returns with the reuniting sisters. After smiling at me through the rolled-down back-seat window, observant Isabel asks, "Are you okay?" I'm touched by her empathy on an intense day for her.

Isabel and Gloria climb out of the jeep and decide to visit the cemetery. The five living siblings will visit the graves of their deceased parents together. Margarita helps Chuy into the car. "You'll be more comfortable in the front," she says. When Chuy sits in the back seat anyway, Margarita helps to accommodate his crutches. I savor the poignant exchange: a former guerrillera concerning herself with the comfort of a crippled soldier from Atlacatl who was injured attempting to kill civilians and FMLN fighters.

Pilar and Ysidro settle into the back seat with Chuy. There's an open spot in the front seat of Lucio's car. I climb in, as instructed. Margarita will stay behind with the Salvadoran journalist. When I comment that I feel bad that Margarita can't join us, Lucio responds, "That's why Pro-Búsqueda needs another car. In a pickup truck, the whole battalion would fit." Lucio's inappropriate joke makes me chuckle.

At the cemetery, Lucio and I watch from a distance as Isabel and Gloria kneel to the ground. No sobbing; just humbly, quietly kneeling. Lucio looks across the cemetery to a uniformed man. "I knew there was a soldier here. I saw the boot prints when we walked in."

I imagine boot prints in the earth floor of the home that Lucio's mother was abducted from. "Does it bother you to be here with a soldier who was in Atlacatl?" I ask.

"Why do you think I'm staying back?" Lucio replies.

We return to the home of the godmother so Isabel and Gloria can say goodbye. Shakira plays on the stereo as Gloria dances with her younger relatives. Margarita and I stand on the edge of the patio, and she tells me the story, as she understands it, of Gloria and Isabel's disappearances. I ask who she believes killed the parents. Chuy swears it was the guerrillas, while Ysidro says it was the Salvadoran military. "We [Pro-Búsqueda] confirmed that it was the military," Margarita says.

I comment that it feels refreshing to hear the truth. Lucio chimes, "We don't know the truth. We deduce it."

"Why were the parents killed?" I ask.

"Because they were a Catholic family and went to church," Margarita replies. "Nothing more than that. The church was linked with the Left in the soldiers' eyes. So, the mother, father, and the nineteen- and seventeen-year-old sisters were killed. Ysidro escaped out the window with the four younger children [Chuy, Pilar, Isabel, Gloria]. The youngest, Isabel and Gloria, were taken to other family members. I don't know how the aunt found them, but she did. She gave them up for adoption in the United States."

At the godmother's home, out comes a black duffel bag full of clothes and toys, gifts from the sisters. Lucio and Marco play basketball versus Margarita and me. With two flat balls that can't be dribbled, we shoot into the rebar hoop, avoiding the barbed-wire clothesline as we play.

At five o'clock, we head to San Salvador. I think about the power of the reunion for Isabel and Gloria—and how in the wordless moments the siblings gelled together. The reunion, though healing, also brought challenges, and Pro-Búsqueda will be available for them if they request support.

Once back in the capital, Margarita and I convince Lucio to take us to Cuscatlán Park, where Pro-Búsqueda hosts a festival in honor of the disappeared Serrano Cruz sisters. The musicians, vendors, and a hundred guests fill the park. Above a grass field beside the war memorial, a Pro-Búsqueda banner hangs between two trees. María Inés munches on an ear of corn and has another one sticking out of her purse. Isabel and Gloria now join a community that celebrates the disappeared children and fights for justice.

One week later, in the chaos of downtown San Salvador, I see a familiar face: Pilar, the older sister of Isabel and Gloria! Her hair is thicker and wavier than her sisters', but the resemblance in their smile is striking. She's selling coffee and sweet bread from a little cart.

Pilar grins as I greet her on a street filled with beauty salons, barbershops, and two-dollar pirated DVDs. "I've been wanting to go to Pro-Búsqueda to get the photographs [from the reencuentro]," she tells me, "but I don't have Pro-Búsqueda's phone number." I show her the tattered Pro-Búsqueda business card that I carry in my coin purse, and she copies down the organization's phone number. Her children mill about on the street and in the nearby beauty salon. I ask how many children she has. "Let's see, how many are they?" Pilar jokes in reply as she smiles to her friend who sweeps in the beauty salon.

Pilar tells me that she's been hurting since the reencuentro. She misses Isabel and Gloria and feels distant from her brothers. "I grew up on my own," she says, mirroring the words the journalist used regarding Gloria. "No one I know has had experiences like mine," she adds. I tell her about the support services and workshops available through Pro-Búsqueda.

Pilar says that Isabel is still volunteering in San Salvador, and they plan to see each other in twelve days. "Isabel said she'll take me to the United States, but I told her that I can't go because of the children. I can't leave them. Isabel said we could bring all of the children. My husband started to cry when I told him." I find myself feeling sad after being with Pilar. It's not just the trauma from the war, being an orphan, the forced separation from her sisters, or the reencuentro. It's that the struggle continues. Pilar is supporting seven children. One coffee from her cart costs twelve cents. How many cups does she sell in a day?

Like Pilar, many of the people I've met in El Salvador are still struggling, two decades after a war when brothers fought brothers. How does a nation recover from the emotional tumult and devastation with so many of its people experiencing financial scarcity? Pilar may have an opportunity to go north to the United States with a sister who promises to take her. But she chooses to keep her immediate family together, even though it might mean sometimes not having enough to feed her children. Isabel, Gloria, and Pilar escaped out the window. The extent to which Isabel and Gloria have the means to help Pilar escape poverty may fluctuate over time, but the reaching itself is an act of love. A symbol of the spiritual wealth of Salvadoran families and the devotion of sisters who've only just met.

13 Meeting Angela

On Monday morning after a fun Sunday beach day with Lucio's and Margarita's families, I'm back at Pro-Búsqueda. Lucio plants me in the meeting room to watch a documentary that will teach me about "the reality of war," he says. *Victoria,* a one-hour film by FMLN's Radio Venceremos, tells a history of combat in a nation bloodied by greed. Just as I'm thinking that war doesn't make sense, in walks joven encontrado Raúl, the receptionist at Pro-Búsqueda whose mother and grandmother died fighting with the FMLN. "I like this song," Raúl says, referring to the movie's musical score. He sits down. "I wish I could've joined the guerrilla force. I was too young, only five years old."

"You don't care that you would have died?"

"No, because I would have died for an ideal," he replies.

The second time Lucio checks on me, the screen depicts government soldiers packing a land mine into the ground. "One of those [mines] killed my dad," Lucio says, then leaves the room.

Many battles later, I look up to see Margarita, Lucio, and Raúl standing in the doorway, peering into the room where I watch the film. "That's a good movie," Margarita comments. She knows the names of all the *comandantes* (commanders). As FMLN rebels on screen break the windows of a well-to-do house with the butts of their guns, Margarita remarks, "I had the pleasure of breaking glass."

The film portrays an FMLN fighter announcing his call to fight: to protect El Salvador from "selling out." I gather he is referring to capitalism, US special interests, neocolonialism, and corporate profiteering. Lucio quips, "It used to be that *we will* sell out. Now it's that *we did* sell out." He feels that his government does not represent the people—that it sold itself to the highest bidder.

Margarita, Lucio, and Raúl name massacres by date and location. A peculiar nostalgia fills the room. Then they leave me to watch in silence again. Between answering Pro-Búsqueda's telephone, Raúl pops his head back in. "There are lots of movies about the war. I wish I could see my mom in one of them. I wish I could see my mom." As bodies, buildings, flags, and cars are desecrated on the screen in flames, Raúl points. "That's over there, at the fountain, two blocks away." Two blocks away and seventeen years in time.

Raúl goes back to his desk in the foyer. Lucio returns after the film ends. "What did you think of the movie?" Lucio asks.

"I think that it's good for me to see the level of violence that existed in this country—and I think that I don't believe in violence." Gandhi, Nelson Mandela, Martin Luther King Jr., and Óscar Romero are my heroes. I tell Lucio about Raúl's wish to have joined the rebels.

"Raúl doesn't know war," Lucio says with a cool shrug. Lucio survived five years running from bombs from ages two to seven while Raúl was safe in an orphanage. Lucio's expressionless face is a reminder of the intense suffering of children during the violence of war.

Earlier in the day, I phoned a joven encontrada recently located by Pro-Búsqueda in Kentucky. Her DNA matched with a father and two siblings in El Salvador, but she's not ready for a reunion. Like Lucio's mother, her mother was assassinated in the war. One sibling who also lives in the United States already had a reencuentro. When I asked the joven encontrada in Kentucky about a reunion, she replied in sweet, southern drawl, "I have a lot to think about." She was at work at a bank and said she'd call later—progress.

After watching the FMLN film and thinking of the young woman in Kentucky, I return to my desk and email the US journalist who attended Isabel and Gloria's reencuentro. I encourage her to include Pro-Búsqueda's contact information in her news article, for readers who may have been separated from their families due to the Salvadoran Civil War. Lucio and I spoke this morning about the right to identity, prescribed in the United Nations Convention on the Rights of the Child, ratified in 1989. Everyone has the right to identity—the right to know one's history and origins—including children adopted transnationally out of a war. The right to identity transcends ideology. It's a right of every child that we must uphold.

Even though Raúl's mother died fighting with the FMLN, because Pro-Búsqueda helped him to reconnect with his family, he understands where he came from. He knows his family's *story*—a story that gives him pride, courage, and meaning in life. The disappeared children still missing do not have that closure. Many were too young at the time of separation to remember their past and believe that their parents willfully abandoned them. They don't understand the struggles of the war or the treachery of many of the transnational adoptions. Fourteen-year-old Sonia from Connecticut and sisters Isabel and Gloria from New York chose to reconnect with their biological families. Whether or not the young woman in Kentucky chooses to reunite, healing has begun. Now she knows she has family in El Salvador and by finding her, Pro-Búsqueda has given her the choice.

One week later, after a visit from my mom to El Salvador, Father Jon asks me to give him another lesson on the forensic genetics software, DNA View. The program uses statistical equations to assess for kinship matches once DNA profiles result from the lab. We installed it on his computer at Pro-Búsqueda two weeks ago, and I began teaching him the forensic math and programming skills needed to run the software. He was a focused student and became distracted only once—when his assistant handed him the newly issued report by the Inter-American Court of Human Rights following up on the Serrano Cruz ruling. After reviewing the hard-copy report, he turned to me and said, "They came down hard on the state." He summarized the court's conclusion: "That the government leaders should *dejen de joder* [stop fucking around]." I chuckled, but he didn't crack a smile. Then Father Jon got right back to studying DNA math.

This morning, I teach Father Jon for three hours. We lean over his desk toward the computer screen as he practices running genetic kinship analyses in the software. It's a pleasure to spend time with him, focused on an important task.

At 11:30 a.m. an incoming phone call on his cell phone interrupts our lesson. He rises from behind his desk and speaks in careful English with the accent of a well-educated Spaniard. Early in the call, slowly and exuding measured calm, he says, "The adoptions were not necessarily illegal but rather illicit, one could say. . . . Could you please repeat that? I have not adequately understood. . . . Why are you asking these questions?"

I surmise that Father Jon is talking about the transnational adoptions that occurred during the war. Lucio has told me that "the people in the US weren't at fault. They were just people who couldn't have kids and wanted to help. The intermediaries were the guilty parties." Lucio explained that a number of adoptions, though illegal in El Salvador, were "irregular" but legal according to US law.

When Father Jon hangs up, he tells me that the call was from the adoptive father of Angela, a Salvadoran-born adoptee raised in the United States. Father Jon fielded what seemed to be a rapid pace of nervous questions. "Angela will be here between 12:00 and 12:30 p.m.," Father Jon informs me. "You can collect her DNA sample and do the interview," he gently commands.

I notify Margarita, the investigator in charge of Angela's case. "Today, I'm leaving at one [o'clock]," Margarita replies, rushing her words and tensing her arms at her side while she speaks. "I have to make some purchases because my husband is leaving for Sweden."

I have ten minutes to eat the sandwich that Lucio's wife, Angélica, made for me yesterday. But I can't get myself to sit because I realize the meaning behind what Margarita has just told me. I find her and ask, "How long is your husband going to Sweden for?"

"For at least one year," she responds. Not a short trip and not for vacation.

Margarita wears a tight, green blouse and black miniskirt. I tease her that she chose the outfit "so he knows what he'll be missing." She grins.

I'm washing the smell of hard-boiled egg off my hands when I hear someone calling me. Angela has arrived. She's speaking on her cell phone to her worried father in the United States. Father Jon walks over to me. "Talk with her," he requests.

I invite Angela to join me in the front office. With a US accent and large brown eyes typical of Salvadorans, Angela appears to be about twenty years old. She has come to begin a search for her biological mother. Sitting across the desk from her, I introduce myself as a volunteer for Pro-Búsqueda. "They asked me to interview you because I speak English." Angela is shaky, crying. She dabs a folded napkin to her cheek. I tell her about Pro-Búsqueda's DNA bank. She's heard about it and agrees to provide a DNA sample. She learned about DNA testing in her anthropology class, she says.

With Angela's eyes still tearing, I collect her DNA sample, scraping the *palito* against the inside of her mouth as I've seen my Pro-Búsqueda colleagues do throughout the countryside. I hand the sample to Margarita, who receives it and then leaves to see her husband off to Sweden.

Angela and I begin the interview. "Some of the questions may be painful. We'll go as slow as you need. When were you last seen by your biological family? Who was responsible for your adoption? Do you have a birthmark? Were you baptized?" We fill out the family tree. Angela knows her original surname and has heard that before her adoption she may have been called Helena. Angela grew up in Berkeley, the town where I've lived for the past eight years! The exchange warms as we discover that our sisters are neighbors—our nephews even attended the same small family-run day care. It feels odd to mention Ashby Street and Walgreens, but it serves an important purpose: establishing trust.

"Angela, I want you to think of me as someone you can ask your questions to," I say as we near the end of the interview. "I know that you're smiling right now, and that is really wonderful to see. And I also know there'll be times when you won't be smiling. You might be crying. You can call me or come to my house in Berkeley." Angela's intent gaze looks at me. "I have been so blessed, fortunate that many Salvadorans have been generous in sharing their stories with me. The least I can do is use the awareness that I have gained to help you, to listen to you. You can talk to me, and I might understand a little more than other people at home."

Angela nods, smiling through tears. "Father Jon Cortina said to me yes-terday on the telephone, 'Wow, you're not freaking out. I would be freaking out,' and I said, 'Don't worry, that will come later.'"

This is Angela's first visit to El Salvador. She has always known that she was adopted as a baby. Her Berkeley parents kept her well informed about Salvadoran politics, history, and culture. She flushed her green card down the toilet when she was three years old, imitating something she saw on a cartoon. It's been an ordeal to prove her existence since, and she's only recently been issued her first passport, one bearing the US eagle. "But I didn't have to pay the ten-dollar tourist visa [to enter El Salvador] because I'm Salvadoran," Angela tells me, with pride.

"As you connect more with your culture, there will be many other ben-efits. This is just the beginning," I reply.

"I never know what to ask," says Angela, alluding to her state of shock. She expects that most of her questions will come later, though there's one issue that perturbs her. When she arrived at the CIS (Centro de Intercambio y Solidaridad), the Spanish-language school for tourists where Ester teaches, Angela learned from Ester that she could search for her biological family, which is how Angela found her way to Pro-Búsqueda. But Angela also over-heard Ester mention that Angela may have been kidnapped. Angela adores and trusts her parents in Berkeley. Could she have been stolen?

Careful to state that I don't know the details of her case, I speak gen-erally about the circumstances that led to transnational adoption in Pro-Búsqueda cases I'm familiar with. In vague terms, I tell of deceitful lawyers and corrupt judges. Angela looks even more confused. So, with-out mentioning names, I say, "Women were told that their children would be taken to a safer place and then returned. Mothers, desperate to save the lives of their children, obliged. So, the adoptions were legal in the paperwork sense, but the mothers had been lied to. In some cases, lawyers even received money for the children, though the mothers had handed over their children with the best of intentions." I pause to gauge Angela's reaction. "I'm not implying that's what happened to you. I just wanted to demystify some of the language you've been hearing."

Angela appears appreciative and much less shaky than when we began the interview. "Yes, I read in some papers that my mother gave me up to save my life."

With the interview completed, we chat. Mexican ranchera music plays on the radio. I remark that she's handling the search amazingly well. Angela smiles and says that her adoptive family "is freaking out," which seems consistent with what I observed when Father Jon tried to calm her frantic dad on the phone. In the fall, Angela will begin university at UC Davis and commute from Berkeley. There are so many changes happening in this young woman's life. I give her *Historias para tener presente*, the book containing the testimonies of Lucio, Andrea, and Amílcar, and remind her that we don't know the extent to which her adoption was connected to the war. Angela thanks me and begins a goodbye.

"Where are you going now and how are you getting there?" I ask.

"I was just going to take a taxi on the street but—" Reading the disapproval on my face, she contemplates aloud, "I suppose that's not a good idea." I give her the phone number of a trustworthy taxi service and then, learning it's a short distance, offer to walk her to her guesthouse.

As we stroll, Angela comments, "It's interesting to be learning about El Salvador's history through the cultural programs at the CIS because, it's like, this is my history too." She asks about my thesis. She plans to major in sociology and wants to understand the factors that lead youth to enter gangs. "I know there's more, beyond the reasons commonly mentioned in the literature." She works with teens at a gang-prevention program in Berkeley and tells me about a term paper she wrote on the notorious Salvadoran gang, MS-13.

Angela says she wants to see me again soon. We plan to stay in touch through email. During our goodbye, I am given immaterial gifts that lighten my spirit: "Thank you so much; you really helped me" and a hug. Little do I know that in the years that follow, I will have the honor of being by Angela's side on her long journey home.

14 Meeting Pedro

After dropping Angela off, I walk with a Pro-Búsqueda employee to an open-air market to buy a chocolate-covered banana. As we cross the boulevard, she says, "A *pandillero* [gang member] sat right next to me on the bus on my way to work today. The *cobrador* [fare collector] had to give him one dollar so he wouldn't assault anyone." I ask why she didn't get off the bus earlier. "We were in an ugly neighborhood." Back at Pro-Búsqueda Marco is out, so I have the psychology office to myself. I type field notes with one hand, holding the chocolate-covered banana in the other. I'm resting with my feet up on the desk when Pedro enters the office. He pulls up a white plastic chair and sits down.

Ester told me about Pedro, the *joven encontrado* who lives at Pro-Búsqueda. During one of our after-dinner talks, she said that the FMLN forced Pedro's parents to abandon him. Then he became involved with drugs and gangs. She once took him, along with a young woman, for a job interview at the UCA. The young woman got a job; Pedro did not. Ester related, "The interviewer saw the scars on Pedro's face and asked if he'd been involved in gangs. He said, 'no.' What was he going to say?"

A few weeks later, when cleaning up after the festival at Cuscatlán Park, Pedro and I folded a Pro-Búsqueda banner together. To me, folding cloth with someone symbolizes friendship. Yet, the whole time, I was cognizant that his hands have done violent acts. That evening, I told Ester that I felt uncomfortable knowing that Pedro had hurt—maybe even killed—people. "*Aw*, it's not his fault," the former guerrillera said. "He was on the street since he was seven. People gave him drugs. He was obligated to do what he did." When we finished folding the banner, Pedro and I exchanged smiles. But we haven't spoken face to face until now.

I eat my chocolate-covered banana and partially listen as Pedro talks about quitting smoking. "It was the first vice I left behind. I used to be so filled with vices," he says, his speech slow and deliberate, his voice gentle and steady. His black hair is combed above his angular jaw and scarred skin, his shirt neatly tucked into his brown pants.

"Pedro, you weren't here on Monday or Tuesday," I say. "Where did you go?"

"I went to see an aunt to ask for her forgiveness. From the world where I come from, it's difficult to ask for forgiveness, but I went to Usulután to see her. That's where I was." Thinking of "the world where he comes from" seems to have shaken him. Pedro looks to the ground and pauses. Then he starts remembering aloud from the day of his rebirth—the day Pro-Búsqueda found him. "I was working at a carnival," he says. "Arsinio from Pro-Búsqueda found me. I was working at the game where you shoot a gun and if you hit a target, you get a prize."

Pedro's stream of consciousness drifts backward to earlier in childhood, to when he escaped his adoptive parents. Ester had told me of their vicious abuse that led him to run away. "I was with my adoptive family until I was seven, and then I just wanted to be free." Then he describes the depravity at the carnival, of *that* world he came from. "When I worked in the carnival, I was so full of drugs."

"What kinds of drugs?"

"Marijuana, coke, crack, and the pill [Valium]. I spent years of my life as if in a dream because I smoked marijuana all the time. My face was very swollen. My skin was pale. I was so sick," Pedro says. "So my boss at the carnival took me to the hospital, but they wouldn't treat me. The doctor said, 'I won't treat him because he's going to die, and then you'll blame me.' My boss pulled out his gun and said, 'Either you treat him, or I shoot you.' So the doctor said that he'd treat me, but if I died, it wasn't his fault. My blood was yellow. It wasn't blood anymore because of all the drugs. After I got out of the hospital," he continues, "I went back to the streets again. That's when I became initiated into the gang. They told me to choose my name. So I chose Goblin."

"What does Goblin mean to you?" I ask.

"Something diabolical. It was such a violent world. I come from a world so full of violence. I lived in a world without laws. I lost all respect for the laws. I evaded the police by giving them so many different names, and I never carried my documents, so they could never bring me in." Pedro adds, "I entered MS when I was nine years old. No one enters that young. I was raised with a boss. And then he died."

I ask what he had to do for his initiation into the gang. He avoids the question by repeating, "So full of violence . . ."

I can't resist asking, "Did you kill anyone?"

"No, these things you can't talk about." He blushes.

I persist. "How many?"

"No, you don't talk about this. I used to spend nights to myself crying." Pedro is twenty-one. The boy whose life he describes was eight, ten, and fifteen, spilling blood with fists, knives, and guns. Sitting alone in this room with him, I don't want to hear more about spilling blood, but I'm intrigued, and Pedro is already deep into telling gang stories.

"This is when my hatred for 18 was born in my heart." Pedro refers to his gang's nemesis, Calle 18 (Eighteenth Street), which was started by Latino immigrants as a street gang in Los Angeles. Pedro's allegiance is to what he calls Salvatrucha, or *eme ese* (MS) for short—also known as Mara (Gang) Salvatrucha, or MS-13. Salvadoran refugees founded MS-13 in the 1980s in Los Angeles to protect themselves from street violence. The civil war and poverty drove migration north in a struggle to survive. Then, as gang-related crime increased in the United States in the 1980s and 1990s, US authorities deported gang members and other youth categorized as "delinquent" to their countries of origin, extending the criminal networks southward.

MS-13 and Calle 18 then took root in Central America and Mexico, employing the guns and tactics of El Salvador's civil war. The US War on Drugs and ongoing demand for narcotics in the United States have exacerbated the crisis. The gang violence that originated in my hometown,

Los Angeles, continues to tear El Salvador apart, contributing to cycles of immigration and violence in the United States and in El Salvador.

Although runaway children like Pedro have, for ages, found a form of community and protection on the street, MS-13 and Calle 18 are not typical street gangs. Their transnational criminal networks use barbaric methods of torture and murder that emulate those of the Atlacatl Battalion of the Salvadoran Civil War. Because of the feud between MS-13 and Calle 18, the streets—and many of the dirt roads—in El Salvador remain dangerous today. But, as Pedro's story reveals, submission to the gang way of life, to the hatred and to the violence, may begin with one person's shattered heart looking for a way to transmute an upbringing of pain into revenge—a revenge that begins to feel necessary for survival.

"Many people have a pain or regret in their heart," Pedro says from across the desk in the psychology office, with his hands pointing to his chest. "But I had hatred. Twenty-six guys from 18 grabbed me. They put a knife to my throat and said, 'See that mud over there? That's where your head is going to be because it's going to come off.' They beat me up. But no, that's not when my hatred for them arose. My hatred was born when I received a fine of 2,500 *colones* for trespassing on the territory of 18. Eight of them came to my house to tell me about the fine. It was 6:30 a.m. They said that I had until 11:00 a.m. to pay the fine, or else I would be finished. I didn't know what to do. I called my boss from the carnival. He said, 'They don't even realize how much trouble they're making for themselves. There's going to be such a big problem.'

"We didn't have much time. Just minutes. It was 10:30 a.m. and my boss still hadn't come. But look how God is. My friend came. He was a clown. I told him, 'Look, I need 2,500 *colones* by 11:00 a.m.' He said that our boss had already collected all the money in the box. He offered to come with me, and when we walked out of the house, the guys from 18 surrounded us. I told them that we were going to have breakfast, and they said, 'It's good that you have breakfast before you go.'" Pedro laughs three beats, and then a nervous smile cracks across his face. "I didn't go to breakfast. We got on the bus and got out of there. That's when I grew to hate 18."

His mind drifts back to the violence. "I used to love to see blood run. It was as if I felt like I was dead if I didn't see blood run." He tells me about an injury to his nose. "This bone was split in two." His jagged nasal bone leads to curved nostrils that flare as he speaks. Bump-bump. If he were a patient, I would touch the crooked aspect of his nose to understand it, but I will not touch Pedro. I feel my own nose instead; bone intact. "There was a big blow to the back of my head. You know, like when you pick up a ball that is flat and it just caves in? That's how the back of my head was." He points to where the skull protects the posterior side of the brain. I wonder if he sustained a head injury. I also wonder why I'm still talking to him—and why I trust him.

"It's God's miracle that the hole in my head healed," Pedro continues. "I don't understand [how it healed]. God did it. God can heal, but man also has to take part. Man has to want the healing. God gives me visions. He talks to me. Just last night he revealed to me that I'm going to be taking a trip to the United States."

"Do you know when you'll be going?"

"God has not yet given me a date."

"Has he revealed to you where you will go?"

Pedro's face brightens. He answers slowly, "To Los Angeles. He told me that I will go to Los Angeles. There's a tall building there. It's white. I think maybe it's the tallest building in Los Angeles. It's next to a freeway. Near there is some land. I will build a house there, a house of God, a church near downtown Los Angeles. My purpose for going is to help clean the air. I get my information from God in my dreams. I'm always thinking how appreciative I am of God. He sent me to see my aunt to ask for forgiveness. He sent me to see a girl once who was sick with brain disease. He told me to put my hand on her for healing." Pedro seems to have transformed his hatred for Calle 18 into a fervent love of God. He describes himself as a holy man who performs miracles. Is he delusional?

Lucio storms into the doorway, announcing, "*Ya vine* [I'm here]." Lucio has just driven back from San Vicente, where he was collecting DNA samples.

My mind's a bit slow, as I've been stuck in the Pedro tractor beam. "What?"

Lucio repeats, "*Ya vine, ya vine.*" It feels as if Lucio somehow knew I was relying on him to give me a sense of safety after listening to Pedro talk about loving to see blood run.

I cannot muster a proper response to Lucio because I'm mesmerized by Pedro's story. I am naive, curious, and a little embarrassed to admit my fascination. This world of violence is foreign to me. Seeing that Pedro and I are talking, Lucio steps back from the doorway and begins to shut the door. '*NO!*' I silently shout inside my head. '*Don't leave me in this room with the door closed.*' Lucio closes the door and then, with his hand still on the doorknob, as if reading my thoughts again, reopens it to halfway and walks off.

Pedro continues to talk to me about his aspirations. He's been quoting the Bible extensively, though he is illiterate. "He has told me that I will read His word." Pedro tells me of his other dreams: to have a carpentry shop and a wife. "But many go to church because they want a blessing. One has to go to church for love of God," he says. Pedro sleeps at Pro-Búsqueda because he doesn't have a home. I don't know how money sweeps his way. It seems that he doesn't care. With a puff of his chest, he tells me that he has a certification in carpentry.

I ask him if his life is in danger. Are the police out to get him? Or 18? He responds that he's safe because "God confuses faces." He relates, "I went to talk to some guys from 18 to tell them about God, but they didn't recognize me. I went with a long-sleeved shirt. I was carrying the Bible, and my hairstyle was different. Then I went to talk to my friends from MS. I told them that I was Goblin. They said, 'Get out of here. Goblin is dead.' And, it's true—God raised me from the dead. He raised me from the dead more than once."

"You were shot?"

"No, I died from intoxication. And God raised me from the dead."

"But how is it that you're still alive?" Surely an opposing gang might have wanted to murder him. Is he a liar, split from reality, or is this all true?

"God confuses faces," he says again.

"Do you own a gun now?" I ask

"No, but I have the right to arm myself at any time. I haven't had a gun since I gave myself to God."

Pedro says, "I eat when God gives me food. Yesterday, I went to the church. I had only three dollars with me. That was all my money. My plan was to give forty cents. Then, when I was about to give the money, I heard

God say that he wanted one dollar. So, I gave one dollar. Today, I was walking back from the bus after visiting my aunt in Usulután. I was near San Luis, and I heard 'Here comes your dollar back,' and I looked on the ground and found a dollar."

"Do you know why you sat down and started talking to me?"

Pedro's smile is wide. "If you listen to God, you know why. Ask God."

Okay, I think to myself, if all this magic spiritual stuff is true, then Lucio will hear me calling him to get me out of this conversation. I want to listen to Pedro's story, but it's turning into a sermon. Pedro's eye contact has been exceptional: eye to eye, except for a few moments when his eyes wandered to the side to think. Then, as Pedro quotes verse after verse, Lucio emerges in the doorway, asking, "Are you staying, or are you coming with me?"

Is he joking? It can't be time to go home . . . but my eyes steal a glance at the clock on the bottom right of the computer screen. It's 5:24 p.m.! Pedro and I have been talking for two hours.

"I'm coming," I reply to Lucio.

Pedro lets out a girlish sigh and says, "I haven't finished talking about God today." Lucio asks Pedro how his daughter is doing, and I exit the room.

An hour later, I'm at Andrea's home. Over dinner, Angélica says that Pedro is "a little crazy." Lucio is convinced that Pedro has never killed anyone. "Pedro spent some time in jail," Lucio says, "because someone blamed him for rape, but she actually consented."

"At least that's Pedro's version," I blurt out.

"But you can trust him," Lucio assures. "Nothing will ever disappear. Sometimes I ask him to buy materials for the backpacks I make." Lucio has a side business selling backpacks that he sews. "I send him downtown with money, and nothing is ever missing when he returns."

"Would you leave him alone in a room with Angélica?"

"No," Lucio replies without hesitation. Today, I gave the maybe-murderer and the probably-rapist my phone number in California because he was talking about his dream to visit Los Angeles. But how would he ever make it to LA?

After Lucio drives me home, I think about Pedro, who seems to carry loneliness and shame. He used to love to see blood run, and now, penniless and pious, scarred but healing, he gets by, powered by his belief in God's voice. He finds the courage to tell his story because he desperately feels a need to be understood. I feel frightened and grateful for the trust Pedro has offered me, and humbled and awed by his ability to find peace in God.

The next morning, I'm in the psychology office when Pedro comes in and pulls up that plastic chair again. "Pedro, do you have any artwork you can show me?" I ask, hoping to avoid the heavier topics. He retrieves two paintings and a wooden craft he carved for Pro-Búsqueda. He sells his paintings. Ceci bought one for six dollars.

"I like this photo," Pedro says, as he hands me the photograph that had been resting on the desk across the room. He points to the image of a smiling young woman with long, black hair, photographed riding the bus. "That's my adoptive sister. We were adopted as twins," he informs me. "Wait." Pedro walks out and moments later returns with a stack of photos. "Here is the day of my reencuentro." An aunt, two Pro-Búsqueda employees, an *abuelita* (grandmother), and a cousin pose beside Pedro, all smiling into the camera. He confirms that this is the aunt who he went to reconcile with earlier this week. I see photos of him in meetings with other jóvenes encontrados.

Father Jon comes in and says he wants to practice DNA View once I finish speaking with Pedro. The Father's face brightens when he sees that Pedro is sharing his cherished photographs. Father Jon steps out of the room. "This is in a hotel in Antigua, Guatemala," Pedro says. "These are two of my closest buddies." Gangbangers. I'm chilled by Pedro's appearance in the photo—the White Sox cap on backward, the faint moustache, and demonic gaze.

MS-13 is notorious for its brutality. Yet Father Jon looked to Pedro with accepting eyes. The priest seems to know of Pedro's sins but is also well aware of the atrocities committed by the nation that orphaned Pedro. Father Jon's acceptance of Pedro mirrors the peace I imagine Pedro finds in God. Love and acceptance, the best balm for the wounds of war.

15   Sandrita and New Separations

After a busy week, Lucio and I pick up pupusas to share with his family. We pull up to his residence at Building 37, where he lives two doors down from Andrea and Amílcar. Lucio's wife, Angélica, is laughing because she accidentally dyed the laundry aqua. It's funny except that it "hurts Lucio in his soul" that his beige pants are now green, "the color of soldiers' uniforms."

We eat pupusas when Andrea arrives. After, Lucio tends to official business: collecting Andrea's DNA for Pro-Búsqueda's genetic bank. Although Andrea's family has been found—she was the first joven encontrada located—proving kinship can contribute to human rights documentation of her disappearance. Lucio instructs Andrea, "Then you remove the cap from the collector—" He interrupts himself, smiles, and says, "I'll do it for you."

With only one arm, Andrea is graceful about her physical limitations. She also has a hip deformity and walks with a limp; she smiles from the chair whenever Angélica and I dance Zumba. Amílcar works night shifts on TACA Airlines' maintenance crew and Andrea has a busy schedule as a social worker with the Supreme Court, so the couple pays Angélica to get their son, Vladi, to school and take care of him until Andrea returns from work. They insisted that Angélica accept money. Whenever Andrea needs assistance, cues are taken naturally, wordlessly. After dinner, Andrea lifts Vladi to go home. She holds the three-year-old against her chest, his sneakers dangling from her fingers. Angélica grabs the miniature Adidas shoes and shoves his feet in.

"We have to take you home now because I'm sleepy," adorable little Michele says to me. We load into Lucio's Nissan sedan. On the drive, Angélica says, "My grandfather isn't well. He's had chest pain for a week. He hasn't eaten since my *abuela* (grandmother) died. He just sits around drinking beer." Angélica lost her grandma one week ago and worries now that her heartbroken grandfather "is just looking for how to kill himself." She invites me for the weekend to Guarjila, Father Jon's parish in Chalatenango, to attend activities for the *novenario*, the nine days of remembrance, to honor her grandmother. Andrea will join too, to visit her parents in Guarjila. We'll leave tomorrow. I fall asleep sitting up in my bed, computer on my lap, hands on the keys.

On Saturday evening, Lucio and his family pick me up, borrowing Pro-Búsqueda's green jeep for our two-hour drive to Guarjila. I climb into the passenger's seat. Michele and Vladi ride in the back, without car seats but with their mothers' laps for protection. Andrea passes my backpack into the trunk compartment with her one arm. To avoid a traffic jam, we detour off the highway. Andrea seems scared as we navigate Apopa's surface streets. Ceci told me that in her Apopa neighborhood, "*La vida vale una quarter* [Life is worth a quarter (twenty-five cents)]." There are roads in Apopa that can't be traversed at certain times of day "because the gangs control them," Lucio says as we drive through. Once we enter Chalatenango, a second detour takes us on an unpaved road with huge potholes. Andrea is terrified of the roads, and Angélica will not get out to pee because she's afraid of the snakes. Is their fear related to war memories?

In the car, I mention Argentina's recent court ruling that declared its amnesty law unconstitutional. "The outcome is good for Argentina, but bad for El Salvador," Lucio comments. By overturning the amnesty law, Argentine military leaders can be prosecuted for the child disappearances of Argentina's 1976–83 Dirty War. In El Salvador, the military still runs the government. Lucio expects that his government will use the case as an excuse to suppress information about the child disappearances. He's certain that his home phone and the phone line at Pro-Búsqueda are tapped. Milto once received a death threat when pursuing a case that involved high military figures, Lucio says. Pro-Búsqueda dropped the case.

At eight o'clock, we pass an open-air cowboy bar as we pull into dusty Guarjila. Andrea's youngest sister, Lena, greets us from the dirt driveway of Andrea's parents' home. Andrea's mother, Santos, a beautiful, stout woman with black hair, wears a flower-patterned cotton dress and white apron. Her huge smile matches Andrea's, as do her streams of vivacious laughter. I meet Andrea's father, a tall, venerable man of the *campo* (countryside), clad in jeans, a button-down cotton shirt, leather boots, and a straw hat.

While the other jóvenes encontrados I've met have lost one or both parents, Andrea is the only joven encontrada I can think of whose parents are both living. She reunited with her entire nuclear family in 1994—two parents and nine brothers and sisters. All of Andrea's siblings, except for teenage Lena, have since immigrated to the United States for economic reasons. Besides Andrea's reunion and brief interactions afterward, the only time she had together with her two parents and nine siblings was before the war. Andrea's family is experiencing a new cycle of family separation, brought on by the poverty and violence of postwar El Salvador.

Lena will also depart for "El Norte" (The North, meaning the United States) once she turns of age. Andrea has a US travel visa but stays in El Salvador because she doesn't want to separate from her parents again, having lived so many years apart from them. Despite the traumas Andrea experienced, she received an education at the orphanage and has a job that, along with Amílcar's work for the airline, places her family in El Salvador's small middle class. She adjusts her daily routine to dodge the violence, and, unlike countless Central Americans, Andrea can afford to stay home.

Andrea hands her mother, Santos, a box of Pollo Campero fried chicken, a fast-food treat from the city. Santos feeds us pupusas greased with pig fat—as Lucio is happy to tell vegetarian me *after* I've eaten one. She also gives us homemade *cuajada* (curd cheese) and tortillas cooked on her outdoor stove. The children play as adults finish eating. When little Vladi chases Abuela Santos's chickens through the yard, it's called *"dando guerra"* (waging war).

After dinner, I walk with Angélica one block along the dirt road under a starry night sky, past bars and food dispensaries, to the home of María, Angélica's biological sister. "I can see that your remittances haven't come," Angélica teases María when we arrive. "There's no toilet paper, no mattress, and no soap." When I dig for toilet paper in my backpack, they chuckle and Angélica tells me she was joking. María's husband has gone to "*Oosa* [USA]" and does send money home.

We settle in for sleep. María, her baby, and her five-year-old daughter pile into one bed. Lucio, Angélica, and Michele sprawl out on a mattress on the floor, and I lay in the twin bed beside them, with barely enough space to step between my bed and their mattress. A seventeen-year-old cousin takes the third bed in the room, sharing it with an eight-year-old named Sandrita. The sleeping arrangements seem crowded compared to what I'm used to, but I recognize that so many people around the globe share close quarters. I feel the family's togetherness, and I feel welcomed.

I awaken at dawn. The jeep is even more jammed with passengers than usual as we drive to the village of Arcatao for the *novenario*. On the ride, I learn about Angélica's family history, and she'll later tell me more in our interview. In the early 1980s, the FMLN forced her father to become a guerrilla fighter, leaving Angélica with her three sisters, pregnant mother, and grandmother. In 1982, upon hearing gunshots, the women and children fled, Angélica five years old at the time. Angélica didn't know how to swim, so when they reached the Sumpul River, she, her mother, and her sister Marta became separated from her grandmother and two sisters, María and Lola.

During the Guinda de Mayo, Angélica hid in the jungle with her mother and her sister Marta. They were pelted by the military's bombs, and shrapnel splintered across the sky and pierced her vulva. She peed blood. Soon after, Angélica heard another explosion. Soldiers took Angélica's mother away in a red pickup truck before killing her and then shoved Angélica and Marta into a helicopter. The helicopter took the sisters to the Salvadoran Red Cross and children received treatment for malaria and other illnesses, she says. The Red Cross then placed Angélica and Marta in an orphanage near San Salvador, where they resided for fifteen years—unaware they had family other than each other. The orphanage told Angélica, Marta, and the other children from the guinda, like Andrea and Elsy, that their parents had deserted them because they weren't loved. No one visited and Angélica felt unlovable because she was an orphan.

In 1994, when Angélica was seventeen, with the help of Pro-Búsqueda, she and Marta reunited with their father, grandparents, and sisters Lola and María, who had been raised by an aunt. Two years after the reunion, leukemia claimed Marta's life. Angélica was devastated. Since reuniting, Angélica has cautiously forged a friendship with her sister María, who rides in the jeep's back seat with her two young girls on her lap. I gather that, like María's husband, their sister Lola is in "*Oosa*" and that Sandrita, the affable child riding in back, is Lola's daughter. In exchange for caring for Sandrita, Lola sends María remittances.

We detour down an unpaved road with sharp switchbacks to collect a sample for Pro-Búsqueda's DNA bank and then proceed to the *novenario*. After winding along dirt roads with wide potholes, we arrive at Arcatao. Women make dough for chicken tamales in huge pots, kneeling to cook on fires over a dirt patio beside a tree. Giant banana leaves dry on the tin roof of the house across the street. Once the leaves dry, the women will cut them to wrap the tamales.

Angélica's *abuelo* (grandfather) walks over to greet Angélica and Lucio. He wears a straw hat and a pink-and-white vertical striped shirt with only two buttons buttoned. He has alcohol on his breath, and cataracts. His dizzy eyes smile when he sees Lucio and Angélica. Lucio greets him as I imagine he would his own grandfather.

We've taken five steps onto the busy, earthen patio when Angélica says, "That man there is my father." She points to the tallest man with a cowboy hat on the patio.

Neither María nor Angélica talk to their father or even make eye contact with him for the entire five hours that we're at the abuelo's small, crowded home, nor does the father approach them. Angélica says that her former orphanage director, though "rigid" and abusive, feels more like a father to her than her own dad, a man she views as a "drunk." After the initial joy of reunion, her father had a new family and visited only when Pro-Búsqueda paid for his journey. "When the money stopped coming, he did too," Angélica told me. He drank a lot, and even more so after Angélica's sister died of leukemia. Growing up as an orphan "alone in the world," Angélica couldn't bear the pain of her father's emotional abandonment after the

Lucio with Angélica's grandfather at the *novenario* event in honor of
Angélica's deceased grandmother. Arcatao, Chalatenango, 2005.
Photo by author.

reunion. The tension Angélica feels toward her dad contrasts with Andrea's
loving relationship with her biological parents, but Angélica's situation is
more typical. Reunions bring hope and then often disillusionment on the
arduous climb to reintegrate relationships, to build loving connections.

Neighbors parade to the abuelo's house, singing church songs and carrying a white statue of the crying Virgin. The procession lifts the statue
across the patio and into the abuelo's cottage, setting it on an altar adorned
with hundreds of tropical flowers, including large red hibiscus. Men decorate vases for more flowers by covering coffee tins with purple streamers
while children glue fancy twists of blue, white, and purple streamers to
hang from the ceiling. I'm told that the *novenario* will culminate at two
in the morning, when the cross is lifted—when Abuelita's memory is honored and her spirit sent to heaven.

While soaking in the beauty of the altar, I meet Aunt Rufina, the relative
who raised Lola and María. As with many families experiencing separation, cousins are considered sisters, and aunts function as mothers out of
necessity. In the home, I converse with eight-year-old Sandrita, an affec-
tionate child who smiles when she speaks. I put my arm around her, pat

Angélica standing with her grandfather, sister, and nieces. Angélica *(third from right)* carries her daughter, Michele, in her arms, as Michele reaches for Sandrita *(far right)*, the girl who will immigrate with a *coyote* to the United States unaccompanied to reunite with her mother. Arcatao, Chalatenango, 2005. Photo by author.

her back, and let her sit on my lap, the way I imagine her mother would if she were here. Sandrita tells me that she doesn't know her mother. Her mother left for the United States a few months after giving birth to Sandrita. On July 28, also my date of departure, Sandrita will depart to travel with a *coyote*, safely I pray, to her mother's arms.

I head back outside. One block down the dirt road, a dozen neighbors sing reverent incantations as they peruse pocket-size leather Bibles. I join the tamale preparation on the abuelo's front patio. It's hard to fold the banana leaf just right. Approximately five hundred tamales will be made and eaten here today. I'm watching the giant vat of boiling, thick corn concoction when one of the chickens running through the yard recklessly jumps in! Soaked in maize and instantly defeathered, the poor chicken flings its body about the cauldron. Seconds later, the creature runs aimlessly in the dirt. Lucio "flies the head off" of the bald chicken with a machete because "it's suffering." The headless body is still writhing. "Just goes to show . . . when it's time to go, it's time to go," says a señora who is cooking.

A cowgirl in a red blouse and black jeans trots by on her horse, steering eight bulls. A bull enters the abuelo's patio. The women carrying children run into the room with the Virgin statue while Angélica's grandfather and dog chase the bull out. As we prepare to leave the *novenario*, Angélica reminds Sandrita to say goodbye to Abuelo. Sandrita might not see him again before she departs for the United States.

In the car to Guarjila, Sandrita sits on my lap. She coughs for most of the ride, a dry cough she's had for at least a year that I presume to be asthma. Will she survive the journey north? I wish I had a stethoscope and medicine to give her.

We reach Guarjila and unload passengers at María's home. The two biological sisters, Angélica and María, don't have much to say to each other. Angélica has told me that Andrea feels more like a sister to her, their sisterhood formed to survive the ordeal of the orphanage. As I say goodbye, I bless Sandrita for a safe journey north. She looks to me with smiling eyes. I hold her outstretched hands. "It's going to be okay."

"Really?" Her eyes ask for confirmation.

"You will be safe. Everything will be okay," I promise, while inwardly praying my words are not falsehood but prophecy.

On our way to San Salvador, we pass a Sunday afternoon rodeo in Guarjila, then pick up Andrea from her parents' home. We detour through Apopa again, at night! Two *mareros* (gang members) ride in the back of a police pickup truck, their faces covered in tattoos. I feel startled by El Salvador's daily dangers and moved by the strength that runs through the women in Angélica's family. Sisters who survived the war together, sisters of blood and sisters of shared experience. Sisters raising children together with limited resources, on violent streets. I think about the bravery of a young girl facing a treacherous journey north to reunite with a mother she doesn't know. Perhaps it's true—we can't control when it's our time to go. But, until then, we can help our loved ones survive, even if that means enduring new separations and nurturing those we cherish, near and far. In a better world, Sandrita would not face this journey. But she does, and her family is strong.

16 La Esperanza

Three days ago, on Friday afternoon, when passing through Pro-Búsqueda's foyer, I asked Raúl, "Has a letter arrived for me from the US?" Before leaving California, I self-addressed an envelope to myself at Pro-Búsqueda so that my boyfriend, Mark, would write at least once while I was gone. That was the first time I thought about it in the one and a half months since I'd left.

"No, Liz. *Al suave es la honda* [Smooth is the way]."

That same Friday, Margarita didn't arrive at the office until four in the afternoon. She'd seen her husband off to Sweden the day before. I gave her the chocolates I'd promised for each of her four children. With a weary smile, she accepted. "I thought I'd cried all my tears because my dad used to drink, and he would mistreat my mother. And then the war came. But it turned out, I had more tears to cry." Margarita didn't cry that day, but her children did. They turned down going to the airport because they felt so sad. When I asked if she'd wanted her husband to go, she responded, "No, I supported the decision, but I didn't ask him to go. His brother is there, so he has a chance." He does not have a job lined up. I commented aloud that the plane ticket must have been expensive and asked about the cost. "$1,200. I took out loans—$2,300 for the airfare, visa, and other expenses. He has to make back what he spent. He will miss the kids a lot, and his mother is very old." In El Salvador, he sells *minutas* (Salvadoran snow cones) for a living.

To console her, I told her that distance kindles love, sharing that my boyfriend, Mark, and I feel closer now than before I left home. The words were barely out of my mouth when Don Jorge, the guard, walked into the office carrying mail. "Elizabeth," he called, holding an envelope addressed with my handwriting and with US stamps. It contained the letter from Mark! I felt joyful yet pensive in the shadow of Margarita's husband's departure.

Margarita then invited me for an overnight visit to her home in the resettlement community La Esperanza de Santa Marta. "We have space for you now," she said. An extra place on the mattress and a spare pair of slippers now that her husband has left. I accepted Margarita's invitation and at the end of Monday's workday, after spending hours with Father Jon drawing pedigrees and constructing primary and alternate hypotheses for the kinship analyses in DNA View, Margarita and I walk together to the bus stop for Route 22. In my purse, I have a water bottle, toothbrush, change of underwear, and clean shirt. Traveling with more is not worth the risk of inviting thievery.

On the bus, we get stuck in a downtown traffic jam. I recall Lucio telling me that once he and Angélica were riding the bus when a *marero* (gang member) with a bloodied face climbed through the window, carrying two stones and threatening to kill a passenger. Somehow the *cobrador* (fare collector) got him off the bus. I ask, "Margarita, do *mareros* ever come on the bus?"

"Yes, they board [the bus] to ask for money." I feel a little nervous but distract myself by admiring the bus's portraits of Jesus, dangly yarn decorations, and rows of Salvadoran commuters. We change buses at the cathedral to a minibus stuffed with passengers. My arm presses against Margarita's. We're crammed so tight that if I fidget the slightest to tie my hair back or to adjust my purse, the man on the other side of me will feel my arm move. I can see in my peripheral vision that he looks at me each time I make the mistake of moving.

At the plaza of Santiago, a hilltop town forty-five minutes west of the capital, I enjoy the panorama, an amazing view of Lake Ilopango and the hills surrounding San Salvador, freshened by a crisp breeze. Families stroll through the stone-paved plaza, eating pupusas and other street food, with the magnificent view as a backdrop. Church bells clang to announce the hour. Margarita and I begin the forty-minute walk downhill to her community. After we buy bread and broccoli, there are no more shops. This is jungle! The teenage boys who trek up the slick, steep, stone path are out of breath.

Margarita points out her cornfield as we walk into La Esperanza. Her son tends the crop, which produces enough corn to feed the family. Roughly the size of three basketball courts, the cornfield slants with the slope of the hill. I admit, my legs feel a little shaky when we arrive. "There's the mango tree that I brought you mangoes from," Margarita says. When we reach the flat terrain populated with homes, Margarita greets all the people she sees.

We pass the tiny school, where I encounter Margarita's youngest daughter, a middle schooler named Elba, along with Nora, Margarita's fourteen-year-old. In Margarita's home, I meet her oldest daughter, Carla, who takes charge when her mother is working. The house feels half-urban and half-rural. The indoor kitchen has a refrigerator and a gas stove, and outside a mud stove rises from the dirt patio near the manual corn grinder and piles of firewood.

A priest founded La Esperanza in the 1980s as a resettlement village for displaced Salvadorans returning from exile. A woman from the United States bought the land and donated it to the church, which then sold it to families for a nominal price. Sixty families live in La Esperanza, a community in the truest sense of the word. Its residents share a modest plantation, which this season is "giving lots of bananas," Margarita tells me. The profit from the community store pays for electricity in the church and other shared expenses. The community used to hire teachers to come to the little school, but since the price of coffee has dropped, doing so has become unaffordable.

I walk alone to the latrine. As I look up the green valley to a lush hillside covered in palm trees and birds-of-paradise, U2's "Bullet the Blue Sky" plays in my head: "I feel a long way from the hills of San Salvador," the live-album opening line calls. Bono wrote the lyrics after visiting El Salvador in 1986. The song thrums about the sky being ripped open through a gaping wound, referring to the bullets and bombs that pelted the women and children of the villages. U2 also paid homage to the mothers of niños desaparecidos in the song, "Mothers of the Disappeared." With a soundtrack playing in my mind, I look across the blanketing blue sky. The people of La Esperanza share a common ideal and are connected to the land in this gorgeous, remote valley. They also share a common history—one of violence and loss that they work together to build past.

Once back with Margarita, I ask about the sleeping arrangements. I want to make sure I'm not taking someone's bed. Margarita says that since her husband left, her son has been sleeping beside her "to take care of" her.

"From what? From drunks?" I ask. The community feels safe.

"I have nightmares," Margarita explains after a pause. "I dream that soldiers are shooting at me or cutting at my neck with my knife. I don't want to sleep when I have the nightmares because then they come back. So, I sit up in bed and drink water or walk to the latrine. I just sit up, afraid to go back to sleep because then I'll be back in the dream."

"Did you have nightmares when you were in the guerrilla force?"

"Of course." The nightmares ended with escape. "Whenever they [soldiers] would come to get me, I always dreamed that I could fly. I just flew away from any danger."

In Margarita's garden, the rose bush her husband, Alonso, planted before he left has not yet blossomed. Elba says the buds will be red roses. I notice a tiny wooden cross growing out of the dirt, its arms tied together by twine. I recall Margarita telling me that, as a guerrillera, she would make a cross to guard her wherever she slept.

At twilight, we amble down a steep path and then up to the church, the heart of the community. Near the church, I meet Margarita's aunt and three cousins. "This is my whole family," Margarita proclaims, her pride sprinkled with sorrow. The friendly cousins tease Margarita that her husband will find another woman in Sweden and not return. We walk back to Margarita's by moonlight and I follow Elba's silhouette along the path.

Upon arriving to Margarita's home, we have a delicious dinner of fresh squash, broccoli, rice, and tortillas cooked by Carla, Margarita's eldest daughter. It is her "shift." The children rotate chores in a cooperative fashion. I still feel hungry, but the pots are empty. Luckily, nature gave the community many bananas. "There are good harvests and there are bad harvests," Margarita said on the walk in.

After dinner, I sit in the rocking chair on the patio, which looks in on the living room TV. Margarita tours me through five photo albums, one of which includes photos of her brother who has lived in Canada since the early 1980s. He was an urban guerrilla fighter and received asylum.

Then Margarita shares with me *Nacido en sangre* (Born in blood), an ethnography of the people of La Esperanza, compiled by a Spanish anthropologist. Margarita's story appears midway in the paperback book. I read the four pages of her testimony, surprised by what I know and what I don't know. Margarita told me a lot of her story, but she didn't relate one of her most critical assignments as a *radioista* (messenger) for the FMLN.

Margarita's written testimony explains that a rumor had begun to circulate that the soldiers were going to attack the *masa* (civilians), who at that point were concentrated into one area. So, Margarita, along with another *radioista*, ran to tell the *masa* to move, to warn of the impending attack. She ran for hours without rest. She ran because she knew that her mother, brother, sister, friends, cousins would die if not informed. She was still running and hadn't yet arrived when she heard shouts and screams from the attack at the Sumpul River. Margarita's mother was killed, and she lost contact with her four brothers. Margarita had told me about running and running, about how it hurt her feet when she lost her shoes, and about the disappearances of her four brothers. She'd told me of her mother's assassination. But she never revealed that it all happened as she carried a message that she could not deliver in time to spare their lives—or to spare her brothers from disappearance.

As I trace her story with my fingertip, she tells me that, although her four brothers are still missing, the death of another brother, a guerrillero killed by the FMLN, is the most painful loss to her. He'd reported the presence of military spies to his superior, she says. But the superior was a military agent who'd infiltrated the FMLN. He threatened Margarita's brother: "If you talk, we'll kill you." So Margarita's brother didn't snitch on the spies. When the FMLN discovered the spy network, they assumed her brother was also a spy and shot him in the back during a battle. Margarita learned this years later from a fighter who was with her brother when he died.

I realize as I read *Nacido en sangre* that all of Margarita's children are named for her siblings. She has four children and five lost brothers—one deceased and four disappeared. Her children are obedient, loving, and cooperative, and it seems that she adores her husband. They will spend one year apart, at least, the first portion of the year just to pay off the expenses of his journey. They'll make one phone call a month; it will be brief because of the costs. They won't email because Alonso cannot write.

Margarita lends me one of her three nightgowns and tries to give me one to keep. Tonight her son will sleep in his own bed because she's not alone. It's a peaceful slumber.

"I'm sorry, Liz, but it's time to wake up." I hear Margarita's voice before my eyes open. Behind the curtain, the sky still holds darkness. We have to *mañanear* (wake up at dawn) to make it to Pro-Búsqueda by seven. I feel about as awake as the morning: peach sky to the northeast, pink to the west. We walk up the steep trail out of the village. Movement awakens my joints and mind. We reach the top (out of the jungle) and the top-top (bus stop in Santiago) within half an hour.

At the peak where the old church bells ring, we rejoin the road for cars and move briskly to get a good seat on the minibus. "No one else from Pro-Búsqueda has done that walk," Margarita says. "They come once a year to celebrate the corn harvest and enter from the other side, via the only road accessible to cars."

On the minibus, with my arm glued to the passenger beside me, I peer out blue-tinted windows. The driver's paper mask protects him from smog. Gangsta rap is playing. At San Salvador's cathedral, we step off the minibus to catch the 22. Margarita runs from the sidewalk toward a car. It's Don Jaime, Pro-Búsqueda's driver, on his way to work too! We hop in his car.

On my overnight visit, I met Margarita's tight-knit family and saw her community, rich in natural beauty and resources. Its name, "La Esperanza," translates to "The Hope." Margarita may never see her missing brothers again and her husband is now far away. But hope—in nurturing her children's future and rebuilding together after a war—replenishes and sustains her. The former guerrillera still has nightmares, but she no longer has to build a new cross of sticks every night. La Esperanza gives her strength that she carries into her day's work at Pro-Búsqueda, that she carries into mothering in the country where bullets ripped through the sky—and still do. She couldn't help her brothers or mother escape. But she finally has a home to escape to. A home that is beautiful, safe, and energizing. Because in community, there is power.

17 Coming Home

After gathering DNA-collection supplies at Pro-Búsqueda, Don Jaime, Margarita, and I set out on a day trip to Cabañas, a department in central El Salvador, bordering Honduras. Don Jaime parks at a corner house one block from the plaza of a charming, dilapidated Cabañas town. The adoptive family of Solomón, a joven encontrado, invites us in. We've come to collect a DNA sample from twenty-five-year-old Solomón to prove suspected kinship with two uncles. He appears healthy and well adjusted. During the interview, shy Solomón recalls aloud his mother's name. She was murdered in the war. His face flushes but he keeps his lips tight, appearing cautious not to reveal emotion in words. He'll leave for the United States soon because, as his adoptive mother says, "Young people have no other option for finding jobs."

Don Jaime asks whether the war passed close by here. *"Ooooo,"* the mother responds, "it's a shame we fixed up the house because you would've seen all the bullet holes." Once we leave, I ask Margarita and Don Jaime about rural Salvadorans' motivation for the wartime adoptions. They explain that the informal adoptions among poor families weren't because families wanted to raise more kids. People took in orphans to spare the adoptees' lives.

Hours away, the next house we visit is not yet constructed, a skeleton of wood sticks around which adobe will be laid. A girl runs barefoot up the dirt road to find Solomón's two presumed uncles. Green pasture and hills surround us. A man rides by on his horse. The uncles, with callused hands and dirt under their fingernails, wear rubber boots and well-worn shirts and pants and have machetes strapped to their waists. Their clothes contrast with Solomón's unwrinkled, turquoise button-down shirt. Class differences form a barrier for international adoptees reuniting with biological families in El Salvador and for many jóvenes encontrados raised in El Salvador. Some adoptive families were of more means, and in Salvadoran orphanages youth like Andrea received an urban education that differentiates them from their biological families. Solomón seems happy with his adoptive family, though his uncles haven't seen what he looks like since he reached waist-high on them—until I show them a digital photo on my camera.

The next day, my last full day with Pro-Búsqueda on this trip, I join a DNA-collection outing to Cabañas, accompanying Canadian journalists filming a documentary on El Salvador's disappeared children. Under roasting sun, we walk through the tendrils of a *pipianera* (squash field) to an abuelita's house. Margarita, wearing a microphone pinned to her Pro-Búsqueda T-shirt, interviews the abuelita, who weeps. When the abuelita cries, her entire body trembles, especially her legs. Once the interview ends and before heading back to San Salvador, I ask if she has a latrine I can use. In response, she puts her arms on my shoulders and grabs me into a hug. "They killed three of my children and my husband. I'm here alone." She cries in my arms and on my shoulder. She's still crying when I have to leave her on the patio—the others have walked most of the way back to the cars and are preparing to depart.

On the drive to San Salvador, Lucio pulls over to inspect an unexploded missile dug into the dirt, eight feet from the road. "This is where it landed," he says, the tonnage of missile too heavy and entrenched to have been manually moved. "They [soldiers] must have forgotten to pack it with explosives." He reads phonetically and I translate the name and location of the factory in the United States where the weapon originated.

The next morning, I ride a bus to the UCA, the Jesuit university where Father Jon teaches, to meet one of my medical school professors. She has come to volunteer on a medical mission and will be sightseeing at the UCA. Brick buildings stand among the UCA's tall trees. A large mural of Archbishop Óscar Romero and the six martyred Jesuit priests adorns a wall. I pay respects to Father Jon's fallen colleagues in the rose garden and enter the Center Monseñor Romero, a memorial to the assassinated Jesuits. The massacred priests' bloodstained clothes are on display. The glass case in the center of the room shows a bullet meant to kill Father Jon. I know about that bullet. When I first met Father Jon, he told me that it crossed through the driver's window of his car, just a few centimeters too high to pierce his skull. He said it was the government's second assassination attempt on his life. So much has come out of Father Jon's being alive, including the successes of Pro-Búsqueda.

Exploring the exhibits, I see my professor. We view graphic photos of the murdered Jesuits that show their desecrated bodies on concrete among dark puddles of blood. She asks me to tell the US delegation she leads of the atrocities of the war. I oblige, citing examples of the horrific violence, but I can't convey all I've heard in a brief museum tour, and the aftermath of violence is complex. It's more violence and years of pain transmuted into desperation to emigrate out of economic necessity, with many people in the United States failing to grasp the role our country played to drive people north. But I do my best to respond, because understanding is important to promoting a humane approach to immigration and to El Salvador.

After the museum visit, we eat at an Americanized Mexican restaurant. I join an overnight excursion, and we dine at a luxury restaurant in a resort at the shore of a crater lake. I miss the El Salvador where I talked with the people. I'd rather be in the home of the abuelita in Cabañas, listening to her, hugging her as she finishes her cry.

The following afternoon, Margarita and Don Jaime retrieve me in Pro-Búsqueda's pickup truck. In the evening, Lucio's and Andrea's families invite me to a generous farewell dinner at Pizza Hut. I leave tomorrow.

After, at Lucio's, I hear the *pha pha pha* of his sewing machine as Lucio prepares a bulk order of backpacks. He dreams of managing a workshop that makes backpacks, a trade inherited from his father, a man, Lucio says, who "cut material from his own pants to sew pants for me." The enterprise can help Pro-Búsqueda raise money and employ jóvenes encontrados. Lucio is teaching Pedro to make backpacks using the sewing machines in

Pro-Búsqueda's back room, where Pedro sleeps. "If I help one person, that is enough," Lucio has told me.

The next day, at Pro-Búsqueda, we organize the DNA samples. Each one gets signed over in the chain of custody to me. I feel honored to transport the 248 samples we collected this summer to California. But, hours before my flight, we realize that the DNA samples are too bulky for my backpack. Lucio goes home to make a duffel bag that will fit the samples "just right."

Father Jon has kind words for me, and I tell him that I hope to see him soon in Berkeley. We don't talk for long though, because he has to prepare for an interview where he'll be discussing a book he hasn't read yet. Like a procrastinating schoolboy, I think to myself, amused. "Whenever you want to come back, you will be welcome," Father Jon says. There's something of a blessing in his eyes and in the way he rests his hands on my shoulders as we say goodbye.

On Pro-Búsqueda's behalf, Ceci gives me a T-shirt with Óscar Romero's image as we gather in the foyer for my farewell. María Inés wants to know why I'm abandoning her and hugs me again. "The good ones always go," she says.

Pedro carries the duffel bag with the DNA samples to the jeep. Yesterday he teased, "I'll keep your bags from you so you can't go." Lucio's family drives me to the airport.

Amílcar finds me in the airplane gangway! Wearing a uniform and security pass around his neck, he says that, as the mechanic assigned the safety check for my plane, he gave it a "little inspection." I joke that I want the plane to have a "big inspection." We exchange goodbyes at the airplane door, and he exits down the stairs onto the tarmac. I arrive at midnight and carry the black duffel bag with DNA samples through US customs without a hitch.

After a night's sleep, I go with my sister to Fruitvale, in Oakland. A man in a sombrero pushes a popsicle cart, bells jangling as he rolls by. A corner stand sells peeled mangoes in plastic bags to eat with chili and salt. I feel like I'm in Central America. Later, at the Berkeley Farmers' Market, a Mexican tamale vendor asks me in Spanish where I've been the past two months. "Don't tell me when you go back to El Salvador," she says. "I'd be too worried. I see so much in the news."

I will go back. Pro-Búsqueda launched its DNA bank and I completed

Mother and son hugging after more than thirty-five years of separation. The reunion is a result of a cold-hit match made through Pro-Búsqueda's DNA bank between a young man raised in Australia and a mother searching for two disappeared boys. San Agustín, Usulután, 2016. Courtesy of Pro-Búsqueda.

my summer fellowship, but my research with the jóvenes encontrados has just begun. Then the tamale vendor adds a phrase I've heard from my Cuban relatives since childhood, *"Estás más gordita* [You're chubbier]." When I left El Salvador, my Salvadoran friends said the same, proud that I liked their pupusas. I laugh. There is home within home.

Cristián, the Chilean geneticist who accompanied me as I began the journey to El Salvador, comes over to my rented Berkeley cottage. We listen to music and crouch on the living-room carpet as I sign over each of the 248 DNA samples in the chain of custody, from me to him. Cristián will deliver the duffel bag to the DNA lab in Richmond, California, for genetic analysis. The samples will reveal "cold hits" that link searching relatives with disappeared children untraceable through adoption records or other means. The batch of samples will also confirm kinship for families who can pursue legal recourse through human rights courts or simply have the peace of mind of knowing without a doubt that they found their missing relative.

Pro-Búsqueda will carry on this wave of DNA collection for several more weeks as the DNA bank we built together continues to grow. Cristián planted seeds for Pro-Búsqueda to someday run the genetic database on its own. Father Jon watered the seeds by inviting the collaboration that led to the DNA bank. We partnered in support of his mission to find all the children disappeared in El Salvador's civil war—for justice and so they may know their family history and have the opportunity for reunion.

PART 2   Fifty Interviews
(Winter 2005–2006)

Father Jon's Legacy

"Father Cortina died this morning from a heart attack upon awakening. His body will be transported to El Salvador and he will be buried." That's the entire content of the email message I receive from Lucio, with the subject "*Malas Noticias* [Bad News]," sent Monday morning, December 12, 2005. It's been four months since my return to Berkeley. Father Jon had a hemorrhagic stroke one week ago while in Guatemala for a conference. He went into a coma after the stroke and hasn't communicated since, except for one instance: On December 8, the date of his seventy-first birthday, when his childhood friend who had arrived from Spain sang "Happy Birthday" to him, tears slid down Father Jon's cheek.

I phone Lucio upon receiving his message. He tells me that in the days that Father Jon was fighting his massive stroke, the UCA aired a special radio show. Lucio was interviewed via his home telephone and told San Salvador, "Without Father Jon the movement to find the disappeared children wouldn't exist. We pray for him." With a voice torn by sadness, Lucio relates to me that the loss is harder for him and Angélica because Father Jon was their only (living) father. It's different for people who have their parents, Lucio says. My eyes fill with tears when Lucio reports, "Guarjila no longer exists. This week it renamed itself Community Jon Cortina."

Father Jon's parishioners wanted to bury his body in Guarjila, but it will be entombed at the UCA instead, in the chapel alongside his friends, the assassinated Jesuit priests. Lucio and I know that Father Jon felt more peace in Guarjila, but history will better remember him at the UCA. "You'll be here in twelve days," Lucio calculates toward the end of our call. I plan to go to El Salvador for two weeks during winter break from medical and public health school classes to interview disappeared children and their relatives about family separation and reunification for my master's thesis.

In my last interaction with Father Jon, I emailed him to request a "letter of support" so that UC Berkeley would approve the formal research interviews. I sent Father Jon's one-sentence reply to my university: "This work is important for Pro-Búsqueda and important for Liz." I feel grateful that he supported my research. The world needs to understand what happens when we separate children from their families. Father Jon taught me and so many others to transform pain into a motivation to serve. He would want us to carry on the work of Pro-Búsqueda in his absence. I move forward with sorrow *and* gratitude, inspired by Father Jon's memory and beckoned by truth.

Twelve days later, at the airport in San Salvador, I see Amílcar, Andrea, and Vladi through the glass wall that separates the airport baggage claim from the rest of El Salvador. I wave, go through customs, and then greet Angélica, Michele, and Lucio. I brought a phone number for a reliable taxi, but my friends surprised me and my boyfriend, Mark, who has joined me on the trip to study Spanish, by receiving us with a two-car entourage.

We stop at a pupusería along the dark highway. Despite the late hour, our Salvadoran friends waited for us to eat dinner. Distance mixes with familiarity as we reconnect past the months and over the wall of cultural divide. Inclusive of Mark, we make Spanglish small talk while eating pupusas on the dark roadside patio. I jump at a loud "boom!" Lucio laughs because it was just a firecracker, but he knows I was imagining much worse.

Forty-five minutes later, we arrive at the entrance of a twenty-home gated community. The private road encircles a central playground, leading to the two-story suburban house where Mark and I will stay. The home, with gleaming tile floors, wireless internet, and maid quarters, belongs to Jenny and Dave, gringo surfer Christian missionaries I met through my friend Allie. In exchange for a place to stay, Mark and I will watch their dog, Listo, while Jenny and Dave are in the United States for the holidays. Jenny hung some of her art before leaving, but they'd just moved in, and most of her paintings lean against the bright white walls. They're expecting their first child; the baby's room contains only a crib. After looking around for two minutes, I hear Angélica say, "Lucio, let's go." I read in her voice and posture discomfort with this upscale, eerily empty home. Perhaps Angélica equates the house with wealth—and wealth with the atrocities of the war. They leave, and Mark and I settle in. The airline lost our luggage, so we have nothing to unpack.

The next morning, Ceci calls and tells me that she and her mom, María Inés, feel so saddened by Father Jon's death that they've been forgetting to eat, and María Inés forgot to take her medication and became ill. Times have been rough, Ceci says. Coping with Father Jon's unexpected death has left everyone bereaved.

A couple of evenings later, I visit Lucio's and Andrea's families to deliver Christmas gifts to the children. When we reach the apartment complex, Vladi is rolling toy cars on the dirt outside his home. Andrea sits in a makeshift beauty salon in her living room. Angélica irons Andrea's hair, with Michele close by. After barely a hello, Amílcar connects his camcorder to the television beside the meter-high Christmas tree and then plays me footage of Father Jon's funeral.

The video shows the residents of Guarjila singing at the UCA's historical chapel. Photos displayed at the mass include one of Father Jon next to Óscar Romero, and there's even one of Father Jon with me. On the screen, the people of Guarjila, the UCA, and Pro-Búsqueda walk outside, parting to allow a path as Father Jon's family arrives from Spain mid-ceremony. His brother embraces a community leader from Guarjila. Father Jon's niece cries. Salvadorans and Spaniards sing together. Attendees parade alongside a coffin covered with flowers that pallbearers carry down the road. I'm still drying tears from watching the video of the funeral procession when Andrea asks, "Who will go first?" She's referring to the interviews for my thesis.

"Angélica first," I say in jest, for she is the shyest. Andrea's mouth drops in playful shock at the joke, but Angélica agrees. I go with it, still eating the chocolate-covered banana Andrea gave me when I arrived. I crouch on the lower bunk of Vladi's bunk bed. Angélica sits on a bed across from me, in the opening of a mosquito net. She says that she doesn't remember her past, but I observe that she remembers a lot. She tells me of her disappearance in the Guinda de Mayo, her injuries, life in the orphanage, and her reunion. I interview Lucio next, followed by Andrea.

After pupusas in Los Planes, we return to our gated home. Lucio and Angélica refuse to come in. "Mommy, *mamita* [little mommy]," Michele pleads. She only says *mamita* when she really wants something. "I want to go in the park." The children are sent to the swing set, but Lucio stands by with his arms folded. Michele and Vladi play, blessed with the innocence of not equating wealth with their grandparents' murder.

On December 31, we go to Guarjila to celebrate New Year's. A procession honoring Father Jon parades down the main street, and graffiti with Father Jon's name covers a stone wall. Andrea's mother feeds us dinner.

Afterward we walk the dirt road to Angélica's sister's home, where we light fireworks while Michele and her little cousin shuffle about in the yard. I learn that Angélica's niece, eight-year-old Sandrita, made the journey to her mother in Maryland. Her family paid the *coyote* $5,000. She lives with her biological mother, "But she's not happy in the United States. All Sandrita does is eat chocolate," Angélica says.

Back at Andrea's parents' place, at eleven on New Year's Eve, I interview her parents, as I have yet to hear their perspective. "You know that war is terrible," Andrea's father begins, "but it's one thing to hear about war and another to suffer it in your own skin." He tells me about the 1982 Guinda de Mayo, when Andrea was seven, and about the shrapnel that cut the air at nine in the morning, severing her arm. FMLN medics attended to Andrea but they had limited supplies and it was a miracle she didn't contract tetanus, her parents say. With nothing to cover her arm, she slept for twenty-four hours. Then they had to flee, but shrapnel had wounded Andrea's hip too and she couldn't walk, her father says. Still bleeding, with her arm bone sticking out, Andrea and her family of twelve faced "bombs from above and from the ground," as they raced to survive.

I ask about the moment Andrea became separated from her family. I know from Andrea's testimony that while running from bombs and bullets, Andrea's father came to a ravine he couldn't cross carrying two children in his arms. Together, the three would die. So, as Andrea has told me without blame, he set Andrea down, the child who could no longer walk, leaving her with "the dead and wounded." He escaped with the other child.

Unlike Andrea, her parents won't discuss her disappearance. They remain quiet and, after a long silence of wearing taut facial expressions, Andrea's father lets out a breath and thanks God that she was taken safely to an orphanage. It seems they still carry guilt and shame. Would it help them to know that Andrea forgives them? It's unclear how much Andrea and her parents have discussed her disappearance.

The tone of Andrea's mother and father changes to joy when they tell me about finding Andrea. Her parents spent years in the refugee camp in Honduras before repatriation to Guarjila. They had limited means and there wasn't yet a process to search for disappeared children. Then, after twelve years of separation, Andrea's parents gained hope that Andrea might be alive when their nephew, a former soldier, told them that he'd "picked up some children" from Chalatenango during the war. Andrea didn't speak with her family again until she was nineteen—at her reen-cuentro in Guarjila, arranged through Father Jon and what would become Pro-Búsqueda.

Andrea told me that her reunion with her parents and nine siblings "felt like a dream come true." Andrea's vivacious laughter mixed into tears only once during our interview together—when she talked about seeing, for the first time, her brother Rutilio, who "had my [Andrea's] face." The odd familiarity felt overwhelming.

Andrea's mother says that at the reunion they "all cried from happiness, hugging her." She adds, "Since we first saw her, she's loved us as if we'd been with her the whole time."

Then Andrea's father speaks to today. "Thanks to God, we're happy because Andrea visits us and we know that she's well."

Andrea's positivity mirrors her parents'. "I always see the present, which is very good now," Andrea said in our interview. Andrea's reunification process is the happiest I've seen, and yet her parents' pain is still so apparent. After the interview, we listen to firecrackers announcing the new year in Guarjila, and we all hug. I climb onto a cot on Andrea's parents' patio and sleep.

I awaken to a new day and new year and stroll to Father Jon's house with Amílcar. The vacant home is still well-kept; even the dirt in front

Top: Family reunion of Andrea *(young woman in T-shirt, back row, fifth from left)* with her biological mother *(far left)*, biological father *(far right)*, siblings, nieces, and nephews. Andrea was the first disappeared child in El Salvador to be found by what became Pro-Búsqueda. Guarjila, Chalatenango, 1994. Courtesy of Pro-Búsqueda.

Bottom: Andrea and her biological mother, Santos, at the mother's home, the day after I interviewed Andrea's parents. Guarjila, Chalatenango, 2006. Photo by author.

is swept tidy. Then we visit the neighbor down the street, Suyapa Serrano Cruz, the woman who won the case at the Inter-American Court of Human Rights. Suyapa has just returned from the airport in San Salvador, where she helped send her friend's daughter off to the United States. Suyapa speaks to us about her sisters' disappearances, whether or not they'd remember the war, why she believes they're alive, and what finding her sisters would have meant to her mother. She says the government pays for her diabetes medicine because of the court sentence.

Amílcar, based on his experience as a disappeared child, assesses aloud whether or not the sisters would remember Suyapa. When I mention that we're headed to picnic at a creek, Suyapa and Amílcar both start talking about all the dead bodies they saw floating down the river during the war. Matter-of-fact war recollections imbue so much everyday conversation, as survivors call back to the moments of carnage that defined a generation's lives—and still do.

When we leave Suyapa's, we swing by Andrea's parents' home to get Andrea and the children. Then, we all walk to the stream, a tributary of the Sumpul River. Our little cooking fire glows on a hillside near the water. My friends cook raw meat, shish kebabs over a fire of sticks and dry leaves from nearby bushes. Tortillas heat on the smoking soil. Guinda skills, I think to myself. Close by, children splash in the stream. Their innocence reminds me of Vladi and Michele swinging on the play structure outside Jenny and Dave's house, with giggles untarnished by the violence promulgated in the siphoning of wealth. Today the blood and corpses are long gone from the waters of the Sumpul River, and children in their underwear swim and laugh.

The innocent children of Guarjila, a village now also known as Community Jon Cortina, will learn of Father Jon's legacy so that parents will never again have to face the horrible choice of whether to carry their wounded child. Father Jon built Guarjila alongside returning refugees amid the gunfire of war. He facilitated the first reunions on Guarjila's soccer field in 1994. He founded Pro-Búsqueda, and he brought Suyapa Serrano Cruz to the human rights tribunal so that the people of El Salvador could be heard. "With Jon Cortina, God passed through Guarjila," the people say.[1] Father Jon found peace in Guarjila, and now Guarjila will always find peace in him.

19 Back at Pro-Búsqueda

I walk into Pro-Búsqueda, excited and nervous, on everyone's first day back after the winter holidays. A larger-than-life headshot of Father Jon smiles at us, hung in the foyer above a vase of flowers and a lit candle. The stove must be broken or out of gas because I see sticks and char on the pavement just outside the kitchen—an alternate way to heat tortillas. A rat runs through the hallway to the foyer. Raúl and Don Jaime catch it between them. Don Jaime stomps on the rat with his cowboy boot and kills it. Raúl dangles it at me, then throws the dead rat behind the couch. Margarita comes over, uses a napkin to pick the rat up by the tail, and puts it in the trash. It feels like kids without parents. The Father watches from his spot on the wall.

Raúl's hair has grown rock-star long since last summer. Pedro appears unchanged, and we exchange a firm handshake. I hug Ceci. María Inés pauses from sweeping to tell me how happy she is to see me, then relates how "horrible" the situation is. She says that she visited Father Jon in the hospital in Guatemala City when he could no longer speak, a little more than a month ago. I talk with Father Jon's assistant, the de facto interim leader, in Father Jon's former office. When I ask about my thesis, she responds that her father-in-law had a stroke too. I feel the absence. Everyone does.

The whole place feels like it has a wind sweeping through it—emptiness and wind. It doesn't have that warmth, fullness, that sense of inevitable triumph that Father Jon brought. Though, we do manage to plan for the interviews. Pro-Búsqueda will invite jóvenes encontrados raised in El Salvador and their relatives to participate, and with my small research grant I'll cover costs for interviewees' travel to San Salvador and for excursions to the countryside for interviews.

In the afternoon, Mark and I ride the bus home. I'd thought that staying at Jenny and Dave's house would give us glimpses of the "other side," but I'm realizing that it's *our* side. I grew up not rich but comfortable, in the country that financed the atrocities that decimated my friends' families. El Salvador's stark divide between the rich and poor puts me on the side of the wealthy. I feel like a bourgeois homeowner. We call the gas company to request a new gas cylinder for the stove, put the empty bottled water canisters on the street, feed the dog, and unpin the machine-washed laundry from the clothesline. The comforts I rely on, such as drinking water that doesn't need to be boiled, remind me to feel grateful for what I have and for my opportunities to serve.

One sunrise and two bus rides later, I meet Don Jaime at Pro-Búsqueda. Our green jeep stops at the gas station, where I pay twenty dollars for gasoline, before heading out to Cabañas and Suchitoto for research interviews. I thank Don Jaime for driving today. "We [Pro-Búsqueda and Liz] need each other," he says, with a sincere, mustached smile. After a highway turnoff onto a bumpy road, I grip the sides of the seat as I get ping-ponged against the seatbelt. Don Jaime remarks that the road has improved so much.

In Santa Marta, Cabañas, I interview the uncle of Armando, one of the jóvenes encontrados raised in the orphanage with Andrea and Angélica. Armando's uncle reclines in a hammock during the interview. He can barely speak, let alone stand. He says he's dying and has already paid for his coffin. He cannot swallow and, judging by the lump in his neck, I'm guessing he has cancer. I record a message for his nephew, Armando, asking for a visit before he dies.

At San Rafael Cedros, I interview Raúl's grandfather. Don Rafael couldn't work in the field today, so he's sitting in a rocking chair on the patio of his planation-like home, facing out over his expansive land. Corn taller than me grows in his fields.

Elderly, energetic Don Rafael has green eyes and light skin, *"chelito"* as Salvadorans say. He wears a white tank top and a silver necklace that dangles low. He feels bitter that his daughter made the "bad decision" of not telling him about the orphanage where she placed Raúl and her other young son when she joined the FMLN alongside her mother, Don Rafael's wife. Soldiers killed both women, and he didn't have a way to reconnect with the boys until Pro-Búsqueda found them nineteen years later.

Don Rafael did his best to give his grandsons a new home in the months after the reunion. He took them in, but, at ages twenty and twenty-three, the boys weren't prepared for rural life. Their hands lacked calluses and they shied away from farm work, Don Rafael says. "The orphanage taught arithmetic, but not how to cut sugarcane or tend to cows." Then Raúl's brother became involved with friends who were "no good," resulting in him leaving for San Salvador. Soon after, Raúl left too. Don Rafael felt he couldn't protect or help the boys, despite their kinship. Though an emotional interview, stoic Don Rafael's face reveals little. When the interview ends, I tell Don Rafael that Raúl will resume university studies in one week. A proud smile escapes his face before he can chase it away.

On our drive to San Salvador, we stop at the bank. Don Jaime has to pay back a loan that will accrue interest tomorrow, a common scenario among my colleagues, I've noticed. At the end of the day, Mark and I are riding home on the bus. The bus stops moving, and everyone aboard darts nervous looks at men attempting to steal money from an armored vehicle just ahead on the road. A SWAT team arrives, and the bus passengers crane their necks to watch a man in a bulletproof vest point his gun in a ready-to-shoot stance while surveying in all directions. Sensing my fear, the man next to me, a middle-aged, chubby Salvadoran, says, "This is normal."

The bus resumes its route, and five stops later I turn to the kind stranger. "It wasn't normal. Everyone was looking. Everyone was nervous."

He smiles at me as if I've just figured out that Santa Claus doesn't exist. "Well, maybe we'll read about it in the paper tomorrow."

I spend the next day in Usulután. In the afternoon, I relax on the couch at Pro-Búsqueda and imagine a count of how many times today sweat drenched my clothes and then evaporated. In the dry flats, I interviewed a former guerrillera who was forced to give up her infant son. The adoptive

father, whom I also interviewed, expressed pride at what his mountaintop
ranch can offer his son, now seventeen years old. The son related feeling
torn between two mothers. He doesn't want to betray the woman who
raised him but wishes his biological mother, whom he views as a "friend,"
would come visit. A few highways over, a widowed adoptive father cried.
In a squeaky, shrill voice, he voiced his fear that his adoptive son will
abandon him by going to live with the biological family. In a confidential
interview, the son asserted his loyalty to his adoptive dad. Reunion brings
vulnerabilities for adoptive parents—and they play a vital role in supporting reunification.

In the evening, I go to Lucio's for enchiladas. Ten minutes after I arrive,
my friends, diligent about helping me gather interviews for my thesis,
declare it's time for me to interview Amílcar, Andrea's husband. As Amílcar
and I sit in his living room, he peruses the interview guide, the only joven
encontrado I interview who requests to do so. Then we turn on the audio
recorder. Amílcar recalls his early childhood as "peaceful." He lived in the
countryside with a river nearby and space to run, raised by a single mother.
"We only ate when my mom could give us food" but were "very happy."

In May 1980, everything changed. The military was killing anyone they
thought supported the rebels, regardless of whether or not the person was
truly culpable, Amílcar says. "There was a massacre, and the soldiers came
and started to shoot at anyone they could find." So, at age five, Amílcar fled
his village with his mother; his eight-year-old brother, Mauricio; and his
baby brother, Vladimir. They sought refuge in Honduras multiple times,
but each time Honduran soldiers sent them back to El Salvador.

Then, another massacre. Amílcar tells me about running from the soldiers and about hearing gunshots as they fled an ambush near where the
Sumpul River forms a border with Honduras. "The river was very full. I
saw many people trying to cross. Many drowned or were shot. Helicopters were shooting from above. The Honduran soldiers on the other side
grabbed people and gave them back to the Salvadoran military." Amílcar,
with his older brother Mauricio and his mother carrying baby Vladimir,
walked downstream, but the river had grown too high to cross. After days
of walking they hid in a shaded thicket, along with the two women in
flight with them. During a brief calm, his mother gave the boys a bit of the
food she carried with her.

Helicopters discovered them and then the soldiers came. "Gunshot by gunshot, it was a lot." Fifteen soldiers surrounded them. "There they killed the two other women, and they killed my mom and my little brother. She had him in her arms and that's how they stayed," Amílcar, my thirty-one-year-old friend with a head of already gray hairs, tells me through tears. "They [soldiers] lifted me up by an arm, and I just closed my eyes. I said I wanted to stay there. I didn't know what I was—if I was human." Soldiers dragged Amílcar and his brother Mauricio away from the corpses. "I saw the bundle of my mother and baby brother."

Then they humiliated Amílcar. The soldiers were cruel. "They made fun of me and urinated on my head. They said I was nothing in this world." Soldiers transported Amílcar and Mauricio in a military vehicle and then delivered them by helicopter to an air force base, where they were given dinner. The boys were taken to a cot in the military clinic to sleep. Amílcar says that Mauricio cried most of the night.

In the morning, their blood-soaked clothes were taken off and probably burned, Amílcar surmises. A commander raised funds to buy the boys new clothes, to meet their "basic needs." As the years passed, the brothers received schooling and an odd home of sorts, sleeping among the dead bodies in the critical care unit of the air force base. While some disappeared children were adopted into soldiers' homes, for Amílcar and Mauricio, the air force base became their residence for the remainder of the war and until adulthood.

The telephone rings. Amílcar doesn't answer it. Now a knock on the door. I see Andrea's smile through the barred window. The kids and Angélica have come too. "The enchiladas are ready," we're told. We break for dinner and then resume.

Amílcar describes walking four kilometers to school with his brother when he was young, and by himself when he grew older. "I threw my whole self to my studies," he tells me. "On the weekends, I didn't have anyone's home to go to, and I didn't have money to buy food. On school days, they served meals, but on the weekends there was no food." All the other students had families to return to. "I felt alone," Amílcar says. The brothers often fought with each other, but it was Mauricio who gave Amílcar a path forward. Mauricio dropped out of school and got a job. "With the little help he gave me, I was able to buy basic necessities during my second year [of high school]," Amílcar says. After graduating high school, in 1993, Amílcar earned a scholarship to study aviation mechanics.

Although Amílcar had an education, he lacked a sense of his origin. "I was always missing something I'd longed for since my childhood: to know my family. I felt that if I could meet a relative, they'd tell me about my mother, which I always needed since childhood." When the war ended, Amílcar searched for clues in Chalatenango about his relatives. He remembered the Sumpul River and his uncle's name. Then, in 1994, at age twenty, he saw a newspaper ad that Father Jon had created just as Pro-Búsqueda formed. When Amílcar read his name and Mauricio's among the list of disappeared children, he telephoned Pro-Búsqueda. His uncle had been searching for them.

Amílcar was one of the first jóvenes encontrados to be reunited. His reunion occurred in 1994, shortly after Andrea's. Meeting his maternal uncle gave him a sense of history, of happiness—a feeling of completeness. "Love from one's family is a vital need. I can no longer find my mother or blood brother." But, by finding his uncle, "what I needed to find, I now have."

I ask Amílcar how he sees himself today. "I'm a child who comes from a family of limited resources, although quite beautiful. I'm a young man who has overcome challenges, thanks to my own effort and because of the opportunity given to me and thanks to God."

I see a man who has suffered to grasp a feeling of belonging. He felt on the fringes at the air force base, barely having money to buy food when hungry, never having family to turn to except for a brother who was also young and struggling. Today Amílcar feels grateful to Pro-Búsqueda—for connecting him to his family, his history, for leading him back to a peace he has not known since early childhood. I admire him for who he is and what he has overcome.

One week later, on the Día de los Reyes (Three Kings' Day) holiday, at Pro-Búsqueda, I interview Mauricio, Amílcar's brother. Mauricio is three years older than Amílcar. Every detail of Mauricio's interview corroborates Amílcar's, even the description of the rain on the day soldiers murdered their mother and of the dinner the military fed them at the air force base the night the boys arrived in bloodstained clothes. Mauricio's lips pucker as he speaks.

He wears a dark-blue polo shirt and resembles his nephew, Vladi, named for their murdered baby brother. Mauricio explains that he has the afternoon off from his job with the air force, so he chose to come to Pro-Búsqueda. I want to understand how he rationalizes working for the military, oiling the machinery that left him an orphan. My silent wish to know is matched by his wish to explain. Money—he has to earn a living somehow. Mauricio describes himself as "someone who fights to get ahead, hardworking." But his heart is with Father Jon and not the state, he says. Though Amílcar and Mauricio share allegiances, Mauricio, as the older brother, has had to bend to circumstance more. As a young man, he forewent his own education to earn wages so Amílcar could study. Now, as an adult, he takes the job he can, the job he was positioned for by virtue of growing up on an air force base, working for pay, not duty, to get by. In war and postwar El Salvador, surviving is success.

I also meet thirty-two-year-old María at Pro-Búsqueda, the only joven I interview who has not yet found her family. She has messy hair, halfway clipped back and wide, lost eyes, and wears a green cotton skirt and a Pro-Búsqueda T-shirt. Her memories begin at age eight, when she was in the care of an abusive adoptive family. At age ten, she began to question whether the "grandma" raising her was really her family. Three days before the adoptive grandmother's death—when María was an adult—the grandmother gave a friend the photo of María's biological family that the grandmother had received when María was handed over to her in the war. María doesn't celebrate a birthday and doesn't know if her biological family is alive. Nine years ago, a friend connected her to Pro-Búsqueda. I hold her hand as she weeps. "Not knowing one's family is like having a wound in your heart, an emptiness that doesn't fill," she says. "If I'm able to find them, I'll feel like I exist. They can tell me the story of my childhood, of when I was born. I'll fill that emptiness that I feel."

Last week María dreamed that she reunited with her mother. She is a niña desaparecida and a mother to a fifteen-, eleven-, and nine-year-old. "Since you didn't have an example of a mother, who taught you how to be a parent?" I ask.

"My suffering taught me," María replies. "I look at the things I lacked, and I think about how I can give them to my children. Not money, because I don't have money," but connecting with her children is what she values most. Pro-Búsqueda's therapies have helped her, and she prays to the spirit of Father Jon, she says. At the end of the interview, I let go of her hand.

The office still holds an emptiness, but less so than when I first returned. María relies on Pro-Búsqueda to help her find that sense of completeness that jóvenes encontrados like Amílcar have described—and that she knows she lacks. The organization is in disarray, but families need and deserve support with searches and with the challenges of reunion, and the world needs to hear what happens when violence and poverty rip families apart. Pro-Búsqueda is grieving but, inspired by Father Jon's memory, the fight for justice and healing presses on.

20 Pedro's Testimony

I've barely put my purse down when I see Pedro, the twenty-two-year-old former MS-13 gang member, at Pro-Búsqueda, and ask if I may interview him. I've interviewed eighteen people and feel comfortable with the process. I've heard fragments of Pedro's story and I'm wary of his violent world, though I recognize the power of gathering his full account. I leave the door to the psychology office ajar and begin by asking Pedro how he became separated from his family.

Pedro looks at me from across the desk, eyes locked on mine. "It was because of the war. I don't know a lot about my parents." The FMLN demanded that his parents, both FMLN fighters, give him up. "I was very young, and my parents couldn't carry me in their arms. You can't carry both a rifle and a child, so they had to choose. But if you abandon the FMLN, they kill you. My dad was told he had to abandon me, and he refused. When he fled, he got caught in a massacre and the military killed him. When my mom realized that my dad had fled, her only choice was to place me in another's arms and keep battling with the rifle, with the hope that she'd see me again. If not, she wouldn't see me again anyway," he says. "That's why she agreed to let me go." Pedro was one month old at the time.

Pedro's grandmother has told him that he was put up for adoption as a baby. Motivated by money, the first family kept him only three days. "God touched" the girl who would become his adoptive sister, he says, when she found him abandoned, leading to Pedro's second adoption. The girl's family took him into their home in Honduras, a family Pedro stayed with until age seven. Pedro says that, when he was three, his paternal grandmother came to retrieve him from his adoptive family in Honduras, causing his adoptive parents to fight because his adoptive father wanted to return him to his biological family, but his adoptive mother had grown too attached.

I'm skeptical the incident occurred because it seems unlikely that Pedro's biological grandmother would have left without him. Pedro's testimony does have some inconsistencies, though I can feel deep truth in the emotions he expresses. Everyone else I meet through Pro-Búsqueda presents information that seems accurate, but aspects of his testimony seem implausible. It's unclear if, at times, he embellishes, or if his extreme trauma or a mental illness has distorted his memories. Regardless, he communicates that he felt distanced from his adoptive parents and even voiced to them as a child his feeling of disconnection. He continues, "I wanted to know my biological family. 'You aren't my parents,' I said to them. I cried."

Pedro experienced extreme abuse at the hands of his adoptive father, stoking mistrust and loneliness. He feels his adoptive father never loved him. His adoptive mother did love him, he says, and sometimes disagreed with the punishments the father inflicted, but she didn't stop him from hurting Pedro. "My dad punished me a lot. If he got angry all of a sudden, he punished me. If he got angry at my mom, he took it out on me. If he had a rock, then he hit me with a rock. If he was carrying a stick, then he hit me with a stick. I would have accepted it if I had done something wrong. With relish, he removed my clothes. He had that habit. He got me naked so the rope lashings would hit me well. He'd take me outdoors to the countryside and hit me."

In response, Pedro threatened to run away. "Every time they punished me, from the time I could talk, I'd say, 'Wait until I grow a little older, and I'm going to leave.' The second time I said that to them, my mother put ground chili in my mouth." But they couldn't stop Pedro from wanting to leave. The abuse was too intense.

Pedro recalls, "I remember once my mom sent me to the vegetable garden to deliver lunch to my dad. When I arrived, my dad said, 'Today, you're going to pay, boy.' He cut a branch from an elm tree, peeled the outer shell, and he said, 'Come here,' so he could hit me [with the branch]. Then he got his belt, grabbed me, and hit me in the head. My head felt like it exploded. When I got to the house, I arrived bathed in blood. My mother asked me what happened. I covered it up by saying I'd fallen. My mom knew that my dad had hit me. He was put in jail.

"Three months later, a police officer came to our home. My dad had been convicted for one year, and the officer had come to ask my mom whether she thought my dad should come home early, to free him or not. She knew that my dad had to return to the farm and work to maintain the family. They had eighteen [biological] children and seven adopted and three grandchildren. So, she told them to let him go. From the day he returned, he didn't care about me anymore. He said, 'I'll be on the farm. I'm going to work for the ones who are my children. I don't love the rest of you.'"

Pedro says that his adoptive family soon moved to Morazán, El Salvador. There "they bought a cow, and with that cow they made my life impossible. It was my responsibility to take the cow to pasture every day. I was deprived of an education because my dad said they didn't have one either. Tending to the cow became my work. They didn't give me shoes. I walked barefoot at noon on paved highways. Those highways burned. I'd peel off pieces of callus from the soles of my feet with a Gillette razor. Eventually, I could walk on thorns and it wouldn't hurt me."

Pedro explains that he would set out each dawn to tend to the cow, walk home midmorning to bring the milk to make cheese, eat lunch, and then take the cow to graze in the paddock. Sometimes it was hard to find the cow. If Pedro returned home later than six in the evening, his father punished him by making him carry a rock all night, and then, in the morning, he'd have to retrieve four heavy barrels of water. "In sum, I always lived a hard life."

Eight months later, his family moved to the department of Usulután, and he continued his responsibility of tending to the cow. "On the day of my seventh birthday, I couldn't find the cow. It was a Friday. I arrived to the paddock at three in the afternoon. There was a big storm. I walked through a lot of mud. By nine at night, I still hadn't found the cow. I knew

I'd get punished, which I didn't want. I started to cry in the paddock, and I asked God to help me."

Pedro pauses his steady narration. As we sit in silence, his eyes water. I wait, then wait more. No tears have formed on Pedro's cheeks, yet as a gesture of support, I dig through my purse to find a tissue. I retrieve a crumpled napkin. When I hand it to him across the desk, it's as if the tissue has given him permission to cry. Tears run over his jagged cheekbones, along the skin of his cheeks. Splotches of tears drop onto his maroon Tommy Hilfiger button-up shirt. I didn't anticipate that I'd ever see Pedro cry. Pedro, formerly of MS-13, crying. Pedro, the joven encontrado. Pedro, a person who has become . . . a friend.

Pedro says that, at midnight, he was still out in that paddock, after hours of searching, crying, and praying to God. A family friend who lived near the paddock found him shivering and took him in. They warmed him and gave him coffee. Once everyone else in the house fell asleep, Pedro slipped out. At three in the morning, he walked toward town to avoid the mud fields. He stumbled into a party, where he encountered one of his adoptive brothers. He had his first cigarette and his first beer. "It was in the middle of the dance party where I started thinking, 'I'm never going home again.' I remembered saying that I'd leave, and that night, I said to myself, 'Today, I am going to fulfill those words.'" After the party, a friend took him in. Pedro set out before dawn. "I left because I was very afraid of my parents. I was too afraid."

Pedro's adoptive father found Pedro scampering down the road in the early morning. "'Where are you going?' he shouted. So, I ran and hid behind a mango tree. By the light I could see my mom behind me. She said, 'Son, come here. We want to talk with you.' I remember that I shouted back, 'It's too late. Don't look for me because you're not going to find me.' I ran to the field where we played on the weekends. My dad came after me with a flashlight. I said to him for the last time, 'Forget about me.' I remember that I raised my hand and said goodbye." Pedro intended to never again see the man who raised him, the man who beat him until blood stained his clothes. "I ran."

Pedro left shoeless. He rode buses. When bus agents asked seven-year-old Pedro, "Where are you going?" he responded, "Farther ahead." All he knew was that he was going *away*. After one week of wandering, he came upon mechanics eating lunch at an auto shop. He asked them for food, and they fed him. He asked for a job. They told Pedro he was too young to work, but took pity on him and allowed him to wash cars and run errands for a few cents. "They tried so hard to get the truth out of me, but I didn't want them to know where I came from." Pedro felt fearful that the men would return him to his adoptive family. After one week, he left.

Pedro wandered on and found a job working the tire swings at a traveling carnival. "I entered a new world." The carnivals were full of gang influences, and he needed to survive—to meet his basic needs. "I worked for my food and the little bit of clothes they bought me." Pedro lied about his name and identity, revealing only that his parents had died in the war. People called him Xavier, and no one asked for papers. "That's how I stayed with that name." He reflects, "From there, I started to wake up more. That was when I started to form into a complete man." His boss at the carnival belonged to the gang Mara Salvatrucha, also known as MS-13. The adults and the illicit activities at the carnival exposed "Xavier" to gangs and drugs, further burying the identity of Pedro, the hopeful, earnest boy, deeper into a past that he preferred to forget.

Pedro's testimony jumps from age seven to age nine. "At age nine, I dedicated myself to gangs. My name was Goblin because I was everywhere." Then our interview halts with a knock on the door, announcing that a joven encontrado has traveled to Pro-Búsqueda from Chalatenango for an interview. I must attend to the joven because he'll need to travel back before dark.

Pedro leaves for the countryside, and six days later I see him again in the hallway at Pro-Búsqueda. We resume the interview. Pedro shuts and locks the door to the psychology office. "No, Pedro, this is Marco's office. We can't lock it," I assert. There's no way I'm going to sit in a locked room with him while he talks about Goblin's thirst for blood. I unlock the door. Pedro insists on sitting on the psychologist's side of the desk, giving me the seat of the patient. With my audio recorder, I replay Pedro's last sentence from where we left off.

Then he continues, "I didn't grow up robbing or begging, but rather in a very diabolical world, very violent. When I say diabolical, I mean because I was in gangs. You know that there's nothing good. Only to kill. Only to see blood run. I craved that a lot. I lost respect for the authorities." Pedro describes his main role as "getting weapons and ammunition." He says, "I was high all the time," and describes taunting the police with phrases like "Do you like me? Am I handsome?" He craved violence, he says again. "It was something even more than diabolical. When I took it out, I took that out from my heart. And, as I repeat to you, I loved to see blood run. It didn't matter if people were getting it out of me, or if I was getting it out of people."

Pedro recounts next about when his boss, whom he viewed as a mentor, died. Pedro was thirteen years old at the time. The boss had told Pedro to observe him, to stay close. Pedro's boss bequeathed his governorship role to Pedro by declaring before the neighborhood gang, "Goblin, come here. They've asked for you. We receive him [Pedro] because we know that the person who can guide our platoon is someone who doesn't have family. Someone who has raised himself. Ask him for arms. Ask him for whatever you want. I hand over my charge to him." One month later, the boss was killed and Pedro assumed the governorship of Zacamil, the neighborhood in San Salvador where Lucio lives. Pedro served in that role for three years.

The recollection seems to shake even Pedro, and his account transitions to when Pro-Búsqueda found him, at age seventeen. He'd been living under pseudonyms and recalls the day his new boss "became angry" when three staff persons from Pro-Búsqueda came looking for a boy named Pedro. Pedro didn't know at the time, but his grandmother had filed a case with Pro-Búsqueda in search of her missing grandson. Pro-Búsqueda followed leads and tracked him down at the carnival.

When Pro-Búsqueda employees whom Pedro had never met approached, Pedro said, "If you're not buying anything, what are you doing here? Get out of here. I suggest that you go." But, Arsinio, an investigator from Pro-Búsqueda, was not deterred. "Arsinio said, 'Pedro, we'll come back a different day.'" Pedro's name connected to his history—to painful memories and to the risk of losing anonymity—and he didn't yet understand that his name also connected him to a family who could love him. Pedro describes his exchange with Arsinio. "I said, 'Please don't call me Pedro! My name is not Pedro.' 'No,' he said, 'You are Pedro, even if you don't like it.' Deep inside, I accepted that, but on the surface, no. I accepted that they call me Pedro, but I didn't trust them."

One week later, the Pro-Búsqueda team appeared again and explained that Pedro's grandmother was searching for him. "I told them I wasn't Pedro." Pedro sent them to find a fictitious Pedro who sold corn. After an abusive adoptive home and a childhood on the streets, he didn't trust the intentions of Pro-Búsqueda or his so-called family.

One more week passed, and the Pro-Búsqueda team returned a third time. The visit prompted Pedro to exchange parting words with his new boss, who was also enmeshed in MS-13. "'If you're going to leave, try not to be seen because it's dangerous, and you should carry arms.' I said to him, 'You're going down, and I'm going up.' He stared at me and said, 'Are you threatening me?' We had a few punches and then I quit." The boss pressured Pedro to help pack up the traveling carnival before quitting. Pedro says that he grabbed his suitcase, moved on to the next town, and then left the carnival.

Pedro soon encountered an older woman who had known his biological parents and observed his resemblance to them. "Upon seeing me, she said, 'Is it true that you're Pedro? Are you the son of Gustavo and Claribel Zepeda, yes or no?'"

After at first denying his parentage, Pedro admitted that she was correct and then asked her for a favor: "Can you call San Salvador for me?"

She placed the call to Pro-Búsqueda, on Pedro's behalf, from her office at city hall, where she had access to a telephone. Pedro awaited the news from Pro-Búsqueda. He felt skeptical but trusted them just enough to reach out. "A bit later, she returned, very happy. 'Pedro, I didn't know that you had family alive,' she said to me. That's when the reality began to sink in that I had a family who cared about me. Because for seventeen years I believed I didn't have family. I knew I had an adoptive family but not a biological family."

The woman explained that, through Pro-Búsqueda, Pedro's biological family was searching for him. Pro-Búsqueda had told him the same at the carnival, but after years of fending for himself he felt leery. The woman observed Pedro's misgivings and advised him to trust his biological family. Pedro responded, "'You don't know me,' I said. 'You know my face, but what I have inside, you don't know.'" Even if his family was well-intentioned, which he doubted, he didn't trust them to accept him and his violent past.

Nevertheless, the woman related Pro-Búsqueda's message: they'd return to find him at six o'clock. Pedro promised to wait—and then left for the next town. Hours later, Pro-Búsqueda found Pedro with his girlfriend's father, in a cornfield. Pedro spotted the Trooper jeep, Pro-Búsqueda's flagship vehicle. "All of a sudden, the Trooper stopped, the same one from before. They were truly searching for me. I was carrying a big stick, and then all of a sudden I saw that they began taking photos. And I learned that it was my family."

Unlike the reencuentros I witnessed last summer, in Pedro's case Pro-Búsqueda didn't plan a reunion event weeks in advance. They brought Pedro's grandmother and aunt to him, surprising him and catching him before he could run. At his reunion, Pedro felt overwhelmed. A powerful tide of emotion—belonging and disconnection—overcame him. "It's very hard. I don't know how to explain it. Almost eighteen years of not knowing about one's family, and then suddenly you're told that you're part of a family that's alive, that they've been looking for you, and you're immediately introduced."

Pedro also felt mistrustful. "In that instant, I thought maybe the government was paying them to say that they were my family. The government was capable of ripping me from my parents' arms when I was so little, so why wouldn't they be capable of paying a family to do that? That's why I didn't trust them."

Despite the uncertainty, after the reunion Pedro went to live with his biological family. When they reached his grandmother's house, Pedro saw Pro-Búsqueda hand her money, which fueled more skepticism. "They think I'm an animal to be fattened!" Pedro thought to himself.

He struggled to adapt to life at his grandmother's rural home. "In the world I grew up in, I wasn't accustomed to sleeping all night. All of a sudden, I was staying with my biological family, and I realized that in the countryside people go to bed early. I saw the first night that they went to sleep at eight. That, to me, felt like a punishment. I thought, 'These people have come to put me in a living hell.'" His grandmother spent three sleepless nights with him. "My grandmother said, 'Look, I understand where you come from, but go to sleep.' After three nights I started to cry because

I felt they had deprived me of my freedom. I was used to controlling my own rolls of cash and, all of a sudden, here, with nothing. One month later, I started to make friends and began drugging myself because I was missing it a lot. I couldn't sleep without the drugs. I had to be smoking pure marijuana or drinking my alcohol. I had to do it so I could sleep."

About a month after moving to his grandmother's home, Pedro's aunt confronted him about his drug use. Pedro responded, "'Yes, I come home *loco* [crazy, high] because that's the only way I can live,' I told her. When my aunt saw I was losing myself too much, she talked with Pro-Búsqueda, and they said they'd put me in a rehabilitation program where I could learn a trade. So, I came to San Salvador, and they put me in a carpentry course."

But upon arriving to the rehabilitation program in San Salvador, Pedro's progress in leaving gangs slid backward. "In the time I was staying with them [Pedro's family], I had distanced myself from gangs and when I arrived to San Salvador, I came with the thought that I didn't want to be in gangs anymore. I had decided to leave the gangs. But when I returned to San Salvador, I found the same thing—there were only gang members [at the rehabilitation program]. So, I had to again choose who I was with. Members of [Calle] 18 and MS were mixed together because they were told they had to recuperate their lives." He could no longer distance himself because gang members seeking to reform or pretending to reform surrounded him. "I was connected [to gangs] on all sides."

Pedro attempted to hide his gang identity but had an altercation with a member of Calle 18 about whether Pedro would put the "little bouillon cube" for chicken flavoring in the rice. "You don't know who you're messing with. I'm not who you imagine," Pedro said, referring to his suppressed identity as an MS-13 fighter. The conflict escalated, and his enemy used Pedro's girlfriend, also a member of Calle 18, to set Pedro up in a trap. The girlfriend invited Pedro on an outing. Stanley, the director of the carpentry program, aware of the plan against Pedro, insisted on joining Pedro when he requested permission to go out. "We walked for a while, and it wasn't my girlfriend—it was my death. Because when we got to the neighborhood, I saw my girlfriend there with 18, and all of a sudden she says, 'Hi, Pedro. How are you?' They surrounded us with knives and guns and said, 'Today, you're going to die.' Stanley had been their director too; they knew him, and he told them, 'Leave him alone.' They let me go. If it wasn't for the director of the carpentry program, they would have killed me." The incident convinced Pedro to reenter gangs. "Well, I'd decided that I would leave gangs. But I felt that served like a wick to activate a bomb. From there, I started in a new role here in the capital."

Pedro returned to the streets for two years. He notes an important difference from when he first joined gangs as a young child to when he became reinvolved as an older adolescent: he now knew he had a family who cared about him. "When I entered gangs at age nine, it was something very carnal, to say it like that. They knew that I didn't have family." But, for a while, the all-consuming gang lifestyle again took hold. Pedro explains, "When one goes around with a gang, it's like everything changes, like you stop being human. You turn into something diabolical, as if you don't have a reason to live." Yet, after two years, knowing he had a family—a grandmother who loved him—gave him the strength to find the church and his way out. Pedro describes a gradual awakening precipitated by realizations and events that led him to renounce gang life again. An unwavering faith in God seems to have lit his path, leading him to exchange his gun for a Bible.

In perhaps his last battle as a gang member, Pedro evaded police and bullets, attributing his survival and freedom to God. "From there, God, as if to finish getting me out [of gangs]—on Good Friday, the police killed two people from 18 in front of my eyes. One of the gang members from 18 was after me, and I was after another, and in the guinda at ten at night, my friend stopped next to me, and the police shot him." He uses the word *guinda* to mean gang battle, a term derived from civilians struggling to survive the civil war. The gang members from Calle 18 got shot: "One was shot in the back, and another one got shot in the foot." Pedro ran. "I had my knife, but not my gun. The only thing I could do was flee because if I stayed there, I'd have sixty years in prison." Only three of Pedro's fellow gang members survived the gangs, he says, but of the three, Pedro is the best off since the other two are in prison—and the rest are dead.

Pedro feels that divine intervention protected him as a reformed evangelical walking the same streets of San Salvador where he waged gang war. "When I left [gangs], I started to congregate in a church." He expected former gang members to recognize him and possibly kill him when he walked to church. But God's protection kept him alive, he relates. He describes an incident when God spared him: "God confused their minds because I see it like a trick. When I returned to the streets, I presented myself as an evangelical, and they didn't recognize me. They wanted to rob me, and all of sudden I found myself face to face with the brother of my [deceased] boss." The young man who'd assumed Pedro's role when he exited the gang threatened to hurt him. So, Pedro revealed his identity as a former MS-13 gang member, but they didn't believe him because they insisted that they saw when Calle 18 shot Goblin. Pedro asked God for guidance and then got the idea to say aloud each of the gang members' names, which convinced them of his identity and saved him.

Pedro perceives his escape from gangs as a miracle, a divine gift, for which he feels indebted. "God has promised to make me invisible to my enemies. From there to now, the only thing I do is walk in the path of God. Just at the time I was getting into gangs again, I saw that God put many of His children on my path so that I would not continue to lose myself." He believes that God granted him salvation for a purpose. "Through the church, now what's left for me to do is give my testimony. God has promised to take me to many churches. Because He has clearly said to me that He got me out of death so that I could share my testimony."

As Pedro's narration wraps up, I weave in a few questions. I ask Pedro how he feels about his relationship with his biological family. He responds that after reuniting with his family, he asked Pro-Búsqueda to run a DNA test. "The result was positive, but there's something in me that doesn't believe it." Pedro has strong faith in God and supernatural occurrences but doubts the DNA test.

I also ask again if he's killed anyone. He responds, "It's one thing to have hands bathed in blood and another to know with certainty that I was the one who did it." Many Salvadoran gang members have tattoos, but he doesn't. I ask him why. He explains that he avoided being "stained" by allowing his fellow gang members to beat him for thirteen seconds, after which he was elected a boss.

Then I ask if he's ever fallen in love. "There are many pretty girls in gangs. Maybe I don't remember. There were a lot." He tells of a romance with a girl from MS-13. "There were so many females I had sex with that I don't remember. Now I know there are more children. I don't know who they are. It's hard. I grew up without knowing who my dad was." I ask about his daughter, as I heard Lucio mention her over the summer. Has he seen her? "Just once. I saw her but I didn't get close to her because I felt like I would hurt her."

I ask again about his family, inquiring whom he feels support from. He tells a long story about, when after being out of gangs for good, he worked for six months as a security guard and in construction, in the countryside near his aunt. He gave his aunt nearly all the money he earned ($23 per week as a guard and $120 per week for construction work), but she took advantage of him. His girlfriend ground corn with his aunt and overhead the aunt saying that Pedro didn't contribute enough money to the household, which the girlfriend then related to Pedro. When Pedro confronted his aunt, she spread rumors that he was gay, which prompted him to return to San Salvador.

In San Salvador, Pedro told Pro-Búsqueda about the situation. "They insisted that I go back to my family, but I told them, 'No, I'd be crazy to return to my family.' So, Pro-Búsqueda gave me the little room to stay in," the room he still inhabits. "It's hard for me to get a job," he adds. His new girlfriend is teaching him to read, and he tells me about struggling to learn to spell his name.

A skilled carpenter, he dreams of having his own workshop. Pedro concludes, "I have three roles that are important for me: the church, building my workshop, and sharing my testimony." He aspires to one day divulge his entire life story. He will share it in churches. That's why he bought an audio recorder, he says. A knock on the door interrupts our conversation. I thank Pedro for the trust he demonstrated with his words and I depart.

When I reflect on Pedro's story, I think about how he personifies the forces that drive children into gangs, the same forces that perpetuate violence in Central America and on the urban streets of Los Angeles. The war separated him from his parents. After running away from an abusive adoptive family, Pedro rose within MS-13 because he had no family to lose—no parents or siblings for enemies to shoot in retaliation or family to agonize over his death. Abandoned as an infant, abused as a child, and then inculcated into street violence, he had a lost-boy identity and couldn't trust his biological family's intentions when they found him again. Today he identifies as a child of God, no longer an orphan because he found spirituality when he had nothing.

The voice of God he hears guides him to goodness. But his old wounds and broken nose remain prominent; his heart seems unhealed. He abstains from gangs and drugs, but I sense that he has not yet found happiness. He hears God speak of acceptance, but he has not yet accepted himself. He hears God speak of the many churches he will visit, but I think the healing will come from reading the scars on his own body and forgiving himself for the scars that he inflicted.

The child of rebel fighters became a rebel himself—a street rebel. And now I understand why, when we first sat down together last summer, he started by telling me about the moment that Pro-Búsqueda found him. It was the beginning of his salvation—his rebirth into becoming Pedro again, a joven encontrado wounded by the war and its aftermath—and he is still rising toward healing.

21 El Norte

Over dinner at Andrea's, I finally meet her friend "El Chino" (Armando), a joven encontrado whose uncle I recently interviewed in Cabañas. Armando has buzz-cut, graying-brown hair, large chocolate eyes, and a Buddha belly. He tells me of his disappearance during the guinda in Santa Marta in Cabañas (which Philippe Bourgois, my anthropology mentor, also survived) and of being in the orphanage with Andrea and Angé-lica. When I play Armando the recorded message from his dying uncle, Armando nods a promise to visit when he has time off from work.

On Saturday, Lucio takes me to suburbs outside San Salvador to meet his friend Julio for an interview. Julio's wife answers the door, holding a newborn in her arms. She offers Lucio and me each an orange while we wait for Julio to return home. I have trouble penetrating the peel, so Lucio gestures to trade oranges with me—his is fully peeled. We eat and Lucio helps himself to a second orange. I do too. The same exchange occurs, and I ask, "How do you peel it so quickly?"

"I'm a guerrillero," Lucio says playfully, taking a bite.

Julio arrives an hour later, carrying two bags of groceries, one with multiple cartons of milk. After introductions, he and I go over to the back patio for an interview. Julio makes sure that I'm in the shade and curls himself on a low stool. He tells of his parents and two brothers killed in the war and of his placement in an orphanage at age four. But, besides that, Julio mostly discusses finances. Until recently, he worked as a security guard by night and as a waiter during the day. Now he doesn't have a job and plans to go to El Norte for three years, to send money home for his wife and baby and to save so he can open a small business when he returns to El Salvador. He wants to know what I think of the idea.

Even if Julio survives the treacherous journey to the United States, there's no guarantee he'll make money. I think of Margarita's husband, who returned early from Sweden because he couldn't find a job. The Zamora family is together again, though now thousands of dollars in debt.

I stay quiet as Julio explains his economic necessity. He makes pillows by hand. Each one takes hours to stuff and sew. He sells them for $10.00, but the materials cost $4.20 per pillow, so he views the pillow business as a hopeless endeavor.

To me, Julio faces a common dilemma of Central Americans. He suffered during the war and was orphaned by it, but his childhood trauma is a distant concern compared to the need to buy milk and pay the baby's doctor's bills. The savings are drying up. Julio feels that if his parents hadn't died, then maybe his financial concerns wouldn't be so dire. What do I think about going north? I still haven't answered. "People say it's dangerous," he remarks. I've had two oranges, and Julio and his wife insist on sending us home with flattened ice-cream-cone honey sandwiches called *empiñadas*. Why am I taking from them? I can afford many pints of milk.

On Sunday, at a pay-by-the-day modest beach club in La Libertad, Vladi and Michele play in the swimming pool. In the cabana, a friendly older woman chats with Lucio and his family as we munch on sandwiches of white bread, orange mayonnaise, and Kraft cheese. She tells them about her brother in El Norte, about the shoes he sent home. How cool to have a brother in El Norte, Angélica remarks. How much money does he send home? How much did he send at Christmas?

On the drive back to San Salvador, we get stuck in traffic. When a fancy, new blue Cadillac Escalade passes us, Lucio says, "I think that car belongs to Osmán."

"Who?" I ask.

"To the *coyote* who took Sandrita," Lucio responds.

"Wow, he has a car that nice?" I say.

"He has five or six cars," Lucio replies. I ask about eight-year-old Sandrita's journey and the dangers she faced. Lucio replies, "In Mexico, you could get robbed and killed. In the United States, at the border too."

"How does a family get the news that their loved one hasn't made it?" I ask.

"They don't hear from them."

It's an unbearable uncertainty already familiar to the families of the disappeared children of Pro-Búsqueda. Sandrita took one month to arrive, Angélica says. She traveled with a twenty-one-year-old woman from Chalatenango and a six-year-old boy. Once a week, Sandrita would call her aunt María, nicknamed "La Morena" for her dark skin. "She was very good about calling. But La Morena could barely eat. She would just cry because Sandrita was like a daughter to her. La Morena was the one who raised her."

I ask why the journey took so long. Angélica explains, "Mexican immigration officers caught her [Sandrita] three times. The *coyote* had to pay to get her out [of custody]. If they don't pay, then they send them back. When I talked to Sandrita on the telephone, she told me that when they caught her, the worst part was that she was given food 'like dog food.'"

We talk about Sandrita's crossing into the United States. "She didn't have to go through the desert," Angélica says with fiery passion. "But my other niece, Martita [Sandrita's sister], had to go through a swamp that she said was up to her neck. Thank God, Sandrita didn't have to walk through that." There was a scare at the Mexico-US border. Sandrita feared for her life. She thought she was going to be left in Mexico forever—until a stranger carried her on his shoulders over the border into Arizona. The *coyote* got Sandrita bused to Phoenix and then to the East Coast, "right to my sister's house [in Maryland]," Angélica says. "But, she's not happy there. She just eats chocolate, cries, and says that she feels encaged."

Like the children lost in the war, it seems that children separated from their families by immigration may also face feelings of abandonment and confusion about family bonds. Sandrita's caregiver-child bond was disrupted when her mother left and then again when she separated from her aunt, the maternal figure who had cared for her since she was one month old. Arriving has been a struggle and though Sandrita will likely adapt, her challenges are not uncommon. Transnational gangs like MS-13 thrive on youngsters hungry for a feeling of family, feeding further separations.

Many Salvadorans were driven north in the 1980s, to the country that sent the bombs. The Salvadoran diaspora population in the United States has increased fivefold since the start of the civil war and continues to grow because of the unrelenting everyday violence and poverty in El Salvador today.[1] An estimated fourteen percent of people of Salvadoran descent live in the United States—and send home $3 billion dollars per year in remittances, contributing one out of every five dollars of the nation's GDP.[2] Thousands of Salvadoran children experience ongoing separation.

I didn't answer Julio's question about whether to emigrate because there is no right answer. Like many Salvadorans, he faces an impossible choice—not in the heat of military gunfire like Andrea's dad, but still in the struggle for his family's survival. For the children disappeared in El Salvador's civil war, separation marked their childhood *and* their transition into adulthood. In today's El Salvador, separations reoccur as many of these same jóvenes are forced to migrate to El Norte. How can a just global society create an opportunity for Julio to earn a living, be safe, and kiss his daughter good night at the end of each day?

•   •   •

The next day, Don Jaime and I trek out to San Vicente. He warns me that we probably won't find Claudio and if we do, he'll most likely be drunk. But Pro-Búsqueda thinks it would be valuable for me to interview him—Claudio has a unique story. I'm lucky to find him sitting on the side of the rural street, talking with friends as we drive up. Claudio wears a simple white T-shirt and shorts, but the T-shirt is bleached bright white and well fitted on his body, his shorts stylish. He invites us into his home, turns off the television, and leaves on the fan. His home appears tidy but has an odor of urine.

Thirty-two-year-old Claudio tells me about getting lost from his family at age five while fleeing a storm of bullets and then facing the guinda on his own. He ran and ran. Finding himself still alone, he made his way into a cave, where he spent the night. He endured hunger, thirst, and fear. Then he was discovered by soldiers, picked up, and taken to an orphanage.

After several years, a French woman reached out to the orphanage and wanted to adopt him. They wrote letters and exchanged photographs. Eventually, ten-year-old Claudio agreed that he wanted her to become his adoptive mother. She came to El Salvador, and they spent two weeks in a hotel together as they metamorphosed into mother and son. Claudio boarded the airplane without looking back to his *tierra* (land), he says, in tears. The guy with the cool persona weeps before me.

He spent seventeen years as Claude—the Frenchman who lived an upper-middle-class life—with education, friends, home, and security.

When Pro-Búsqueda sent Claudio a letter telling him that his biological mother had been found, twenty-seven-year-old Claudio traveled to El Salvador for a short visit to meet her. They had a tearful reunion but when Claudio went back to France, he felt discontented. A few months later, he quit his corporate job and returned to El Salvador. He says he left his comfortable French life because in France, "Everything is based on the material." He prefers El Salvador, where "the people are poor and live for what they'll eat tomorrow."

Today, five years since the reunion, Claudio has a Salvadoran wife and baby. He relishes the simplicity of the countryside. But he's "allergic," so he cannot do the difficult work of farmers tending to corn and bean crops. Being in the countryside is boring—he says boring three times for emphasis—and life in San Salvador is too expensive. Claudio seems stuck between two worlds. He speaks French better than Spanish and struggles to form sentences in his native tongue. His "mother from France" comes to visit him and presumably sends him money. His relationship with his (biological) mother has soured since she doesn't approve of her daughter-in-law. Claudio says it's materialism that hurts him, but I think his pain stems from the rupture of the parent-child bond and confusion about who he is and where he belongs, layering on top of wounds from the war. "I have two identities," Claudio says. His friends in El Salvador call him "El Francés" (French Guy). He has two countries and two mothers, but he never feels *home*.

Don Jaime asks him to speak to me in French. His statement is a description of the corruption in El Salvador. Despite his wish that conditions in El Salvador will improve, he concludes, "*On peut pas le changer. C'est moi meme qui change la vie* [We can't change it. It's me who changes my life]." At the end of the interview, he asks me if the recording device I'm using is an iPod. He's the first person after over forty interviews to notice that I'm using this overly priced, trendy device. Claudio, who complained of the materialism of France, asks me how many CDs the iPod holds. I respond and he comments, "I have to get one of those."

.   .   .

Before Don Jaime and I leave Pro-Búsqueda for my last day of interviews, which will be in Chalatenango, we decide that my boyfriend, Mark, will go to the bank machine to withdraw money from my account to pay the interview transcriptionist. Ceci sends Pedro with Mark as a bodyguard. "*Te vas* [Are you going], Pedro?" Don Jaime asks him.

"If they don't catch me, I'll go," Pedro replies, laughing a crazy laugh as he walks through the street to catch up with Mark. The wolf protects the hens but the wolf is no longer a wolf. He howls.

With the motor of the red pickup truck running in Pro-Búsqueda's driveway, Don Jaime and I encounter a joven encontrado headed to Chalatenango to visit his mother. We give him a ride. From the back seat, he tells me that he still considers himself an orphan, though at meals his mother serves him the largest portion of chicken because she's making up for the years that she couldn't express her affection to him.

In Los Ranchos, Chalatenango, I interview Francisca Romero, survivor of the Guinda de Mayo, mother of Elsy, and cofounder of Pro-Búsqueda. Today's the day Francisca places her hand on my shoulder and asks me to tell the people of "Norteamérica" (North America) what happened in El Salvador when the children were disappeared. As I load in the truck, she yells, "Go see Maida!" A short drive down the road, I meet Maida, another cofounder of Pro-Búsqueda and the mother of Juan Carlos. Maida's home is set among abundant land and foliage with fruit-bearing trees. Inside, trays with dough ready for baking spread on the table across a tiled patio. Forty-year-old Maida tells me about running from bullets and then hiding by a stream, where soldiers found her and ripped six-month-old Juan Carlos out of her arms, a baby she gave birth to at age sixteen.

When Juan Carlos was twelve years old, mother and son reunited, thanks to Andrea being found in the same orphanage. Juan Carlos took well to his younger siblings, but Maida "annoyed" him, she says, and she felt rejected. Over time, they learned to accept each other. She had to come to terms with his resentment about their separation and his maltreatment in the orphanage. Juan Carlos also shared his happy memories, and they learned to find balance and comfort in Maida offering a mother's guidance, including when laced with criticism. Finding the trust to share a loving mother-son relationship took years, Maida relates.

Maida encouraged Juan Carlos to "take charge of the house." So, Juan Carlos recently left for the United States. "There's no work. No opportunity here," she explains. He went six months ago, shortly after I heard him speak at the nunnery last summer. He lives with his stepfather in Virginia. "He already sent his first five dollars home." He sent five dollars to each of the children at Christmastime. "He says he's going to work hard so that we have what we need." He's helping his family, but Juan Carlos and Maida are now separated again.

After the interview, Maida insists on making us lunch, pineapple juice and scrambled eggs that taste like smoke. "I wish you'd told me that you were coming," she says, apologizing that she didn't prepare chicken and that the sweet breads are still baking. She offers us jars of honey.

While we eat on Maida's spacious, shaded patio, she tells us that it took Juan Carlos two months to reach Virginia. After he arrived, he told her that when he was crossing the desert, he heard mothers crying and it made him think of her. He also saw corpses: a deceased young woman holding a dead infant in her arms. And he met a little boy who was lost and alone. Since Juan Carlos didn't have money to pay the *coyote* for the boy to join their group, he gave the boy water and crackers and left him behind in the desert.

Maida made the journey north six years ago, to her husband in Virginia. As we eat lunch, Maida tells of the tears she shed on her way to the United States. "I was upset about three things. One, I was leaving small children. Two, when I phoned my husband from Mexico, he told me that he had a new woman. And, three, I walked one day and two nights. The walking, the hunger, the elements made me cry." Maida felt vanquished, especially after learning of her husband's infidelity. "When I heard that my husband had another woman, I didn't know what to do. I asked God, 'Do I go back now, or do I keep on going?' I realized that from the North, at least I could help my children, so I continued."

"Sometimes you have to run from the authorities," Maida says. "The *coyotes* are very good. As soon as they see a vehicle they say, 'Hide. Run.' That's how people get lost. Everyone runs in different directions, and you have to hug the earth."

"And then is there a pickup truck waiting for you?" I ask.

"Yes, a van." All sixteen people in Maida's group made it to the van. "You know how the *coyotes* are. They get their money and dump you off," she says. "The *coyote* sent me with a Guatemalan man and said, 'This one goes to Virginia.' I arrived at two in the morning. I called my husband, but he didn't come. By five, my husband still hadn't come. I telephoned my brother-in-law, and he delivered me to my husband's home. I was nervous because you know what they say about America. I figured my husband would have a beautiful woman, courteous, well-mannered—at least with a nice figure. When my husband saw me, he reached his arms out for a big hug, and I shoved him away. I saw her, a *vieja panzona* [fat, old lady] just like me, from San Miguel, and I said to my husband, '¡Ni te mejorraste! [You didn't even do better!]. You could've traded me for something better, but you got the same!" Maida gives a victorious grin, and Don Jaime and I laugh. Maida continues, "I told my husband, either you get her out of here, or I'm going. He came with me."

When it's time for us to leave, Maida says, "Please come back for the sweet breads." We thank her for her generosity and roll on to the next town, dusty Guarjila. We pass the store where Andrea buys me chocolate-covered bananas. Graffiti in the town plaza reads, "Jon Cortina lives" and "Comunidad Jon Cortina."

I interview José, a *joven encontrado* raised in the same orphanage as Elsy, Andrea, Juan Carlos, and Armando. At five years old, José had just traded places with his grandmother to hide him deeper under a bed when soldiers shot her. Sometimes, as a child at the orphanage, José would speak of the war with his friends. José shares one of the more painful *guinda* memories of Armando, the *joven encontrado* whose uncle is dying. "Soldiers used to make him [Armando] stand on top of a hill and shout, '¡Mamá!' The mothers who were hiding would shout, 'Son!'" With the mothers' locations revealed, soldiers would shoot the mothers. Philippe has shared similar horrific stories from that same attack.

When José left the orphanage at age eighteen, he became involved in gangs. But finding his mother through Pro-Búsqueda allowed him to learn "who I am and where I come from." It gave him the hope and sense of belonging he needed to exit MS-13. He left the gang and moved to the countryside to recuperate from drug addiction and be near his mother. It feels fitting that my last interviewee is a young man whose family reunion pivoted him from despair to hope—from gangs to a family life reintegrated in a resettlement community: Guarjila. José is a fruit vendor and out of gratitude for Pro-Búsqueda, he sends us home with bananas and a bag of oranges.

It's Friday afternoon, and Don Jaime speeds back to Pro-Búsqueda. After a bus ride home, Listo the dog greets me with the pillow he chewed on today. I organize the audio recordings of the interviews and burn them to a CD for transcription. I completed fifty interviews: twenty-six jóvenes encontrados, fourteen of their biological relatives, three adoptive relatives, three individuals searching for missing children, one joven searching for her family, and three Pro-Búsqueda employees as key informants. All the interviewees spoke of identity and loss—the pain of family separation, the long-term challenges of reunification, and the peace that came with knowing the truth—or in continuing to fight to discover it.

The next day, Lucio's and Andrea's families take me on a fun farewell outing to a waterpark, and we enjoy a magenta sunset at an oceanside restaurant. Back at Jenny and Dave's house, I say goodbye to my friends. The almost-full moon hangs like a pendant above us. "Come here," three-year-old Michele says, asking me to kneel before her. I do and she jumps into my lap. She looks up at me with imploring eyes. "Is where you're going ugly?"

"No, it's not. But, Michele, the most beautiful is to be with your own family."

At the airport, early the next day, Lucio asks, "Will you return?"

"Yes, but I don't know when." Inside the terminal, I look around. There are Salvadorans boarding my flight who may have hugged their mother and father farewell for the last time. Immigration driven by poverty and violence tears this country apart. I pray that I may do right with the powerful testimonies given to me, to honor Francisca's request and ensure that people in El Norte know what happened and is still happening in El Salvador.

PART 3 Angela's Story (2006–2020)

Three days after returning from El Salvador, on my first day of classes after winter break, I walk in the door of my Berkeley cottage and sit to check email. Angela, the young woman raised in Berkeley whose DNA I collected last summer, has replied to my message. A few weeks after Angela's July 2005 visit to El Salvador, Pro-Búsqueda traced adoption records and then used word of mouth to track down a woman presumed to be Angela's biological mother. Confident in the match and with the DNA test still pending, Pro-Búsqueda asked me to inform Angela that they found her biological mother. I notified Angela, and we've been emailing since. Marco, Pro-Búsqueda's psychologist, has been shepherding communications with Blanca, her biological mother, and checking in with Angela, but the mother and daughter have not yet had contact with each other.

Before I left El Salvador, Marco had given me a letter for Angela from Blanca. Angela wants to come by and get the letter. "How about right now?" her email proposes. Within the hour, Angela is in my living room. I hand her the envelope with the handwritten note from Blanca. (Angela later gives me permission to share it.) Blanca wrote, "Dear Angela, Perhaps I am someone unknown to you but I love you more than I love my own life. Please forgive me for giving you up but maybe it was not my fault.

189

May God bless you." Also included in the envelope is a short note from Angela's brother: "I would love to meet you." Angela stashes the envelope in her purse, saying she feels "overwhelmed" and will read the letter later.

Before Angela leaves, I pull up on my computer a digital photograph that Marco asked me to show her of Blanca and her brother, Ricardo, standing in Pro-Búsqueda's courtyard. Angela's nose wrinkles as she leans in toward the screen. "She's so short," she says.

"Or your brother is tall."

I send Angela the photo electronically and, after a hug goodbye, ask if she'd like to get together and talk. "Yes, I really would," she says.

Two weeks later, Angela and I meet at a café on Telegraph Avenue. I relay the message Marco asked me to give Angela: Blanca is a kind woman who wants to meet her and is happy to know that Angela is safe and has a good life in the United States. Over lunch, Angela tells me about growing up in Berkeley. Kids at school called her a "bad Mexican" for not speaking Spanish. As a Cuban-American of Jewish descent, I tell her, "When I say that I'm *not* Latina, I feel like I'm lying. When I say that I *am* Latina, I feel like I'm lying." Sitting at this corner table that Angela chose, I realize that I'm helping to bridge Angela to her own culture, and she helps me to see the dual identities in myself.

Angela describes her tight-knit adoptive family. Her brother, also adopted but born in the United States, is jealous that Angela found Blanca. Angela lives with her adoptive parents, works, and commutes one hour from Berkeley to attend her classes at UC Davis because she doesn't want to be a financial burden on her parents. She earned a competitive scholarship that twenty applicants of thirty thousand receive. Angela's wit and sharp thinking are apparent in her speech. I wonder, would the world recognize her brilliance if she'd grown up barefoot in rural Chalatenango? I ask Angela about the possibility of someday meeting Blanca. "I need to marinate with my feelings," she concludes at the end of our lunch. When we say goodbye, I encourage Angela to phone me soon so we can meet again.

As the weeks go by, my strongest connection to El Salvador becomes my new friend Angela. The DNA bank continues to grow, with Cristián, the forensic geneticist, at the helm. Cristián and his DOJ geneticist colleagues will travel to El Salvador to present the results of the DNA analyses from the samples we collected last summer. They will also solidify Pro-Búsqueda's independence in maintaining the DNA database on its own. Yet the latest news from Pro-Búsqueda is disturbing. The organization's electricity was cut off and their internet blocked. Persons entering and leaving the office are being surveilled—even photographed—and employees of Pro-Búsqueda are receiving calls at home from unidentified callers demanding information about the activities of the organization. The harassment coincides with the one-year anniversary of the Inter-American Court of Human Rights decision in favor of the Serrano Cruz family.

The conservative ARENA party, still in charge of the government, fails to comply with the demands of reparation. The Inter-American Court gave the government one year to obey, and time has run out. Worried about the safety of my friends in El Salvador, I write an op-ed for the *San Francisco Chronicle* about the movement to find the disappeared children, the intimidation of Pro-Búsqueda, and the opportunity to facilitate amends—by finding the remaining missing children.[1] Presumably, many hundreds to thousands are still missing.

Three months after I gave Angela the letter from Blanca, Angela and I sit on the curb a few blocks from my home, nibbling on lemon poppy-seed muffins we got at the Farmers' Market. "I'm not ready to call [Blanca]," Angela says. She did read Blanca's letter, and Blanca and Ricardo have since sent a few more. When we met last month, Angela told me that she felt afraid to go to El Salvador, citing death threats by MS-13 to her close friend's brother. Angela's friend lives in Berkeley, and his brother is in El Salvador. Today, Angela voices her concerns about a telephone reunion with her biological mother. She fears she won't be able to form words over the telephone and that Blanca will mistake silence for indifference.

Another month later, in May 2006, UC Berkeley issues a press release about Angela to promote the collaborative work between its Human Rights Center and Pro-Búsqueda. Angela is happy to be featured, as she wants to support the search for the disappeared children. The press release quotes Angela's response to a reporter who asked why she contacted Pro-Búsqueda: "It's not like I'm trying to find a family. I have one. I'm trying to find myself in relation to my family." Angela searches for the truth of her family origin—for her place among two families, two cultures, and two nations.

Two weeks later, in June 2006, I see Angela and her adoptive dad, Jerry, who arrives on bicycle, for a press conference at the UC Berkeley Human Rights Center highlighting Angela and the Pro-Búsqueda DNA bank project. Angela looks beautiful and radiant as she tells her story to the press.

"Which family would you choose?" an insensitive journalist asks.

Angela gives a dimpled yet worn smile. "I can't change the past. I'm just incredibly grateful for the opportunities that I have." She tells the world that her adoptive parents supported her every step of her life.

The microphone passes to me. "I'm here to convey two lessons I learned from the disappeared children and their families while in El Salvador. One: they want their stories told; they want people in the US to know what happened. And two: there's more work to do—more children to find, more families to reunite, more located young adults who need psychological attention." I describe the process of DNA collection—about the cornfields and dirt roads and the relatives of the disappeared I met while gathering samples for the DNA bank.

Jerry speaks, choking on a tear. "Angela was not stolen," he says in a way that makes the press laugh because from the loving way he talks, it seems like the possibility furthest from the truth. "We [now] understand that there were irregularities with the adoption agency. I could no longer find them listed in the phone book. I checked last month." He tells the story of Angela's adoption: "My wife and I couldn't have children of our own. We were told a girl was born. 'Do you want to come down to El Salvador to pick up your daughter?'" the adoption agency asked. Jerry's honest expression warms the room.

Angela's story makes it to the Associated Press, TV news channels, and international outlets, creating a positive feedback loop. As more people learn about Pro-Búsqueda, Salvadoran-born adoptees around the globe step forward, and more disappeared children can be found.

I intermittently speak with my friends in El Salvador to share updates. By phone, Andrea tells me that Sandrita, Angélica's niece in Maryland, still "wants to come back to El Salvador but can't because her mom is settled in the United States." She also says, "I feel sad for El Chino [Armando]. His uncle died last month." I ask if Armando visited his uncle. He did, Andrea confirms. Reunions have a life cycle that, like life, evolves over time. For those who want to reunify, it is important to seize the moments available.

Inquiries have been coming in since the press conference and my op-ed. Some go straight to Pro-Búsqueda, some to the UC Berkeley Human Rights Center, and a few to my inbox. I've been emailing with Yvette, a college student born in Usulután, who had what she describes as a "sketchy" adoption and was raised in the United States. I connect her with Angela for mutual support. Angela tells me in a North Berkeley park that they "talked a lot about identity. What does it mean to be Salvadoran?"

Yvette's quandary typifies what many transnational adoptees may experience. She feels uncertain about whether to search for her biological family. Until learning about Pro-Búsqueda, she believed that her biological mother was dead and did not realize a search would be possible. She worries how she would reconcile finding a family she cannot support financially or emotionally, in her own challenging transition to adulthood. "What are my responsibilities to them? Legally, I know I have none but morally, how can I ignore them?" she asked me. I don't hear from Yvette again, but I'm hopeful that her healing was facilitated by the knowledge that she had the opportunity to search. Father Jon would have wanted her to know she had that choice.

Later in June, my pounding heart catches when I read the email subject: "Hit Confirmation Fillingim," sent from one of the DOJ geneticists, referencing Angela's last name. Blanca's DNA sample, mailed from El Salvador and run in the DOJ lab in Richmond, California, against the sample I collected from Angela last summer, was indeed "indicative of a maternal relationship." The UC Berkeley Human Rights Center publicizes the match because more awareness about the DNA bank may lead more adoptees to come forward. With the match confirmed, now all that remains is for mother and daughter to reconnect, for the first time since Angela's birth.

Summer passes. When classes resume in September, Angela asks if we can meet at our favorite taqueria, one block from UC Berkeley's campus. It's been nine months since I gave her Blanca's letter. As we munch on tortilla chips, Angela surprises me with her words: "I want to call Blanca, and I want you to be there."

One week later, the telephone in my living room rings. Angela's eyes say she doesn't want to be the one to pick up the phone. I answer and then push the orange button so we can hear Marco on speaker phone. He helped coordinate the reunion phone call. "Are you excited?" Marco asks Angela, with university-polished English.

"Nervous and scared," Angela replies.

"Perfect," he says, in an even tone. Angela and I look to each other and giggle, our mouths away from the phone.

A moment of transition and then Blanca's first words to Angela: "Daughter, I love you. I cried so much. I missed you. God bless you. Thank you for finding us."

Angela sits in my red IKEA swivel chair, wearing a low-cut *Animal House* "College" T-shirt, with her cheek glued to the receiver. Angela says in sweet Spanish: "I'm really happy. I'm glad to know you. Thank you." Then I translate her additional words for her mother: "I was always wondering who I look like. Now I know that I look like you. You were always with me."

"Your mother is crying very much," Marco says. "She's really happy." His words float.

"Thank you." Angela replies. I get up to get a camera, but I see Angela crying, so I reroute to grab tissues.

Blanca responds, "No, it's me who should be thankful to you. It was so hard to give you up for adoption. It hurt my heart. I cried for years, then you found me, and the pain came out."

Marco speaks above Blanca's choking tears. "Think about living in war," he says to Angela. "It's hard to survive. Just before we called, she was talking about how she had to give you up because of the war."

Next, Angela's sixteen-year-old brother, Ricardo, speaks. We have trouble hearing him through the echoing phone connection, but Angela understands when he says, "I love you so much. Come visit." I snap a few photos.

Angela says to Ricardo, "Congratulations on your graduation." She paid close attention to the information he conveyed in letters.

"Angela, your Spanish is really good," Marco comments.

"I like to think so. I'm a Spanish major," she replies, grinning.

Blanca tells Angela that she has a travel visa, permission to leave El Sal-

vador for the United States. "I'm serious about the visa," Blanca adds, with
a tone turned stern. Gone is the cooing, gentle adoring, melting of years of
longing. Now it's a burning, a piercing, as Angela will later describe. Then
the motherly, tender longing returns to the fore. Blanca wishes "blessings"
on Angela's adoptive parents. "All of your successes, I'm so proud of you for
all your successes," she says to Angela. "Thank God. Thank you for searching for me. You never would have had those successes [*if you had stayed
in El Salvador*]." Unspoken words finish her thought. Blanca mentions
the travel visa again. The forcefulness with which she presents the idea of
a California reunion a few weeks from now makes Angela tense. Her eyes
tell me she doesn't like this.

"*Whoa*, tiger," Angela whispers to me as she exhales ecstatic and nervous giggles.

The line is choppy but I'm able to translate more of Blanca's words. I
have the advantage of knowing what mothers say in reunion: "God bless
you." "Forgive me."

"She's really happy," Marco says. "You don't know how happy."

"Oh, I think I know," Angela replies. Her wide smile speaks of an overwhelming shared joy.

Blanca, sounding fierce, speaks again. "I'm really not kidding. I'm serious, Angela. I want to see you."

Marco repeats "the surprise," as he calls it. "Your mother has a visa to
come to the US."

"I need to think about it," Angela says. "Thank you. Liz and I will talk
about it. Goodbye." The call ends abruptly because Angela doesn't want to
commit to a visit next month. Angela decompresses as she swivels in the
chair. "*Whoa*, my mom is hard-core."

Angela and I discuss the possibility of Blanca coming to California versus Angela going to El Salvador for a reencuentro, possibly in December
when classes end. Blanca's forceful words about meeting soon in California dominated the coos and tears that characterize other reencuentros
I've attended. Perhaps the underlying expression is the same—daughter
come back to me—but her determination and almost ferocity took both
Angela and me by surprise. Angela feels nervous about declining Blanca's
proposal of traveling to California for a reencuentro because she does not

want to offend Blanca. I tell her it's all about how she presents it—and remind her that, though Blanca wants to meet, Angela can control the pace of reunion. Both parties must choose to reunite.

Angela cheers up as she recalls celebrating her twenty-first birthday in Las Vegas with her friends. I walk Angela to the street corner. "Thank you for being there for me," she says when we hug goodbye.

In late October, one month after Angela spoke with Blanca, Angela arrives at my door. I ask if she's talked with anyone about her call with Blanca. "*Yah,* my [adoptive] mom wanted to know every detail," Angela says. "My dad finally said, 'Leave her alone.'"

We discuss a winter trip together to El Salvador for Angela's reunion. Angela told me over a recent taco lunch that she wanted me to be the one to travel with her. If her adoptive family went, she'd feel responsible for taking care of them. She observed the productive response to the press conference and wants the press to join for the in-person reunion "because there are people like Yvette who don't have support. I want them to hear my story," remarkable young Angela says.

Three weeks pass with Angela not returning my calls or emails. Then my cell phone rings. "I've been scared," Angela says. We decide to meet. It is now late November. Over tacos, we talk about her recent wild trip to "La Bega" (Cuban pronunciation of Las Vegas). A handful of tortilla chips later, I bring up El Salvador. "What are you most afraid of?"

"Blanca's expectations," Angela replies. "That she wants too much too quickly. That she'll touch me too much—I know it sounds bad. It's like [ripping off] a Band-Aid. I just want to get this [reunion] over with." We finish lunch, drop coins in the parking meter, and find Wi-Fi to purchase our plane tickets. Over the next days, I coordinate logistics for the reunion with Marco.

Four weeks later, in December 2006, we've completed our final exams, Angela has sent out her graduate school applications, and we each have suitcases by our front doors, set for a dawn departure back to El Salvador. Through Angela and Blanca, I will watch from up close an entire reunion process unfold.

23 Return to El Salvador

Angela and her parents arrive in early-morning darkness outside my Berkeley home to take us to the airport. I feel committed to supporting Angela, and we're all a bit nervous about her reunion. Angela and I will visit El Salvador for two weeks. A film crew from PBS's *NewsHour with Jim Lehrer* will accompany us at the reunion and for the days surrounding the event. On our ride to the airport, as we cross the Bay Bridge, I ask how it went when PBS interviewed Angela's parents yesterday at their home. "They don't get it," Gretta responds. "Jerry and I did the best we could to make sure that everything was perfect," she says, referring to Angela's adoption process. "There was a lot we didn't know about what was happening in El Salvador then."

I give a sympathetic, taut smile and release a soft sigh. "Well, it was hard to know what was happening because the US government and the Salvadoran government colluded to ensure that the public didn't know about the atrocities," I say. And the illicit nature of the transnational adoptions, as suspected by Father Jon, has never been revealed to the public and certainly was unclear in the 1980s.

When we reach the airport, Angela hugs her parents goodbye, then drags her suitcase between terminals as if it had wheels. After we check in for our flight, we wander to a dessert shop. As we sit to pass time, Angela's witty quips about society and passersby keep me laughing. Taking account of the water I've spit onto my shirt, I set the ground rule between us: "No making me laugh when I'm drinking!"

As the conversation opens further, Angela tells me about her adoptive family. She says that her brother, also adopted, is African American and one year older than her. Her sister, fourteen years older than Angela, is Jerry's biological daughter from a previous marriage. Once Gretta and Jerry married, they pursued adoption so they could have children together. The "six-month rule" agonized them. Angela explains that the rule stipulates that biological parents have six months to reclaim parental rights of a child and halt an adoption. Gretta and Jerry waited five months and twenty-nine days for an infant, Angela says. On the last day, the mother decided to keep the baby and forego the adoption. Gretta and Jerry then placed themselves on a waiting list to adopt a child from El Salvador. When the stipulated six months was up for a candidate child in El Salvador, the couple traveled south with their toddler son to retrieve the baby, whom they named Angela, for the esteemed civil rights activist and philosopher Angela Davis.

Angela's stories convey a happy childhood, one in which she felt nurtured. Once, when Angela was in elementary school, her father took her to see Angela Davis speak. After the talk, Angela tapped Dr. Davis and said, "Excuse me, I have something to tell you." Angela Davis looked down and little Angela elaborated, "My parents named me after you because you are so wonderful." With that, she received a kiss on the cheek from her namesake.

On the flight to El Salvador, Angela and I share an *Us Weekly* entertainment magazine, and she tutors me on pop culture. Hours later, we emerge sweaty from the stuffy plane. The PBS crew has already arrived and films us as we step out of the gateway. Outside, at midnight in San Salvador, Marco picks us up. In the car, Marco shares that Pedro is married and has moved away. Pro-Búsqueda staff are exhausted from day-to-day work and from activities honoring the one-year anniversary of Father Jon's death, Marco says. He drops us off at the small, family-run guesthouse where Angela stayed last summer.

The next morning, Angela and I walk to Pro-Búsqueda. Marco tells

Angela that her reencuentro will be at the home of Blanca's parents, in Ilobasco, a municipality in Cabañas. When we see Ester, we hug and chat. "Ester, how are you?" I ask.

"Trying to be a flexible mother," the former guerrillera responds. "Mélida is sixteen years old. The hardest is when her boyfriends are in the neighborhood." Ester is serving as Pro-Búsqueda's interim executive director. The organization makes steady progress in its mission to support the disappeared children. I remind Ester about my ethnography. Ester tells me to use her real name for a potential book. "We're still guerrilleras," she says. "Without rifles, but still guerrilleras." The comment seems to have awoken memories. With her head shaking no, lips curling into a scowl, she talks about "seeing so many dead bodies" in the war and "taking guns away from people who were dead."

In the foyer, Angela and I meet a joven encontrada newly reunited with her biological mother only two weeks ago. Roxy, a tiny woman raised in Texas who reminds me of a hummingbird, hones in on Angela as a Pro-Búsqueda staff member introduces us. "Where are you in the process?" Roxy asks Angela.

"I'll meet my mother tomorrow," Angela responds.

Roxy nods. "Are your parents support—" Roxy interrupts her own words, the term *parent* not so simple anymore. "How are your *parents in the US*?" Roxy asks Angela.

Angela nods and smiles because when Roxy said "parents," Angela knew that Roxy was referring to the couple who raised her. Angela says her parents are doing well and that they support the reunion.

"Roxy, do you have any advice for Angela?" I ask.

She nods, still fluttering around Angela. "Stay in your comfort zone."

A bit later, Angela, Ceci, and I head out for chocolate-covered bananas. Ceci says that her mother, María Inés, feels too sick to come to work today. She also has good news: she's been emailing with Andrés in Italy, the brother in the photo on her screensaver. "He gets the emails translated. He asks me questions like, 'How did I escape [the war]? What did we eat during the war?'" Andrés wrote that he hasn't yet chosen a destination for his January vacation, which Ceci and her mother assumed meant he might come to El Salvador. Marco advised that the idea of Andrés visiting "must be born from him," but María Inés's hopefulness could not be dimmed. "My mom is already preparing the house for his visit," Ceci says, as we cross Boulevard de los Héroes back toward Pro-Búsqueda.

I deliver Angela to the psychology office for a private moment with Marco to prepare her for the reencuentro. In the hallway, I see Margarita and tell her I've missed her. She takes my arms and says she's happy to see me. Earlier this week, I phoned her to ask if she'd escort the news crew to Guarjila. I told her that PBS's *NewsHour* has wide viewership in the United States, meaning that their reporting might help locate lost children. "I hope that among them is one of my brothers," Margarita said. "We have to maintain faith."

A bit later, a PBS crew member knocks on Marco's door. They ask to film a conversation between Angela and Marco. "B shots" include Angela looking serious, then smiling, and me nodding in support as Angela "listens." Then, with cameras still rolling, Angela tells Marco, "We got you ice cream because you were grumpy," just as I've taken a gulp of yogurt drink. Angela is breaking our fundamental rule: Don't make me laugh when I'm drinking, especially when I have a mouthful of yogurt shake!

When Angela returns to the foyer, I stay with Marco. "Blanca's character is *muy fuerte* [very strong]," he tells me, visibly anxious about the reunion.

"Do you think she'll be difficult with Angela?" I ask.

"No, no. With Angela she will be *un amor* [a love]." Marco adds, "Angela is holding her feelings in. When these two meet, there's going to be an explosion—a supernova."

Two hours later, at a pupusería, Angela recounts what happened when Ester first told her about Pro-Búsqueda. "She scared me when I first met her," Angela says. "She was working at the CIS [language school]. She saw the name of the lawyer involved in my adoption and said to someone, 'I know about that lawyer. He did bad things. He probably stole her.' Ester didn't know that I understood so much Spanish." Ester's unsettling assertion did lead Angela to Pro-Búsqueda but also made her fear that she'd discover that her adoptive parents were somehow complicit kidnappers. Although Pro-Búsqueda has helped Angela to understand the circumstances of adoptions like hers, the deeper answers she needs will have to come from Blanca.

Over our meal of pupusas, we talk about *closure*, a concept Angela refers to in the context of healing and moving on from a traumatic experience. Angela witnessed Ester's quick retreat into war stories. "If one does not have closure from the war, then one is still living the war," wise Angela comments. She relates a story she read in a Latin American literature course: "A soldier died in a war, and after his death his mother is sent home a lead box that she can't open. She goes to many people to help her open the box because she can't have peace until it's opened." The lead box is a metaphor for the tremendous pain of uncertainty, of not having closure after the death of a loved one. It can also be a metaphor for the uncertain process of reunification, such as when mother and daughter reunite after so many years. I imagine darkness sealed inside a lead box impermeable to light that only a reunion can open. Tomorrow Angela will meet Blanca, and Angela's life, her identity—the way she perceives herself in the world—will never be the same.

24 Angela's Reunion

We turn off from the highway at San José Las Flores and pass the eatery with the smoky kitchen where I've eaten a dozen times. A bumpy, unpaved road takes us to the rural home of Blanca's parents. I've attended several reunions, but Angela's feels different. She has become a friend, we both fear what she may learn about her adoption, and I brace for the culture clash and class divide I've felt at reunions, especially of transnational adoptees.

Marco parks, as does the PBS van, which followed behind us. Margarita and Marco climb out of our jeep. The PBS crew unloads. Angela and I wait in the jeep because the film crew and photographer want to get in position to film Angela's arrival. When we step out, the sound guy clips a microphone pack to the waistband of Angela's skirt. Then, Angela, Marco, and I walk to a wired gate decorated with streamers, behind which Blanca awaits. We walk single file up the narrow dirt path, Angela leading us to the home that will receive her.

Now Angela's looking at Blanca, the woman in the red blouse who stands apart from the rest of the family, who stands beside her tall son with spiked hair, black slacks, sage-green shirt, and tie. Blanca cries. Angela walks over to her. Marco manages to squeeze in a quick introduction, as I know was his plan: "Angela, this is your mother." They're hugging, Blanca crying. Ricardo watches from a few steps away. Blanca cries more; Angela does not cry at all. I hear Blanca's words rolling like a rushing river, fervent but not as emotional as that first phone call, perhaps because of the onlookers. The PBS camera operator moves to get shots of The Hug from multiple angles.

After two minutes, Angela lets go of her mother, whose tears landed on Angela's shoulders, to greet Ricardo. With a triumphant smile, Angela gives a super excited "Hi, nice to meet you" in Spanish to her seventeen-year-old brother, followed by an exuberant hug. Then she gives Ricardo a blue-stuffed smiley flower she bought at a gift shop at the San Francisco airport. Other relatives—grandparents, three uncles and their wives, and cousins—watch.

Angela is escorted to a couch on the patio of Blanca's parents' humble ranch. The patio, with one mud wall and an aluminum ceiling, functions like a North American living room. It separates the kitchen and its mud stove from the two bedrooms that comprise the home. The room adjacent to the bedroom has a large wooden weaving loom powered by foot pedals.

Angela sits on the patio between her mother and brother, who now has his arm around her. Angela's Spanish is excellent, and her emotional strength and composure admirable. I keep a respectful distance and take in our surroundings. A squash vine wraps its tendrils up the poles just outside the kitchen. The kitchen sink and its reserve of water are full. A kernelless cob of corn plugs a drain in the sink. Four toothbrushes are tucked into an apron-like garment strapped to the pole beside the sink that I lean against. Chickens and chicks run about the patio, magenta blossoms and tall agaves fill the garden, and an expanse of fertile earth stretches out around us.

I hear Angela say to Blanca, "I have a letter for you from my parents." Then Angela gives them more gifts. To Ricardo, she gives a San Francisco Giants baseball cap. To Blanca, a coffee-table book about Berkeley. "This is where I live," Angela tells them, as she opens right to the glossy page that shows a photo of her performing an Aztec dance at her high school graduation. Mother, brother, and sister-daughter talk excitedly. Then, perspiring Angela is introduced to three adorable *primitos* (little cousins). She gives them stickers and kneels down low for hugs.

Someone suggests that Angela meet her grandparents. Her grandfather, aged beyond gray, leans against the wall to the bedroom, about six feet from Angela. So far, he hasn't said a word. She walks over to him with a brilliant smile, says hello, embraces him, and offers him a small gift: kitchen towels and a San Francisco key chain bought at the airport. He smiles and thanks her.

Next, Angela is shuffled to her grandmother. The film crew follows as Angela scuttles into the kitchen to meet the short woman at the mud stove making tortillas. Angela beams as her grandmother shows her how to take a ball of dough, form it into a ball, flatten it between her hands, and then set it in the adobe oven to heat in the fire. Angela announces, "My tortilla is ugly." The young cousins are close by, giggling. Angela presses one tortilla between her palms and then retires, leaving the heat of the kitchen and her grandmother's side.

On the patio, there's mostly silence, except for Angela creating joy wherever she steps. The PBS crew and Pro-Búsqueda staff and volunteers, including me and my thesis mentor, Eric Stover, hang to the side—as does the rest of the family (uncles and aunts, grandpa, cousins). Blanca hurriedly provides the guests, Angela first, with Coca Cola and Sprite. With steel posture, Blanca thanks me. "I know you helped her a lot," she says, almost austere, before she steps away to bring me a Sprite.

Then, Blanca, Angela, and Ricardo, accompanied by only Marco and young cousins, set off for a walk to a river. Ricardo shelters her from the sun with a rain umbrella held like a parasol. While the newly reunited family meanders along the river, I talk to Angela's grandfather, Don César. Thin, with drooping shoulders, he leans against the wall. I give him a wallet-sized photo showing Angela speaking with Blanca and Ricardo by telephone for the first time. He grins and tucks the photo in the front pocket of his shirt. I invite him to sit beside me. We sit together as he stares off over the land, looking toward the river where Angela is now walking.

No-toothed Spanish is difficult for me to understand, but I do my best to listen to Angela's grandfather's reminiscences about the war, about when "they dragged them out of the house," his faintly audible words say. "There were dead bodies in the street." Each time I start talking, Angela's grandfather interrupts to mention the dead bodies in the streets during the war.

Then, wanting to gather information for Angela, I manage to ask, "Did you know that Angela existed?"

"Yes," he replies. "They searched for her, but Blanca told me she wasn't sure if Angela had died." He talks again about the corpses dragged out in the street and then switches topics to his high cholesterol and heart problems.

Angela's grandfather strolls across the patio with me to the kitchen, where Angela's grandmother heats tortillas above the flames. He shows his wife the photo of Angela that I gave him. She smiles the generation of smiles that I see in Angela's face and shoves the photo in the pocket of her apron. "This goes in the pile of family pictures. Angela looks exactly like Blanca did when she was that age."

I say to Angela's grandmother, "I realize that today is a beautiful day for you and your family, and it's also probably difficult because it brings memories."

Still busy with tortillas, she pauses, avoids eye contact, and then looks at me. "Yes, what you say is true."

"Did you know about Angela?"

Her eyes get wide and sad. "We thought she'd died."

"Do you know where her father is?"

"No, I asked Blanca yesterday, and she says she doesn't know what happened to him." Angela's grandmother, Rosa, shakes her head, a gesture of mixed sorrow and joy, and repeats this refrain: "God knows what He does. God is great." Then I speak with Angela's grandfather again, about the crops and flowers growing on their land.

Angela and her entourage return from their walk by the river. PBS interviews Blanca inside the grandparents' home while Angela joins Ricardo, self-described as a clean-cut young man who aspires to be a minister. He tells Angela about his close childhood friend, a fifteen-year-old baker who got mixed up in gangs and was shot to death two years ago. We all sit to eat lunch on the patio. Ricardo leads us in a rushed prayer (Angela giggles when her brother looks to her and says, "The faster we pray, the faster we eat"), and lunch commences. With a spoon, I scoop out the fly treading in my soup. A bountiful basket of steaming tortillas serves as the centerpiece of the table.

After awkward, icebreaker conservation, Blanca turns to Angela. "I want to ask you something. You can say no. There's no pressure, but I'd really like it if you came to my church tomorrow." Marco and I look at each other. Marco warned us she'd ask and said the masses at Blanca's church last hours. People go into trances and speak in tongues. Blanca wishes to present Angela to her church community, but Angela looks miserable while Blanca continues, "You have three choices: you can come to mass at eight [in the morning], eleven, or four." I know Angela doesn't want to attend, and I also know she fears disappointing Blanca. We shuffle onto another topic, the issue of attending mass hanging in the air as Angela hugs her brother goodbye before he leaves for a church event.

Lunch ends. I request to snap a photograph of Angela in the garden as an excuse to confer with her about the mass. "I want to go at the end," Angela determines.

When we return to the table, Blanca repeats the Sunday mass schedule. I relay that we'd like to attend the end of a mass. Blanca seems confused. I negotiate, "The 8:00 a.m. mass ends at 9:30 a.m., so we'll arrive at 9:15 a.m.," which Blanca wants to push to 9:05 a.m. Marco has other commitments, so it will be just me and Angela coming to the church tomorrow.

Somehow it's universally understood that the reencuentro is winding down. It's three o'clock. I rest on the couch on the patio and flip through the coffee-table book of Berkeley that Angela's adoptive mother sent as a gift for Blanca. I see a photo of my street corner in Berkeley and, for a moment, fantasize about walking into the page. I show the photo to a British volunteer with Pro-Búsqueda. She's attended a handful of reencuentros and says, "I've never seen a joven guide the reencuentro as gracefully as Angela did." Angela took control, soothed everyone, and made people laugh.

The *NewsHour* crew pulls Angela aside for an interview. Blanca and I stand together as the reporter interviews Angela for her "post-reencuentro" thoughts. During the ten-minute interview, the correspondent asks Angela if her reunion affects her sense of identity. Angela replies that meeting her family in El Salvador has allowed her "to solidify the two sides that created me."

I survey the scene before we leave. In the kitchen, the dog is eating a chick he killed ten minutes ago, bones crunching as he chews. Smoke from the cooking fire wafts into light beams streaking the gray air. Eric Stover, who helped Father Jon begin the DNA work, gives Angela a blanket he bought today from Angela's uncle that the uncle wove in their wooden loom.

Angela hugs and kisses her biological family members goodbye, then walks with me back up the dirt road where Pro-Búsqueda's jeep awaits. We will drive Blanca back to the city. I offer Blanca the passenger seat before climbing in. A huge smile overcomes Blanca when she declines. "No, right here," she says and taps Angela's leg. Angela and Blanca hold hands, legs squeezed against each other in the crowded back seat.

The highway winds us past verdant volcanoes and trucks overstuffed with goods and passengers. At Angela's request, we stop at a wooden shack on the side of the highway for sugarcane and then after driving more, reach Soyapango, a high-crime suburb of San Salvador.

When we arrive at Blanca's street, because of the risk of car theft, Blanca pays the thirty-five cents to park Pro-Búsqueda's jeep in a lot protected by a seven-foot chain-link fence. We walk three long minutes down a narrow pedestrian alley between two rows of homes. Margarita clings to her purse. Blanca shows off Angela to neighbors and then, twenty paces ahead of us, announces, "This is where the gang members are." In a hushed voice, she tells us that she made the announcement loudly to chase the neighborhood *mareros* (gang members) away.

Blanca's concrete home stands as one of the last in the row. Her slender living room blends into a kitchen. Two curtains, drawn closed, separate the living room from the two bedrooms. "Perfect for two," Margarita says. A machete hangs by a string at a door leading from the kitchen to a small, enclosed backyard. The tropical decorations lead Angela and Blanca to realize that they have the same favorite fruit: pineapple. Blanca offers us chicken tamales.

Angela jokes with her brother Ricardo, and then asks for a picture with him. I snap a photo of Ricardo standing in the front doorway, and Angela jumps in from behind, giving her brother bunny ears. "He's so tall," Angela says. Now I snap a photo with Blanca in the doorway as well. The family appears complete. At four o'clock, Marco drives Angela and me back to our guesthouse.

Later, Angela and I walk to the supermarket at San Luis to grab dinner before it gets dark. Angela tells me that during the walk by the river, they talked about "Ricardo's childhood." Angela still doesn't know if she

Angela on the day of her reunion with her biological mother, Blanca, and her brother, Ricardo, in the doorway of her mother's home. Soyapango, San Salvador, 2006. Photo by author.

and Ricardo have the same father. "I love Ricardo," Angela says. "I felt so comfortable with him." I notice she's not saying the same about Blanca.

Tomorrow we will spend the day with Blanca. "Think about what you want to know," I advise as we rush our footsteps before nightfall. We talk about Angela's fear of upsetting Blanca and that she deserves to know the truth surrounding her adoption. We eat tamales at the guesthouse and watch a sappy Hollywood movie about a mother learning to accept her daughter's rebellious ice skating. If only Angela had cried at the reencuentro, then I wouldn't have all these silly stray tears to let out! It worries me that Angela hasn't cried today. One thing I can say: at least Angela doesn't hide from joy.

After an intense day, it's finally time for bed. On our first two nights in El Salvador, instead of the top sheet the guesthouse provided, Angela used a bath towel she brought from California as a blanket because "it smells like home." Tonight, Angela sleeps draped under the blue blanket woven by her biological uncle, the lavender towel folded by her head. Both families are a part of her, comforting her in the knowledge of who she is and where she comes from.

25 Blanca and Ricardo

The taxi driver gets lost on the way to the Brotherhood of Jerusalem Church. When we do arrive, we spot well-dressed Ricardo, with gooped hair, in the driveway, running "security." Ricardo directs us to the open doors of the church. Inside, Angela and I are passed among six church ladies who, with hushed commotion, direct us to the two empty seats beside Blanca. Blanca beams and Angela gives a nervous hello as the minister leads the congregation in prayer. I quietly cue Angela to bow her head like the assembled worshippers. We drop our knees to the kneeler in front of the bench, emulating the large group of congregants.

After an electric band rocks the congregation, the minister speaks in a serious tone about Blanca, sharing the fulfilled prophecy proclaimed in the church months ago that someone looking for Blanca would come from far away. Since Angela refused Blanca's request to go on stage "to be presented" to the congregation, Blanca scribbled the name "Angela" on a piece of paper she gave the minister before the mass. "Angela, please rise," the minister decrees. Angela stands, appearing embarrassed by the attention, especially when the congregation applauds. "Blanca hadn't seen her daughter for twenty years," he says. "Proof that dreams do come true."

After one more song, the mass ends and church ladies swarm to greet

Angela. "*Mucho gusto* [Nice to meet you]," charming Angela says, offering generous smiles and hugs to each of Blanca's many friends. Angela acts polite and caring, honoring the importance of the moment for Blanca, despite feeling uncomfortable. At the doorway leading out of the church, I'm given a handshake and a glare and am asked if I accept Christ.

Outside of the church, pupusas heat on the grill. Blanca hands Ricardo the Bible she keeps in her purse. On the adjacent concrete, friends of Ricardo's approach to meet Angela, our interactions brief because of a planned quick departure. Then the four of us (Angela, Blanca, Ricardo, me) climb into the waiting taxi for an outing to the shopping mall near our guesthouse so we can spend time together at a safer location.

In the open-air portion of the Metrocentro mall, I sit on a low slate wall surrounding potted trees, with Angela beside me. Our group of four splinters into a two and two configuration. Passing time as Blanca and Angela converse, I ask Ricardo if he has a girlfriend. Stories of his love life captivate me for twenty minutes. His most recent breakup was three days ago. He met his ex-girlfriend through church and although she cheated on him, he'd "never speak badly about a girl." Angela's back presses against mine. Hopefully, having me and Ricardo near helps calm her nerves about speaking with Blanca. I know Ricardo serves as a support for Blanca. Ricardo tells me that, for a while, he was hanging with the wrong crowd and joined "the mafia." I hadn't guessed that this pious, woman-respecting, sister-adoring teen had a violent past.

Ricardo says that he never knew his biological father. His father left when Blanca was still pregnant. Blanca's "lover," a man Ricardo accepted as his own father, raised him but was shot when Ricardo was twelve. "Why was my dad shot?" (Ricardo likes to move stories along with rhetorical questions.) A man had borrowed a plot of land from Ricardo's stepfather and, instead of paying back the money he owed, hired an assassin to take out the stepfather and Blanca. The assassin killed the stepfather and shot Blanca four times. "She has the bullets in her arms. She can show you," Ricardo insists. One bullet remains lodged near her heart.

Ricardo's eyes grow cold and distant. "I thought I saw that man again," he says, referring to the man who hired the assassin. Angela's back still presses against mine. I feel her warmth radiating through her cotton T-shirt and listen as Ricardo continues. "I wanted revenge." So he joined "the mafia," which, he explains, is distinct from gangs. He describes the "special training" he received. "They took me to the countryside and taught me how to fire a gun, how to make bombs. They shot a dog, and they made me watch the dog die. And they said, 'Imagine that this [dying dog] is the man who killed your father.'" They were preparing Ricardo for murder. Ricardo doesn't think he ever killed anyone (Ricardo offered this, I didn't ask). But a number of times he ran from bullets. He and his friends stole cars, participated in "weapons trade" to gangs, and as a "*coyote* for cell phones," he would steal, hack, and then sell cell phones on the black market.

"I wanted to kill him. I wanted revenge," Ricardo confesses, speaking from the wound of a boy who lost his father. "Once, I was on a bus, and he boarded the bus. I had a gun. I reached for it," Ricardo says, grabbing toward the left-side pocket of his jeans as he speaks, making me fear that the mall security might notice us and attack. I manage to sit still. Ricardo continues, "I was about to shoot him. He'd boarded the bus to sell chewing gum. But then I heard someone say, '*Papi* [Daddy],' so I didn't shoot. It was his two-year-old son next to him." In that moment, Ricardo decided not to leave another boy fatherless. Ricardo feels relief that life spared him from committing murder on that bus. His friends in "the mafia" made plans to break into the man's home and shoot the family. "But the funny thing is," Ricardo says, "it was a special squad of the police that killed him. They killed the boy too."

I absorb Ricardo's revelations. Perhaps encouraged by my empathetic eyes or provoked by the transformative reunion process he finds himself in or the human urge to expunge tragedy by voicing struggles—for whatever reason, Ricardo is gifting me with his story. I listen as he talks about his near kidnapping after his involvement with "the mafia" and then of having to stay home for three years because of the dangers on the streets. His narration attunes me to the poverty and its twin, violence, that he and Blanca face—that Angela will inevitably confront. Angela has not yet reached the part of the reunification process where she feels responsible for rescuing her biological family from poverty, across distance, and over the wall they're building on the Mexico-US border. I don't have the foresight and courage to warn her of this.

After lunch at a chain restaurant in the shopping mall, Ricardo says he'd like to go for a short walk. I jump at the chance for an escape. We leave Angela to speak more with Blanca. As Ricardo and I peruse the supermarket, I ask, "Does Blanca work?"

"She helps the neighbor at the little store," Ricardo replies, referring to the tiny shop that sells oil, crackers, eggs, soda, and candy to other neighbors.

That doesn't seem like enough. "How do you two get by?" I ask, at the grocery store checkout line. Ricardo explains that they live off the money Blanca receives each month from a man who is slowly purchasing their plot of land. I wonder, what will happen when the payments stop, when they're landless and without steady income?

When Ricardo and I return to the restaurant, Blanca tells Angela about her previous work as a seamstress. Blanca lost her job one year ago when the factory closed because US taxes were too high, Blanca says. She talks about conditions at the factory. "They would lock the doors if you weren't there by eight in the morning." I ask Blanca where she learned to sew. "At a sewing academy, but I didn't learn much there. I learned by working." She tells us about her boss's scrutiny for imperfections. He would hold up a dress she'd sewn and demand to know, "What's wrong with this?" Though her boss had unreasonable expectations and wanted shortcuts, Blanca was assertive. "I can do this stitch, if that's what you want. But it won't come out well that way," she'd tell her boss.

To demonstrate imperfections, Blanca grabs the teddy bear that Ricardo just gave Angela. "One paw is bigger than the other," Blanca points out. She's right! I wouldn't have noticed. "And one ear is shorter than the other," she says, tracing the stuffed bear's ear with her finger. Right again!

Angela slips out with Ricardo. Blanca tells me that in production in the factory assembly line, my T-shirt "passed through many hands." Her eyes squint as she examines the shirt. It took "two minutes, at most," to sew by machine. "I worked from eight until six. And if we were behind on an order, we worked again from eight at night until four in the morning." When Angela returns, she gives Blanca a small, white teddy bear holding a pillow embroidered with the words, "I love you." Blanca receives the gift with a shy smile from her seat across the table.

Three hours later, we walk out of the restaurant. As we stroll, I ask Ricardo how he found the church. He responds by describing once watching an evangelical program on television. "They were singing. The people on the show seemed so happy," he says. "I wanted to be that happy. I felt a warmth in my heart I hadn't felt before."

As evening approaches, Angela offers to pay for a taxi to take Blanca and Ricardo home. The first taxi driver we hail refuses. "Some drivers don't go to Soyapango because it's too dangerous," Blanca explains. Angela pays the next cab driver seven dollars to take Blanca and Ricardo home. As the taxi pulls away from the curb, Angela promises that she'll call soon.

Angela and I have three more days in El Salvador, but we haven't planned past the present. The future feels uncertain, as does Blanca and Angela's reconnection. Where will Angela fit in the new family? How will she respond as she learns of her brother's violent past and of the bullet lodged near her mother's heart? Blanca and Ricardo's vulnerability to poverty and violence heighten the stakes of their fledgling relationship with Angela. I trust Angela's goodness—and Blanca and Ricardo's as well. But incongruent expectations often complicate the moments after reunion. Reunion marks the beginning of an identity but also the end of a simpler way of viewing oneself. How Angela views herself relates to how she connects with the world.

Before our trip, Angela told the reporter that she was trying to find herself in relation to her family. Now that she's found her biological family—and through them a part of herself—she weaves together new relationships. After reunion, for Angela and for all jóvenes encontrados, a new set of challenges and opportunity begin. Blanca and Ricardo are becoming a part of Angela's social fabric, not just her DNA.

26 Remittance

The following afternoon, Amílcar picks up Angela and me in his beat-up, gray Honda Civic with Andrea, Vladi, and Andrea's mother for pupusas at Los Planes. Lucio's family has already arrived at the mountaintop pupusería. Angélica braided little Michele's hair into a wreath. We enjoy a delicious meal overlooking the glimmering teal lights of San Salvador. When Lucio drives us back into the city, I ask him why his family moved to a new home with the same layout, only twenty paces from the previous one. He explains that they were renting and had an opportunity to buy, borrowing money from Andrea. I remark aloud that I'd love to live in the apartment between Andrea's and Lucio's two ground-floor homes.

"You would never move to El Salvador," Lucio says. "You can't anyway. My government wouldn't let you immigrate." Angela is listening to the humor and tension. Then Lucio rebuts his own joke, maybe for Angela's sake, saying there aren't rules here, and anyone can live where they want to. I comment that at the public hospital in San Francisco where I'll train, I'll likely encounter many Salvadorans. "That's good," Lucio responds. "Do me a favor, Liz. If you see a *mojado* [undocumented immigrant], don't tell on them. Hide them," he quips.

Lucio drops us off at the guesthouse. Tonight Angela sleeps snuggling with the teddy bear from Ricardo, her body under the blue blanket her uncle made, the lavender towel close by.

·   ·   ·   ·   ·

Blanca "tried to have an abortion," Angela blurts the next morning as we're about to enter a movie theater.

"How do you know that?" I ask.

"It says so in the adoption papers. She went to the clinic, but it was too late." I'm glad Blanca didn't have an abortion, though I can understand, given the circumstances of poverty and war, why she might have wanted one. I respond with consoling eyes.

Today, on our last full day in El Salvador, Angela will say goodbye to Blanca. Angela and I went to a matinee movie to pass time and for respite. Angela continually processes the reunion, piecing the experience together with information she gathered years ago from reading her adoption records. "She didn't want to see me after I was born," Angela says as we walk back from the movie. "A nurse wrote it in my adoption papers. It says, 'Mother does not ask about the baby.'" I think about how hard it must have been for Blanca to give Angela up.

At the guesthouse, Angela phones Blanca and invites her to meet us at the San Luis shopping center, which is walking distance from us and safer than Blanca's neighborhood. When Blanca and Ricardo arrive at Mister Donut, we greet one another with hugs and kisses on the cheek. Blanca gives Angela a sealed letter. Ricardo gives Angela a porcelain lamb and a homemade picture frame like the one Angela admired at their home.

After a lull in conversation, I ask Blanca if she craved any special foods when pregnant with Angela. Blanca smiles and replies that she ate mainly fruit during the pregnancy. "Especially pineapple, watermelon, and mango—when I could find ones that were ripe." I ask what Angela was like in the womb. Blanca smiles again. "She and Ricardo were both very active. The doctor said it was a sign that they were healthy." Blanca's grin widens more. "Sometimes you could see little hands."

I dare to comment, with Angela listening, "Those hours after Angela was born must have been so special and so hard for you. How long did you spend with Angela after she was born?"

"Twenty-four hours," Blanca replies. Then she talks about her excruciating childbirth.

Next we switch to discussing politics and shuffle seats. We've been at the restaurant for well over an hour. It's probably 1:30 p.m. and I'd promised Angela that the visit would end by 2:30 p.m. I lean in and say to Blanca, "I think that Angela wants to ask you questions. But she's afraid to ask because she doesn't want to hurt you."

"Oh, no," Blanca says with a loud whisper. "I already told her to ask me anything she wants. I told her to ask me *everything* she wants to know." I'm still looking at Blanca, unsure of how to proceed, when she throws her arms around Angela's shoulder and declares to Ricardo, "It's my turn now. I get to have her now." Blanca gives Angela a squeeze and motions a *shoo* to me and Ricardo.

As the glass door to Mister Donut shuts behind us, I ask Ricardo, who is five years younger than Angela, what he knows about Angela's adoption. Ricardo says, "My mom gave Angela up for adoption for economic reasons, and there was the war. The years of the war were hard, and her family didn't support her." He tells me in a serious voice about how Blanca suffered after she gave Angela up for adoption. "She heard later that babies who were given up for adoption were dismembered and their parts sold." We pause at the horror of the imagery.

As we walk farther up the road, Ricardo comments that he feels glad to have Angela in his life. "I'm happy. I feel like she's a sister and a friend." For a moment, he struggles with words, his speech slow and spread in thought. "I'm glad she's there—I mean, I wish she'd never left. I wish we could've been a family, the three of us. My whole life I wanted someone to play with. I was lonely. But I'm also glad she didn't stay because she wouldn't have had opportunities here." I feel humbled by his generous words.

We've circled the block now. As we cross the street to the lady who sells chocolate-covered bananas from the "dairy products" shop in front of her home, Ricardo tells me what meeting his sister has meant to him. "People in the neighborhood heard about my sister coming [from the United States], and they would come up to me and ask, 'What are you going to get from her?' I want to punch them. I don't expect anything material from my sister." Ricardo just wanted to meet Angela, to know his kin.

A number of Ricardo's friends have parents in the United States who send them goods. He tells me of his friend who "wears his new shoes and ruins them," failing to appreciate the parents' sacrifices. "I know that in the United States parents work hard to send back money. They work long hours and save as much as they can, sometimes not eating to send what they can to their family here. And this friend eats whatever he wants, whenever he wants."

"Did anything ever lack for you?" I ask. "Did you ever not have enough food?"

In the honest sun, sitting on the curb as we munch chocolate-covered bananas, he says, "Of course there were times we didn't have food." He lets out a hybrid between a laugh and a sigh, and then is quick to add, "But not recently." Shame evades Ricardo. He makes the most of what he has. "Sometimes I wanted name-brand clothes or shoes, and I couldn't get them, but I think I dress well." He does, especially given his limited means. He shrugs as his eyes refer to his black T-shirt that stands out against the collar of the yellow shirt layered underneath. And he wears electric-blue rimmed sunglasses, slick pants, tidy sneakers (not name brand), and once again the well-gooped spiky hair cut short on the sides. There's no doubt that the boy has style.

"Do you ever think about going to the US?"

"Sure. To visit, to know Angela's world. But not to stay." He reiterates that he doesn't expect anything material from his sister. "*Solamente quiero ser un amigo a mi hermana y amarla y quererla* [I only want to be a friend to my sister and to love her]." Ricardo's elegant words roll into my ears just as I near my last bites of chocolate-covered banana. Then I get the sudden, distinct feeling that Angela needs me right now. I don't understand the urgency, but I scramble toward the dairy-products shop with Ricardo following, across the street to the commercial center, and back through the glass doors of Mister Donut, where Blanca and Angela, daughter and mother, stranger and stranger, sit facing one another. Angela smiles upon seeing us. Whatever conversation they were having is halted, and the four of us walk to an internet café to create email accounts for Blanca and Ricardo so that they can write to Angela after she leaves.

While Angela goes to a computer with Ricardo, Blanca tells me what an amazing young woman Angela is. "I admire Angela. She is wonderful, and I realize that a big part of that is because of the parents who adopted her. They formed her." Blanca expresses her gratitude to Gretta and Jerry as she stands beside me in the internet café. "She didn't have to come back and find me." The gift of knowing that Angela is alive, let alone thriving, of seeing her in the flesh, is more than Blanca ever thought possible to ask for. The glass door to the internet café opens as a customer walks in. I brush Blanca toward me so she doesn't get jammed by the opening door as she continues speaking. "If I had known she would have gone into the care of another before the parents who adopted her had her, I never would have given her up." Blanca refers to the six-month period during which Angela was under the care of a foster parent in San Salvador.

I ask why it would have mattered.

Blanca's mouth drops, and she turns to me as if she will say something shocking. "I repented." She holds her eyes wide for long seconds after she's exhaled these words.

My quizzical eyes ask her to elaborate.

"I went back to look for the [adoption] lawyer, but he had moved his office, and I couldn't find him." Blanca says that if she had known then about the six-month rule and been able to find the attorney, she would have cancelled the adoption.

After the internet café, we wander to the sidewalk, its concrete wet from the stains left by supermarket trash bags. It's 2:30 p.m.—our exit time. Blanca and Ricardo will catch the bus in the opposite direction, away from the stench. Blanca's strong arms envelop Angela into a hug. Ricardo and I watch, then hug goodbye. Blanca lets go of Angela. She hugs me, thanks me, and says goodbye. Ricardo and I wait as Blanca scoops herself into Angela's arms again, crying with her head bolstered by Angela's shoulder. I look to Ricardo. He waits, knowing he will have to support his mother once the hugging is done.

Angela and I walk away, past my favorite pupusería. "She told me about my father." Angela wants to blurt out all she learned in her exchange with Blanca, expel it quickly. "He was studying to be a civil engineer. She met him when she was working at the factory. They would take their lunch break in the same restaurant every day. That's how they met. She says I look a lot like him. They broke up before she found out she was pregnant. She doesn't know where he is. She thinks that, because of his education, he's probably in the United States by now." There's more. "She told me that his name was Alberto Alvaro. Or Alvaro Alberto. She said, 'I don't remember which one went first.'" I laugh at the painful bareness of Blanca's revelation. After all of Angela's searching, Blanca cannot even remember the father's name. Angela laughs too. She has no leads to find her biological father—and never does. We've walked two blocks, and Angela is still ripping off the Band-Aid. "She asked me for $1,000," Angela continues. "She thinks I have $1,000 lying around."

"What did you say?" I inquire.

"I didn't answer. I didn't have to answer because you showed up." I had apparently come back just in time. "Thank God you came back."

"I got this feeling you needed me, so I came quickly." I now understand the topic of the interrupted conversation: money, the modern Salvadoran tradition bred of necessity—remittances.

"She wants it to pay lawyers' fees so she can sue someone over the *terreno* [plot of land]," referring to the same land that killed Ricardo's dad. Blanca promised Angela that if she secures the land, it will bring prosperity to Blanca and Ricardo and that she'll pay Angela back. But after everything Angela and I have heard about corrupt lawyers, $1,000 for legal fees in San Salvador sounds like a poor use of money. $1,000 is six months' wages for a typical Salvadoran.

So that's how Blanca sent her daughter away. To soothe Angela, I share Ricardo's caring words. "That's amazing, because at the exact same time I was with Ricardo and he was telling me the opposite. He was saying he doesn't expect anything from you. He just wants to love you."

I don't think Angela hears me. She's fuming. I attempt to defend Blanca. "I'm sure she didn't realize that this would hurt you. She has the responsibility of putting food on the table. And it's probably cultural too. That's what families do here. I'm sure she wouldn't have wanted to hurt you, but try to understand."

I could have warned Angela about the "burden" that seems to follow so many reunions. "I'm sorry she asked," I add. "But it's good that it came up sooner rather than later."

Furious Angela doesn't want to hear any of this. "Blanca saw pictures of my [adoptive] parents before putting me up for adoption. She [Blanca] knew that they were both social workers. She said she didn't have support from her family. She knew they wouldn't support her because I wasn't a boy, and she felt I would be in good hands with my [adoptive] parents." We're crossing the street. "I feel dirty," Angela says, as we walk on the road to our guesthouse. "I feel like an object."

"She told me that she went back to look for you," I respond. "She didn't know about the six-month rule, but she regretted her decision to give you up for adoption. She tried to find you, but the lawyer had moved offices."

"THANK GOD." There's spirit in Angela's livid breath. "THANK GOD THE LAWYER MOVED. Is that bad?" Angela deflates with worry. "I can't ever tell my parents that she went back to look for me. They would feel so bad. And I can't tell them about the money either because they would give it to her. They're so nice. Maybe she didn't go back," Angela postulates.

I convey disbelief. Blanca had seemed sincere to me.

"Maybe God gave her the ability to act." Angela's referencing Blanca's religiosity and the fact that Blanca did not search for her after the adoption. We've made it to the front gate of the guesthouse. As we walk through it, Angela, alluding again to the $1,000, says, "I feel like a whore."

At 5:00 p.m. Lucio picks me and Angela up for enchiladas. At Lucio's, Michele styles our hair with her doll's brush while Vladi shapes figurines with orange cooking dough. "Salvadoran Play-Doh," Angela tells me. After we eat orange enchiladas, the children scatter to play. I sit at the table with the four jóvenes encontrados: Angélica, Lucio, Andrea, and Angela. I'd hoped their shared past would help Angela, but she hasn't mentioned Blanca or Ricardo. Finally, out comes a peep from Angela about her reunion. Angela shares that her mother put her up for adoption for "economic reasons" and that a couple from the United States adopted her. The adoption was arranged before Angela's birth, and the reunion occurred last Saturday. Today was the goodbye, Angela relates.

"That's the hardest part. The reencuentro is the pleasant part. What comes after is what's hard," Lucio says.

Angela, Angélica, and Andrea squeeze onto a bench at the kitchen table; Lucio and I sit on the opposite side. The three jóvenes want to hear Angela's story, but she's being quiet. So, Andrea begins to tell her own story. Angela knows of the war but hasn't yet soaked in firsthand accounts. Andrea talks about the shrapnel that cut off her arm and mutilated her hip and even shares that, at one moment, her father left her because "he couldn't carry all of us. God knows that he did what he needed to. I don't fault him. I blame the war."

"My aunt is crying," Michele announces. Andrea smiles through the tears that swim down her cheek. Angélica hushes Michele while Angela listens with wide, absorbing eyes.

Now it's Angélica's turn. She begins by saying she doesn't remember the war. Then she talks about the shrapnel that pierced her vulva at age five, about being stuffed into a helicopter, about life at the orphanage, and about meeting her "worthless" father, who drank and visited only when Pro-Búsqueda paid his bus fare from Chalatenango.

Now it's time for Lucio's story. He recounts his mother's murder and tells of his years running from bombs and bullets with his dad and of the orphanages he was shuffled between. He concludes with an assertion of how much his wife and daughter mean to him.

Then the focus turns back to Angela. She avoids telling the jóvenes what burdens her: Blanca's request for money. But with small clues— mostly through words unsaid, I think—the jóvenes pick up on Angela's pain and sense of responsibility for her poverty-stricken family. Angela did not speak with enthusiasm about her biological family. "You don't owe them anything. You can't resolve their life," Lucio offers.

Perhaps sensing what Angela needs to hear, Andrea relates, "I gave my parents money. I gave them $1,000 so they could have a store like my mom wanted. But, with so many children, they ate all the soda and snacks, so that didn't work," Andrea says with off-kilter laughter. (I notice the coincidence that Angela too was asked for $1,000. Still, Angela chooses to not reveal this.) Andrea also tells of Amílcar's sour experience with giving his biological father money. One helps out when one can, Andrea says beneath pained laughter. Only give if you want to, don't expect the money to do much, and certainly don't expect to ever get it back, Andrea conveys.

Angélica's turn: "I was in the orphanage receiving an education, and my father wanted things from me," presumably money. But she realized she needed to focus on herself.

Lucio talks about the shocking state of poverty he found his sister and her children living in, crammed in a shack without a toilet or a latrine. After their reunion, with the help of a US volunteer at Pro-Búsqueda, Lucio raised funds to build his sister a house. Doing so made him realize he couldn't keep supplying their livelihood. He has his own family, and handouts aren't sustainable. Lucio asks Angela rhetorically, "If you give them money, what will that resolve for them?" Angela nods. A little money here and there won't fix their poverty, and it's not your responsibility to repair their lives, he says to Angela. He mentions a family he worked with at Pro-Búsqueda who was reuniting with their biological son, an international adoptee. When the family told Lucio that they wanted to ask the son for money, Lucio discouraged it, warning that the request might drive the son away. The biological family asked anyway, and the relationship between the Salvadoran family and son stayed frigid. "We don't have much," Lucio tells Angela, "but, to me, this is a palace." My eyes scan the blue walls of Lucio's small home. "We have everything we need. We have Andrea nearby. We have neighbors that come over. We have a sense of community." Andrea nods in agreement.

A banging noise followed by the rattling of a car comes from what sounds to be just a few meters in front of the home. "Look to make sure that my car's not being broken into," Lucio calls to Angélica's teenage niece, who sits by the window. He wants her to reach her arm up, pull back the curtain, and peek but, mesmerized by the TV, she doesn't. "Look to make sure that my car isn't being broken into," Lucio repeats. Four-year-old Michele, who is near the door, takes command. She opens the front door while the banging continues and peers outside. Then she turns back to her father and wags her finger to indicate no. Little Michele checking for burglars!

Midway through our visit, Lucio sees me scratching. "We have fleas here," he says. Regardless, I can see that, to him, his home is a palace where he has the honor of being a father and a husband.

Angela seems relieved when, at ten o'clock, Lucio drives us back to the guesthouse. As we pack our suitcases, Angela talks about how dangerous Lucio's neighborhood seemed. "Did you see the graffiti?" I shake my head in response. "It said 'M.S.'" I replay in my mind's eye the drive to Lucio's apartment, one I've made many times. I can see large, black spray-painted letters on a cement wall. Angela and Mark both commented on the dilapidated buildings, tin roofs, and graffiti in Lucio's neighborhood, signals of danger that I must have blocked out because I needed one place in San Salvador to feel safe. Angela and I laugh at the memory of adorable little Michele poking her head out her front door to check for gang members.

Laugher soothes but Angela still feels upset about her interaction with Blanca, and the stories the jóvenes told from the war, laden with trauma, layer on top. Still packing, Angela asks to hear "her song," "Angie," by the Rolling Stones (I feel honored that I was the first to play it for her). As Mick Jagger sings, "I still love you, baby," Angela dries her eyes. The lyrics remind us how precious it is to be alive, and they resonate—no one could say that Angela and Blanca never tried. We fall asleep listening to music, Angela draping herself with the blanket her uncle wove.

In the morning, Lucio and his family drive us to the airport. On the way, Angélica points out the public hospital where Michele was born. Angela comments that she was born in a private hospital in San Salvador. Lucio says that means that her adoptive parents likely paid the hospital fees for the birth. As we ride along the highway past the coconut vendor, on the topic of money, Angela heaves, "She asked me for money. She asked me for $1,000."

Angélica's immediate response: "I knew it. I could tell. I told Lucio last night, 'She doesn't seem happy. Maybe her mother asked her for money.' Tss," Angélica expresses. "How shameful. And $1,000 is no small amount."

"You don't owe them anything," Lucio remarks. "When you can help your mother, you will. If you give, give because you want to. Give because it arises from your heart. If you don't want to give, don't give." Lucio, still focusing on the road ahead, adds, "And how can you love them? You're barely beginning to get to know one another. You can't obligate someone to love. Love never comes from obligation." Angela listens and absorbs the words.

When we reach the airport terminal, Lucio asks me, "When are you coming back?"

"When there are mangoes, this season or next."

After a smooth flight, at our layover in Houston, the US customs agent asks Angela, "What was the purpose of your visit to El Salvador?"

"Visiting family," Angela replies, unemotional and assured. Salvadoran-American—it seems that's how she now sees herself. Life placed us both in a situation in which we had a *choice* over what aspects of our identities we nurtured. I dream in Spanish and English. Though I live a US life of white privilege, my cultural roots extend deep into Latin America. In Angela, I've found a true friend, one I joke with in Spanglish and who walked with me in El Salvador slums and ritzy San Salvador shopping centers.

The San Francisco–bound plane leaves us at almost the same gate we departed from two weeks ago. We descend the escalator to baggage claim. Angela runs into Gretta's open arms, broadened by a large, warm winter coat. Jerry looks on with a huge smile. It's midnight and Christmas is less than a week away. Before we even exit the parking garage, Angela tears the Band-Aid off. "Blanca worked in a sweatshop, and she asked me for $1,000."

Gretta's immediate response matches my initial reaction: to defend Blanca. "She must really need it if she asked."

In the first ten minutes of the ride, Angela tells her parents that Blanca has a bullet near her heart, that Ricardo's stepfather was murdered, and that Blanca and Ricardo's situation is bleak and dangerous. As we drive north on Highway 101, Angela asserts, "We're not giving her that money. She wants the money to pay for lawyers for a lawsuit, but in a culture ruled by gangs it would be worthless."

"She is your mother," Gretta replies.

"No, she's not my mother. *You* are my mother."

"Well, we're both your mothers," Gretta says, as Angela's "*harummph*" fills the car.

I can sense that Angela wants permission from her well-meaning parents to be angry. She struggles to reconcile her two worlds. We arrive at Parker Street, and Angela's parents walk me to my front door.

The next morning, jetlagged, I lock up my bike on campus for a press conference on Angela's reunion. As soon as I enter the UC Berkeley Human Rights Center, I see Angela. She grabs me into a happy hug, and I hear the sound of reporters snapping photos. Angela tells me that she and her parents "stayed up late talking."

When the press conference begins, a journalist asks Angela, "How do you feel now that you found your family?"

Angela tells America, "Like a weight lifted off my shoulders." They seem to love when Angela talks about making tortillas with her grandmother and when she holds up the blanket her uncle wove. Angela has looked to me a number of times for support as she fields questions. A reporter inquires about Angela's father. "My mom met him through her work at the sweatshop."

Then a reporter asks Angela's adoptive father, Jerry, how he feels about Angela's reunion with Blanca. He tells the crowd of reporters, "No one can ever have too much love."

.   .   .   .   .

Five days later, on the day after Christmas, Angela and I have lunch together at a café. Angela's story splashed through the Associated Press and many other outlets in the United States and abroad. I congratulate and thank her for raising awareness about the disappeared children. Angela says that even her experience of shopping has changed, the thought of sweatshops salient in her mind. "Imagine, I could be wearing something that Blanca made."

The next day, I receive an email from a Salvadoran-born young woman raised in Rhode Island who heard Angela's story on the news. The young woman is "very interested" in learning more about the DNA, she writes. She states that she has always wondered about her past and if she could still have family in El Salvador. We speak on the telephone, her own young children raucous in the background. I give her the contact information for Pro-Búsqueda so she can initiate a search. Other inquiries pour in.

On the last day of the year, Angela emails me to request a letter of support for her sociology doctoral application. She sends me the personal statement she submitted just before we departed for her reunion. Her essay opens with a question a journalist posed to her during the first press conference: "If you had to choose a family, which one would you choose?"

Angela's answer: "A friend of mine, who had a similar experience of growing up Latina and white, gave me an important piece of advice. It is not about choosing a side. . . . It is about being the bridge between the two sides. . . . My biological family gave me a beautiful culture and heritage. My [adoptive] family gave me the sense of working for social justice and ameliorating inequalities especially when you have the social power to do so. It is the coalescing of these two sides that empowers me to work for a better society by working to create a greater interpersonal understanding and knowledge." Angela wrote the essay after she was matched by DNA but before she even met Blanca. She's still working out her own sense of identity—and untangling her relationship with her biological mother. But just knowing they could meet brought her peace and enhanced her motivation to serve others, exactly as Father Jon would have wanted.

28 Berkeley Days Between

In January 2007, one month after Angela and I returned from El Salvador, Cristián emails that the Salvadoran government approved the DNA bank, meaning that the Supreme Court DNA lab I visited with Father Jon and Cristián can assist with processing samples. "Father Jon would have loved to see this great dream achieved," Cristián writes.

I phone Angela. She still hasn't spoken with Blanca since our return. I tell her that the young woman from Rhode Island who wrote me after the media coverage of Angela's reunion called Pro-Búsqueda to initiate a search. "See, that's why I'm glad I turned my life into a puppet show," Angela says. Angela has lost touch with Ricardo, so I give her the email address of one of Ricardo's friends. Minutes after our call, Angela forwards me the graduate school acceptance notice she just received from UC Berkeley. Two days later, she emails telling me that Blanca called. "We talked about nothing really. The connection was bad, so I couldn't really understand. Needless to say, the situation was awkward."

In July 2007, seven months after our return, Angela and I meet in the Berkeley Rose Garden. "They keep asking for money," Angela groans. "I keep going back to Lucio's advice not to throw money at the situation. I don't have $500 lying around. What does she think? That I shit golden eggs?" Economics erode the fledgling trust even before it has a chance to form.

Ten days later, Angela and I see each other at a UC Berkeley Human Rights Center dinner in honor of Ester, who flew in from El Salvador. Pro-Búsqueda continues steadily advancing its mission—still without government financial support. I brought my mom, a social worker, to the dinner. My mom speaks with Angela and advises her to tell Blanca what she wants: a relationship and not to be asked for money again.

Four days later, I meet my mom and boyfriend, Mark, for dinner at a bustling taqueria in San Francisco's Mission District. I walk buried in thought after the filling meal, my head facing the sidewalk. "Look who it is!" my mom exclaims. Ester, along with a staff member from the UC Berkeley Human Rights Center, stands on the sidewalk at 24th and Mission Street. Ester looks underdressed for San Francisco summer fog. My mom offers her sweater and the HRC staff member says, "We're going to see the murals on Balmy [Street]. Do you want to come?"

Ester and I, serendipitously united, walk to an alley painted with murals that pay tribute to El Salvador. The last mural shows a soldier ripping a child from a mother's arms beside a decorated bus with "Chalatenango" written on the front as the Sumpul River bleeds with bodies, and children swim downstream next to a letter sent to accompany *remesas* (remittances). Ester and I stand silently together soaking in the vibrant display of the past thirty years of history. Just as in the interviews I've gathered, the mural connects the Salvadoran Civil War and child disappearances to new family separations caused by immigration.

By the spring of 2009, Angela has gone almost two years since speaking with Blanca. Angela hasn't reached out, and she's ignored Blanca's occasional phone calls to her adoptive parents' home. I'm planning to return to El Salvador in the summer to present my thesis findings, and Angela has asked to join. Angela's unsure if she'll see Ricardo because she feels she can't see him without notifying Blanca. She also plans to launch her graduate school–dissertation research on "jóvenes encontrados who were appropriated internationally."

Two months later, Angela and I meet on the UC Berkeley campus, now with flights booked for El Salvador for when school gets out. Angela asks, "What do you think would be a good gift for Blanca? I was thinking of getting Ricardo a Cal T-shirt" (Cal is the nickname for UC Berkeley). Angela adds facetiously, "I'd like to get Blanca a T-shirt that says, 'Cal Birth Mom.'"

I ask if she'll want to see Blanca when we're in El Salvador. "I want to see Ricardo, but not Blanca," she replies. Guilt weighs on her face. I respond that I'd like to see Blanca regardless of whether Angela sees her. "I was hoping you'd say that," Angela replies. "It would be messed up to be in the country and not let her know." I stand up and hug Angela. After our visit, Angela emails Pro-Búsqueda to ask for help with reaching Blanca.

Two weeks later and ten days before our return to El Salvador, I arrive home from my medical school graduation to an email forwarded from Angela, containing a message from Pro-Búsqueda's new psychologist:

Hello Angela,

Yesterday, I visited your mom (Blanca Rosales) and your brother Ricardo. They're still living in the same place. When we told them that you are coming to the country, they got very excited. They said they've tried to contact you over the last while, but couldn't reach you because they were calling your parents and your parents said you no longer live with them. They say that your parents have been very kind to them, but that they don't understand much because of the language. YOUR MOM AND RICARDO SAY THAT FOR THEM THE BEST GIFT THAT THEY CAN RECEIVE IS YOU.

Ricardo is working and doing very well.

See you soon,
Alexis

29 Angela's El Salvador

On our first full day in El Salvador, Angela and I head out early to San Vicente with Pro-Búsqueda's psychologist to see Claudio, the French-Salvadoran. I seek Claudio to give him a short, nonfiction story that I wrote about him based on our interview.

Claudio reeks of alcohol and has a dirt-smeared face. His wife kicked him out and won't let him see their baby. Sprawled on a hammock on his biological mother's patio, he seems so different from the sharp-minded young man in bleach-bright clothes I interviewed two years ago. I show Claudio the bound story and read his own sage words aloud. When I get to the French part, I pause and ask if he wants to read. *"C'est moi meme qui change la vie* [Only I can change my life]." Claudio's mouth drops open as if he cannot believe his own wisdom. He thanks me for the copy of his story, poses for a photograph, and then comments on Angela's lighter skin: "That's what I looked like when I came back from France."

Claudio asks to use Pro-Búsqueda's cell phone to call his *maman* ("mother" in French). Minutes later, his *maman* phones back with news of plane tickets purchased for her visit next week. His teenage sister comments that Claudio wishes both his moms lived in the same place. His adoptive mom adores their biological mother, calls her *mamá*, the sister says. Meanwhile, Claudio's biological mother groans to me that her daughter-in-law takes all the money that the adoptive mom sends from France.

Claudio pulls his hair as he paces. He fears that his "*mamá de* Francia" (mom from France) will be angry when she discovers that, of the $1,000 she gave him to open a store, the store exists but without commodities to sell. The scenario bears a striking parallel to what Andrea described about giving money for a store and is the same amount Blanca asked of Angela.

Claudio's uncle comments that Angela looks miserable. He points to her huge, swollen mosquito bites and says that she's "allergic," like Claudio.

The Pro-Búsqueda psychologist reminds Claudio that the organization's doors are open. When he wants help with his drinking habit, they will be glad to receive him.

Claudio shakes my hand. "Be careful out there on the streets," he says in farewell.

As we drive away, Angela sighs. "As a researcher, that was fascinating. It was also depressing. He has a lot of issues to work through, and he may never get to them." Angela is right. Claudio seems to have a fraught sense of identity and intense childhood trauma likely at the root of his drinking and malcontent. I have the impression that he still feels torn between two mothers and two countries, and it impacts his parenting and functioning as an adult.

What about Angela? Two years after reunion, returning to El Salvador is a brave step in reconciliation. Angela says she came for her thesis, but she clearly also wants a connection with Blanca and Ricardo. Regardless of whether Angela ever gives the $1,000—and if she does, if it is lost or misused—she must address her hurt, her confusion, and her healing as a person with roots in the United States *and* El Salvador, building a daughter-mother relationship in a nation still in the footprint of war.

At 2:24 a.m. an earthquake awakens Angela and me in our guesthouse. Like Claudio, Angela turns to her adoptive mother for comfort via a phone call. "Mommy, there was an earthquake, and I just wanted to hear your voice." While Angela's relationship with her adoptive mother is strong, her relationship with Blanca is faltering. I think Angela timed her trip with mine to feel safer and to feel supported as she works to mend her relationship with Blanca.

Hours later, we're back at Pro-Búsqueda. I'm in the kitchen with María Inés when Angela comes to me crying. "Blanca called. She said she saw the doctor and is getting [blood-test] results on Sunday." More tears fall. "I felt like she was about to ask me for money again."

I lead Angela to the unkempt grassy yard. Ester sees Angela's tears, hugs her, and sits beside her. "This is normal. You can't solve Blanca's problems," Ester says, seeking to defuse the pressure Angela feels about money. She reasons, "If you give Blanca money today, then Blanca will still need money tomorrow. But it's very common. It's not your fault. It's not her fault. The problem is the problem."

In the afternoon, I talk to Margarita in the hallway. Her daughter attends university and her family is well, she says. I will leave El Salvador soon to start pediatrics residency at Stanford. I tell her that Angela will stay the summer. Margarita cuts off my rambling about Angela's plans. "Liz, I understand the message: '*Cuídamela* [Take care of her for me].' I will."

The next morning in front of Mister Donut, their prearranged meeting location, Angela spots Blanca and Ricardo. It's been two and a half years since Angela and Blanca last saw each other. Angela still fears Blanca. In their first call, Angela felt pressured about Blanca's US visa and, since the reunion, the requests for money. Angela hugs Ricardo, who wears a tie, white shirt and slacks and sports his trademark hairdo—and she ignores Blanca, who breathes slightly heavily and occasionally coughs.

Angela sits across from Ricardo and chirps happily with him, so I focus on Blanca. Middle-aged Blanca tells me about her congestive heart failure and depression, the decline in her health evident. Blanca was feeling "very low," but the news of Angela's arrival made her feel happier again, she says. Despite Angela's reserve toward Blanca, Blanca appreciates the joy of having her daughter at her side, albeit temporary and strained.

When Blanca overhears Ricardo mention his girlfriend to Angela, Blanca interrupts to say the girlfriend is no good for Ricardo. "She led him away from the church, and that's dangerous. One doesn't play with God." The girlfriend pushed her once, Blanca says, shoving Angela's arm to demonstrate. Blanca shares the sad news that Angela's little cousin, the son of the uncle who makes blankets, died last year of a brain tumor. Still addressing Angela, Blanca adds, "Ricardo cried for three days when you left."

Ricardo looks to Angela with an adoring gaze. "Angela, you mean so much to us. We want to get to know you." He describes their finances as sufficient, then states, "There's no amount of gold in the world that compares to how much you mean to us." Ricardo seems keenly aware of what caused the second separation from his sister.

We go for ice cream. I sit on a bench beside Blanca as she retells the story from a few years ago of hearing from a *seer* at her church that someone who looked like her would come searching for her and that she'd receive a message in a manila envelope. Pro-Búsqueda arrived within months with a manila envelope containing photographs of Angela, bringing the news that Angela wanted to meet her. Blanca asks Angela to come to her home to meet more of her church friends. Blanca says her home is safer now because many of the neighborhood gang members have been jailed or killed. Angela's eyes look to me to say "no way." Unlike before, Blanca does not push. She makes a request and lets it go.

I ask Ricardo about his work schedule. With an excited smile, he tells us that he'll be working a catering gig this weekend, serving the outgoing and incoming presidents of El Salvador. Mauricio Funes has been elected as the country's first-ever FMLN president. Ester has taught me not to trust politicians from either side, but the change in political power does signify that El Salvador has entered a new era. As history marches forward, the FMLN finally has its chance to lead.

Angela and I hug Blanca and Ricardo goodbye, then head to Pro-Búsqueda. I see Ester, who tells me that Pedro got married at Pro-Búsqueda, then went north with his wife. They didn't use a *coyote* and got stuck in Mexico for a year. Pedro now lives with his wife and baby in New York. Ester asks if I would call him, but I don't follow up.

On Saturday, Andrea and Amílcar take Angela and me to La Libertad for a day at the beach, replete with swimming, mariachis, dinner, and sunset. Andrea and Amílcar now have a toddler, Vladi's little sister. I watch mesmerized as Andrea changes her daughter's diaper and pulls on the girl's dress while keeping the squirmy, youngster giggling, all with just one hand.

In the evening, Angela talks about how she felt seeing Blanca. "She's so needy. . . ." I respond that Blanca is a strong woman who did a selfless act. El Salvador's persistent violence and Blanca's poverty intensify the challenges of family reintegration. The constant need to protect oneself can feel depleting. I love El Salvador but at the end of each day, I feel relieved and count down the days I need to stay alive before my flight north. The tourist T-shirt Angela had pointed out with amusement at Los Planes felt fitting to us: "I survived El Salvador without getting shot."

Angela recalls my earlier mention of the theory of a "primal wound of adoption."[1] The requests for money magnify Angela's hurt from the adoption, and she also feels gratitude for her good life. She navigates her reunification while developing as a graduate student and a young adult. I commend her courage and generosity in not giving up on Blanca. Blanca cares about Angela much more than any money she might receive. Blanca didn't say it today—she let Ricardo convey the words—but I know that Angela's smile truly does mean more to her than gold.

The next day, we meet Blanca at a café in Metrocentro. I see Angela becoming more comfortable with asking Blanca questions about her family history. Blanca says that she was born outside of La Ester in Chalatenango, one kilometer from the nearest house. Blanca relates a story from her childhood that gives insight into the stern character that cloaks her generosity. One day, when Blanca's father was away, she and her sisters locked the door of their home to keep a "crazy beggar" out. When the father returned, he was furious at his daughters for not opening the home to feed the man. "If you ever do that again, I'll hit you hard," Blanca's father had said. Blanca relates that, during the war, the FMLN shot her uncle in front of his daughter for refusing to join the guerrilla force. Then the army came and turned their straw home "into a sieve with all the bullets they shot into it." Angela's not understanding, so I stop to translate, which Blanca encourages. I can see that Blanca doesn't forgive the FMLN or the military.

As Chalatenango became more dangerous, the family migrated to Panchimalco, at the foot of the hills of Puerta del Diablo, on the edges of San Salvador. She worked in a factory, making garments for JCPenney and Walmart under harsh conditions. "I had to make five thousand dresses a month. They would randomly check ten. If one came out with problems, maybe that was okay. If two came out with mistakes, then they'd throw the whole thing out and . . ." Blanca laments that she no longer has the energy to work in the factories.

Blanca's parents moved to Ilobasco, the site of the reunion. She mentions an attack in the capital that she evaded because she'd gone to visit her parents the day before. Blanca moved to Soyapango and became pregnant when she was a factory worker. "I gave Angela up for adoption because bullets would hit babies on the street and kill them. Children who were a little older would get drafted." Her watery, reddened eyes look to Angela. "But one matures with the years. I realize now—I regret it. I regret giving Angi up," she says, using Angela's nickname.

"You did the hardest, most generous act a mother can do," I tell Blanca. "You gave Angela opportunity. It was difficult. I'm not saying that all babies are better off in the United States than in El Salvador, but in those circumstances adoption made sense. Everything Angela has in the US is because of the opportunities you let her have."

"Yes, I'm so grateful for her opportunities. For her education." Blanca keeps her features steady, her tense body relaxing a little. "A friend was telling me the other day, 'I think you did the right thing.'" I see in Angela's facial expressions her growing compassion for Blanca, as Angela comes to understand the choicelessness of Blanca's decision.

When Angela steps away to the bathroom, I ask Blanca how they're doing financially. I explain that it creates a barrier for Angela when they ask for money. Pro-Búsqueda has conveyed Angela's wishes, and I reinforce it. "Angela is a student with debt," I explain. "She feels responsible for her parents at home too."

"I just want to get to know her," Blanca replies.

When Angela returns, we all walk to the taxi depot. Angela gives Blanca forty dollars, twenty for bus rides and another twenty for a birthday gift.

"Don't you need this money?" Blanca asks, attempting to decline the cash.

"Thanks for coming to Metrocentro to meet us," Angela says in response. "Sorry, I didn't know what to get you as a gift."

Blanca gives me a blanket woven by her brother, like the one Angela has. "*De corazón* [from my heart]," she insists as we say goodbye. I won't see her again—but Angela will.

After seeing Blanca and Ricardo off, Angela and I take a cab to meet Ceci for pupusas. Ceci cries about her difficult communications with Andrés in Italy. The intensity of María Inés's yearning seems to have contributed to driving him away. Angela cries too as she observes the sister left behind.

The next morning, Angela and I are working side by side at Pro-Búsqueda when two Quebecois parents and their Salvadoran-born, petite, green-eyed daughter, Elmy, enter the room. Relieved to speak English, they describe their case. As a young girl, Elmy survived a shoot-out in an FMLN security house during the war. Milto explains that soldiers killed the adults but "pardoned" the lives of the children when security houses were discovered. The family has come to El Salvador from Quebec for three days to explore Elmy's history—to trace her roots and seek her biological family.

Elmy's adoptive brother refused to come to Pro-Búsqueda today but asked that they initiate a search on his behalf. "You're my mother," he'd told his mom on the ride from the airport. The adoptive mother cries as she tells us that they know thirty-four Canadian families who adopted children from El Salvador during the war. Angela spends hours translating the investigative exchange between the family and Milto, who will lead the search at Pro-Búsqueda.

Over lunch, Angela shares her story with the family, and the adoptive father proposes a toast. That afternoon, I say goodbye to Angela and others at Pro-Búsqueda and then watch the green hills slip by as I ride in a taxi to the airport. Angela will remain in El Salvador for two more months.

Near midnight, upon my arrival in California, the US customs agent forces me to pull out each item from my backpack for inspection, scrutinizing, I imagine, for drug smuggling because I mentioned that I'd gone to El Salvador "to see friends." He seems to find it suspicious that I could have friends in El Salvador and visit without criminal intent. If only he understood that the true crimes were committed in the era of the civil war and in the years after, when the United States failed to make reparations, to apply pressure, or to actively assist in the search for the disappeared children. I repack my luggage, transformed by my time in El Salvador, and walk into the night air to rest before the new day, when I will begin residency to become a pediatrician.

I carry a full heart into the next stage of my professional journey, knowing that tonight Angela sleeps in "the thumb of Central America," in an El Salvador she can relate to as part of her heritage. She will call Blanca again. Angela understands her family origins and the circumstances around her adoption. Her identity is now clear. She's loved by two mothers and understands both worlds. She uses that love and knowledge to help others. Together, we built a bridge, and now Angela walks on the other side, in an El Salvador she navigates on her own.

30 Onward

Two and a half years pass. Angela and I have stayed connected over email and social media, but only rarely, as she's been focusing on her doctoral training in sociology, and I've been busy at the hospital. Only six months remain before I complete my pediatrics residency. Mark and I married two years ago, and we're expecting our first child. I know that Angela keeps in touch with Ricardo and that she had a successful summer in El Salvador after I left, spending time at Pro-Búsqueda as a volunteer, conducting sociology research, and visiting with her brother. Blanca's illness and the dangers of her neighborhood made it harder for Angela to see her, but they still maintain a connection, though mostly through Ricardo.

During the winter holidays in late 2011, I'm surprised by an evite celebrating Angela. The invitation reads, "Baby Shower for Angela and Mike." Gretta, Angela's adoptive mom, is listed as the event host. I scan posts on Angela's Facebook page. A few friends congratulated her on her marriage several months ago. I notice the date of Angela's baby shower—in three weeks, one day after my own baby shower!

I reach out to Angela, and one week later she knocks on my front door in Palo Alto, along with Mike, a young man of Filipino and German descent. Seven months expecting, I hug Angela, who is eight months into her pregnancy. Angela looks radiant, warm in a loose cotton short-sleeved shirt despite the winter weather. She wraps and rewraps a stylish scarf around her neck. We sit on my living room floor and catch up. We last saw each other in the summer of 2009, when Angela stayed in El Salvador for two months volunteering with Pro-Búsqueda after I left for home. She returned to El Salvador in March 2011, on Pro-Búsqueda's invitation, to commemorate the Day of the Disappeared Child. Angela helped translate during a breakfast with Mauricio Funes, the FMLN president of El Salvador, whose inauguration ceremony Angela and I had watched in 2009 livestreamed to a fancy San Salvador hotel.

Angela's third trip to El Salvador after her reencuentro was planned as a two-month research trip, starting in June 2011, seven months ago. "I cried in the airport, and I cried the whole flight down," Angela recalls. At first, she attributed her vomiting and fatigue to the "usual stress" she feels when going to El Salvador but after a positive pregnancy test, she phoned her adoptive sister and said, "I have to come home." Angela's abbreviated trip included a short visit with her grandparents in Ilobasco. She saw Ricardo but not Blanca because Blanca was taking care of a relative's child and Angela had a sudden departure. Angela's adoptive parents took the news of her pregnancy well—she told them at the airport baggage claim. Two months later, a friend who was an ordained minister married Angela and Mike in Angela's childhood living room.

Over the Mexican fast food I was craving, I reflect aloud, "I wonder what it means that you found out you were pregnant in El Salvador."

"I don't know. I'm still contemplating the symbolism of that." Angela has already chosen a middle name for her unborn daughter: Malaya, which in Tagalog means "to be free."

⸱ ⸱ ⸱

One year later, I receive an email from Angela, now a mother to a beautiful baby girl. It's been seven years since Angela's reencuentro. We last spoke on the visit with Mike, when we were both pregnant. Angela writes to share an update from Ricardo: "Blanca passed away on Monday. He said that Blanca died of a heart issue." I reply with loving condolences. The bullet lodged near Blanca's heart may have sped her demise—we will never know. I'm glad for the time that Angela and Blanca had together, that Blanca's heart endured long enough for her to know her daughter. The relationship with Blanca brought Angela pain, but it also brought peace from knowing her biological family and the identity she could not have reached any other way—an opportunity for healing that every disappeared child deserves.

One month later, on November 14, 2013, I receive disturbing news about an attack at Pro-Búsqueda. As reported by the Los Angeles Times, gunmen raided the office and set fire to the agency's archives.[1] The attack occurred six weeks after the archbishop of El Salvador abruptly closed Tutela Legal, a Salvadoran-based human rights organization that documented the civil war massacres. It's unclear why the archdiocese shuttered the agency, but the timing coincides with the Salvadoran government's revisiting its amnesty law. If the amnesty law is overturned, top military and even some FMLN leaders could face prosecution for crimes committed during the war. Much of the evidence of the war crimes exists in these two organizations.

The Los Angeles Times reports that at 4:45 a.m. three gunmen attacked Pro-Búsqueda's driver as he walked into the office, pointing a gun to his neck and threatening to kill him. Once inside, the gunmen assaulted the night security guard and tied his hands behind his back. The attackers opened cabinets, confiscating laptops and desktop computers. One computer contained legal information for a Supreme Court case about the forced disappearances that was scheduled to be held three days prior—but was delayed when military officials failed to appear. The assailants doused three Pro-Búsqueda filing cabinets with gasoline and set them on fire.

The news article quotes Ester, who described the attack as a "clear sabotage of our work." The assailants destroyed 80 percent of Pro-Búsqueda's documentation. I recall holding the manila folders that contained photographs, adoption records, and other evidence—much of it now destroyed. Digital backups of the information do not exist. The information that I hold—the voice recordings, the written testimonies, and the stories of reunion—is so precious. Someone does not want this information shared, but I will do all I can to bring it to light.

As time passes, I stay connected to Pro-Búsqueda and my friends in El Salvador. I publish two research articles analyzing the fifty interviews, but mostly day-to-day work and parenting keep me busy for five years. I complete fellowship training to become a professor of pediatrics and, informed by my time in El Salvador, transition to domestic research on youth incarceration—an issue also fed by poverty, violence, and for some of my patients and research participants, family separation due to immigration.

In July 2018, with a humanitarian crisis at the US-Mexico border, where immigration officials are separating children from their families as a matter of policy, I'm asked to speak about the harmful effects of family separation on children's well-being. I appear on Jonathan Van Ness's *Getting Curious* podcast to discuss lifelong negative impacts of the toxic stress created by forced separation and the inevitable challenges of family reunification—all lessons I learned from spending time with and listening to the disappeared Salvadoran children and their families.[2] I argue the importance of keeping children with their families whenever possible and of supporting families in prompt reunification when separation does occur, guided by the best interest of the child.

In August 2018, I open my laptop to dig into my untorched archives. It's finally time to write the book about El Salvador's disappeared children. I've taken a retreat from work to revisit the field notes and interview transcripts. My career as a physician and researcher is on track, and my children, a six-year-old daughter and four-year-old son, are old enough to spare me a few moments at my computer. One hour into writing, I receive an unexpected text from a medical school classmate living in Washington State, whom I haven't heard from in years. She's just realized that she's been providing obstetric care to *the* Angela I talked about after every time I went to El Salvador. Moments later, Angela emails me. Her baby boy was due last Friday. With happy tears in my eyes, I send well wishes for a smooth birth. I check on Angela over the next several days.

Two days after our last text exchange, I sit on the couch, thinking I'd like to see a photo of Angela's baby, as I haven't heard from her since she went to the hospital for induction. When I pull out my phone to text her, it pings with a new message from Angela. Two photos! The two photos make the entire process of supporting Angela in reconnecting to her culture and identity worthwhile. In the first photo, Angela's six-year-old daughter, clad in blue pajamas and seated in an armchair, beams as she holds her newborn brother, still swaddled in his hospital baby blanket. In the second photo, Angela's adoptive father, Jerry, sits in the same armchair, smiling with eyes closed as he holds the newborn bundle while Angela's daughter—the new big sister—leans onto the armrest as she grins with arms wrapped around her baby brother.

Now a mother in a family of four, Angela brings a strong sense of identity to adulthood, to parenting, and to her work as a sociology professor. Her daughter has already traveled with her to El Salvador, to meet her family and know their roots—to enjoy her right to identity, inscribed in the United Nations Convention on the Rights of the Child.

Months later, on October 14, 2018, the Catholic Church canonizes Archbishop Óscar Romero. In 1980, weeks before his assassination, Romero had told a reporter, "I do not believe in death without resurrection. If I'm killed, I shall arise again in the Salvadoran people."[3] Fallen hero and divine messenger, Saint Óscar Romero served as a mentor and guide for Father Jon Cortina. Their spirit inspires Pro-Búsqueda's ongoing work. Margarita and María Inés are the only employees who remain from my first summer in El Salvador, but the organization still facilitates reunions, has a robust DNA bank, leads human rights cases, and hosts commemoration events in El Salvador and on social media that spread internationally to honor the disappeared children and their families.

Now, in July 2020, amid the global COVID-19 pandemic, I focus on fulfilling Francisca's request—to tell what happened in El Salvador. I think about key figures who shaped the movement to find the disappeared Salvadoran children. Father Jon, a hero and man of faith, survived the war after risking his life many times to help the people and then created and led Pro-Búsqueda with such strong leadership that his vision carries on today. Cristián, the Chilean forensic geneticist, harnessed the power of science in turning DNA into a tool for justice. The guerrillera, Margarita, battles on to locate the missing children. So many—too many to name— have been courageous, dedicated, and effective in contributing to the important work of Pro-Búsqueda.

I recall Lucio telling me in 2005 about an elderly woman he met while collecting DNA samples. She knew Lucio's grandmother and described her as a "good person." As he drove his Nissan on the urban streets of San Salvador, Lucio recounted the memories that the old woman had shared with him. Then he turned to me, emphatic and anguished, and said, "What am I going to tell Michele when she asks where *her* grandparents are? Every child has a right to have grandparents." Michele, daughter of two jóvenes encontrados, was three years old at the time.

A few weeks ago, in 2020, Michele, now a teenager, posted a Father's Day wish on Facebook for Lucio. She thanked him for his love, for working hard to provide for their family, for the good example he sets. She concluded, "I know my grandparents would be proud." Michele is now the age that Lucio and Angélica were when they left orphanages to reunite with their families. They rebelled because they felt lost until they came to better understand and accept themselves, thanks to Pro-Búsqueda and their evolving knowledge of their roots and life history. Then they found each other and formed a family. Lucio and Angélica's vision to keep their family together, despite experiencing economic hardship and living in a dangerous city, has proven valuable. Michele knows her family origins and that she is loved. Lucio and Angélica, child survivors of the war, broke the cycle of family separation.

As a global community, we must support family connections. So that Michele and her generation can someday raise healthy children and Lucio and Angélica's contemporaries can enjoy being grandparents. So that youth can feel fulfilled in their identity, with the means to exist and thrive. Feeling loved and with a strong sense of self, Michele and the millions of young people she represents can lead us all to a healthier future.

Afterword

In learning about the experiences of El Salvador's disappeared children, I observed patterns that I believe have relevance to all marginalized communities impacted by family separation. Here I summarize salient observations and potential implications.

PHASES OF FAMILY SEPARATION AND REUNIFICATION

The experiences of the jóvenes encontrados and their families elucidate distinct phases of the separation and reunification process: pre-disappearance, disappearance, separation, searching, reunion, and reintegration.[1] Recognizing the commonalities within the phases may be useful to other settings.

Pre-disappearance. Nostalgia and happiness about family togetherness imbued memories from before the war. The jóvenes encontrados and their families described themselves as poor and also discussed the dangers in the countryside, the horrors of the war, and the sacrifices parents made to help children survive.

Disappearance. Whether separated: forced at military gunpoint, coerced or inspired by the FMLN, or through informal domestic or formal transnational adoption, all the jóvenes encontrados and their families experienced a deep sense of irresolvable trauma related to the disappearance event.

Separation. Trauma from prolonged family separation extended the psychological injury of war, leading to lifelong repercussions on well-being. Youth and their relatives conveyed the longing and intense pain characteristic of *ambiguous loss*, when the whereabouts or condition of a missing loved one are unknown.[2] Pedro, the former MS-13 gang member, exemplified how scars from forced separation, war, and childhood abuse intermingled to lead him to a dangerous, destructive life on the streets. Like Pedro, many of the youth felt lonely, abandoned, and incomplete during their separation. Parents, like María Inés, felt an unquenched yearning filled with anguish and sorrow, interspersed with occasional hopefulness that they might someday see their children again or at least extinguish the uncertainty of the loss.

Searching. For families and youth actively engaged in a search, the process involved a constant negotiation between hope and despair. The act of searching began to restore a sense of agency. For the disappeared Salvadoran children and their families, searches occurred with the instrumental support of Pro-Búsqueda.

Reunion. Reunion was a potent, transformative event in the lives of each of the disappeared children and family members whom I met. During a reunion event, youth experienced overwhelming joy tempered by revisiting traumas (from the war and separation) and the challenge of reconnecting anew with biological relatives. Feelings of love *and* anger, acceptance *and* abandonment, were common for youth. Knowing they had the opportunity to reconnect extinguished the ambiguous loss and restored a sense of agency. Related to that agency, reunion events operated on a continuum in terms of the physical and emotional approach to reconnecting. Some jóvenes encontrados, especially international adoptees, chose to not meet their biological families. Others, like Andrés, María Inés's son in Italy, had a phone reunion. Through letters and telephone communication, Andrés obtained answers about his family, the war, and the circumstances of his adoption. Finally, many jóvenes encontrados, like Angela and the "French-Salvadoran" Claudio/Claude, chose an in-person reunion. For some, reunion sparked longer-term relationships. Pro-Búsqueda seeks to give disappeared children the opportunity to reunite and to know the truth of their origin. As long as *choice* was present in the reunion process, healing could begin.

Reintegration. I observed that family reunion marked the beginning of a long-term process of family reintegration, in which all the jóvenes encontrados faced decisions about their role and new relationships with their biological families. The uncertainties of family reintegration mirrored the ambiguity of separation. *Ambiguous reunification* refers to the long process in which the jóvenes encontrados struggled to fit in with their families.[3] Reconnecting, although difficult and uncertain, also presented an invaluable opportunity for healing and growth. Angela's relationship with her biological mother was painful *and* rewarding. Jóvenes encontrados from abroad and within El Salvador faced cultural and class barriers when interacting with their biological families. For many, however, reconnecting with biological relatives enriched their social fabric and enabled them to better understand their identity. On the long journey home, *home* meant identity and family connection. Encouragement and acceptance of fragile, re-formed relationships by biological and adoptive families was paramount.

Across the phases of separation and reunification, the experiences of the disappeared Salvadoran children and their families elucidate the vital importance of nurturing family connections and preventing separation whenever possible and of supporting families throughout the arduous process of reunification.

LOOKING BEYOND

Authors have described family separations and reunions since even before the written word. When Homer's Odysseus sailed away to fight in the Trojan War, he left behind an infant son, Telemachus. Homer's *Odyssey* describes Telemachus's search for his father after twenty years of separation, amid questions around his father's fate. In his coming of age, Telemachus faces longing, uncertainty, and a hunger for identity that can only be resolved by family reunion.

The experiences of the disappeared children separated in El Salvador's civil war transcend time, context, and setting. The fundamental nature of the parent-child bond and the quest for identity inherent to all humans may explain the universality underlying the Salvadoran families' experiences with separation and reunification. Children need connection with loving caregivers as an essential requisite for healthy development—and all people with a missing child or relative yearn to know whether their loved one is alive or deceased and when, if ever, they will reconnect.

Separations span the globe. In 1943, Anne Frank wrote of the Holocaust in her diary, "Terrible things are happening outside.... Families are torn apart; men, women, and children are separated. Children come home from school to find that their parents have disappeared."[4] The quote recently went viral when tweeted in connection to children in the United States returning home from school to find parents deported after US Immigration and Customs Enforcement (ICE) raids.[5] The unremitting violence and poverty in El Salvador feed ongoing and now intergenerational cycles of family separation caused by immigration and the disappearances inflicted by gangs. All of Andrea's eight older siblings have emigrated to the United States out of economic necessity, creating new separations in her family. As we saw through Sandrita, the unaccompanied minor who traveled to El Norte on her own, prolonged separations caused by immigration negatively impact child well-being and too often have become a necessity for survival. The gang violence in El Salvador and throughout Central America's "northern triangle" leads to what has become a new usage of the term *desaparecido*—someone expected to have been killed by gangs because they went missing and their body was never seen again. Families of desaparecidos lost by gangs likely experience a similar emotional pendulum of hope and despair as the families torn apart by the war.

Millions of families in the United States alone are experiencing ongoing family separation. After the US Civil War ended formal slavery, hundreds of parents placed newspaper ads to find children sold in the slave trade decades earlier. Today, thousands of new family separations occur each day in the United States due to mass incarceration. An estimated 2.7 million US children—including one in nine Black children—have a parent who is currently incarcerated, and parental incarceration is a major determinant of children's health.[6] Additionally, the massive foster care system utilizes family separation in a last-ditch effort to support families in need. Over four hundred thousand children are in out-of-home care in the US foster care system on a given day, with insufficient support for reunification.[7] Dollars and policy paradigms that keep families together and that ease reunifications are likely to have outsized benefits for society.

DNA AND IDENTITY

In instances of separation where the whereabouts of missing family members are unknown, DNA has proven to be a critical tool. For the healing process of family reunification to begin, a match must first be made, and DNA can expedite identification of a match or can link separated family members untraceable through other means. In the application of DNA for family reunification, DNA can and should be used with appropriate safeguards in the best interest of the child.[8] Technology exists such that there should never again be children experiencing prolonged, needless separations because they are lost. Thus, the global application of DNA in the search for disappeared or missing children becomes a moral imperative.

I co-lead DNA Bridge, a consortium formed in December 2020 to apply DNA as a tool to reunify migrant children forcibly separated from their families under the Trump administration's zero-tolerance policy.[9] As a collaboration of geneticists, physicians, and human rights advocates, we are developing a technical, logistical, and ethical framework for using DNA to reunify migrant families experiencing forced separation. The thousands of unaccompanied migrant children crossing the US-Mexico border monthly further indicate a potential need to apply DNA technology for identifying children through a DNA database approach that can connect them to searching relatives. As our global society faces increasing challenges due to climate change, widening inequality, and resource scarcity, family separations related to war, disasters, and immigration are likely to increase—and DNA may become an increasingly useful tool for family reunification. The experiences of El Salvador's disappeared children with loss and regained identities motivate me in this work.

RIGHT TO IDENTITY

My experiences with the child survivors of El Salvador's civil war have guided me to focus on one central right: Article 8 of the United Nations Convention on the Rights of the Child (a treaty signed by 192 member states, with the United States the sole exception). Aligned with Pro-Búsqueda's mission, Article 8 calls for the preservation of children's right to identity, including nationality, name, and family relations—and its restoration if violated.[10]

The right to identity may be best understood in its absence. Violations of the right to identity create psychological trauma, while reunion begins to resolve that trauma. When we *preserve* children's right to identity, we bend the arc of the universe toward justice and healing. Michele, the teenage daughter of jóvenes encontrados Lucio and Angélica, has grown up with her identity intact, in part because Pro-Búsqueda helped restore her parents' sense of identity. As Armando, the joven encontrado raised in the orphanage with Angélica, has said, "When I found my family, my life changed 180 degrees. It was the incentive I needed to try to give meaning to my existence.... I had a history, a reason for being."[11] The right to identity is so important that its abrogation made a priest spout profanities at the government's defiance of an international human rights court's decree. Illuminated by Father Jon's vision and action, may we persevere in protecting children's right to identity, a tenet interdependent with all the fundamental rights that every child needs and deserves.

Acknowledgments

On behalf of the community of Pro-Búsqueda and all children and families experiencing family separation, thank you for receiving the stories of the disappeared children of El Salvador.

Five years prior to my time at Pro-Búsqueda in the summer of 2005, I was studying abroad for a year in Latin America. That year, I once rode on a public bus through El Salvador. In the dark of night, a Salvadoran police officer in black military boots pulled us over, stepped aboard and looked around, and then called for me and my friend, "the Americans," to get off the bus. One row in front of where we sat in the back, a grandmotherly Central American woman stood up and asserted, "*TODOS SOMOS AMERICANOS. NOSOTROS VIVIMOS EN EL CORAZÓN DE AMÉRICA* [We're all Americans. We live in the heart of America]." The officer backed down, and our bus rolled on, dropping off a burlap sack of beans in San Salvador, and reaching our destination, Guatemala, by dawn. Not only did the woman protect us—facing risk and no benefit to herself, but she also showed me the collective spirit of Latin Americans to refuse to bow down to unjust dominance. I thank her.

"I have a strength, and that strength is called the Salvadoran people," Father Jon Cortina once said. Thank you to every staff and community member I interacted with through Pro-Búsqueda. I admire your strength, diligence, and devotion. I extend special gratitude to my friends Lucio, Angélica, Andrea, Amílcar, Angela, Ceci, María Inés, Ester, Margarita, Marco, Patricia, Raúl, and so many others. *Les queiro y les admiro.* Father Jon Cortina's and Cristián Orrego's presence in my life and in the movement to find the niños desaparecidos was a blessing. Thank you to everyone who shared their story with me, especially Pedro, for your trust. *Reunion* includes only your first names because of the conditions of repression that you still live in. The jóvenes encontrados and their families may not have expected me to recollect so much. I hope that I have done justice to your powerful lived experience and apologize if I shared anything you preferred unwritten. I also apologize on behalf of my native United States of America for the injustices wrought on peoples of the world, especially in El Salvador. I truly hope for reparation. The people of El Salvador and my friend Allie inspire me with their generosity and beautiful spirit. Thank you all for being a part of my life.

To my thesis committee chair, Eric Stover, this work would not have been possible without you and the UC Berkeley Human Rights Center. You guided me to Pro-Búsqueda, supported my master's thesis process, helped me to find the "essence of writing," and connected me to DNA Bridge. Your MacArthur award and Nobel Peace Prize through Physicians for Human Rights are well deserved. I admire your extraordinary contributions to human rights and the use of DNA to find desaparecidos. You have shaped my career, and I thank you.

Philippe Bourgois, my anthropology mentor and academic *"padrino"* (godfather), as my mother calls you, I am so grateful for your continued support. Thank you for answering the phone whenever I called and for telling me to write field notes in 2005 and for reading them. It felt fated to bump into you in 2015, both of us new faculty at UCLA, because we knew this book needed to be written. You never settled with the injustice you experienced during the war, not because it was horrific for you but because of the suffering you saw around you. You are a talented ethnographer and an astonishing person. I hope that readers will appreciate your testimony in the appendix to help us understand why *nunca más*, never again, may we allow such barbarities to occur—or the same violence in disguise in its aftermath. The children's drawings you gathered and share in *Reunion* further demonstrate your commitment, through decades of service, to make sure the families' stories are heard and innocence reclaimed. I also thank your lovely Laurie Hart.

Thank you to my colleagues and friends who have supported the birth of this ethnography. My friends have nourished me on so many adventures abroad and at home and abroad again. Special thanks to Peter, Paul, and Moira (Szilagyi, Chung, and Szilagyi), Carol Mangione, Ken Wells, Bob Brook, Karen Sokal-Guiterrez, Lisa Chamberlain, Neal Halfon, Barbara Moscicki, Laura Abrams, Eraka Bath, Rebecca Dudovitz, and so many others who have taught me and lit my way. I extend gratitude to UC Berkeley, UCSF, Stanford, and the UCLA Department of Pediatrics. I thank book doulas Andrea Lampros, Jonathan Cobb, Naomi Schneider, and the entire University of California Press team. Thank you to Bill Nelson for the maps. Tom White, Sara Katsanis, and our DNA Bridge consortium—thank you for helping me bring lessons from the past into the present. Laura Shortt and Marcela Krejčí, I am so grateful for your expert eye in preparing the photos and selecting children's drawings.

I thank my parents for lifting me up across all the stages of my life. To my siblings, the five of us, I love you. Mark, my husband, best friend, and secret book coach, I am grateful for your infinite support. Finally, I thank my children, Zoe and Jonah, my inspiration. I wish for you and all your peers worldwide a present day and a future in which your rights as developing humans are met so that you and the planet's children can flourish into adulthood.

· · · · ·

From Philippe: Thank you, Liz (Elizabeth), for inviting me to write the foreword for this terrific book and then for asking me, as I struggled with my own traumas from the Salvadoran Civil War, to share my survivor's testimony. When I melted down trying to write it, you saved it just in time by proposing I reframe it in photo-ethnographic form (appendix A). You regularly checked in on me and generously edited and reedited my umpteen versions of each of those documents. Thank you also to Mark Halpert (Liz's husband), Laurie Kain Hart (Philippe's wife), and Meredith Steinberg, who manages my research office with patience and cheer. Finally, thank you to all the survivors/sufferers and compañero/a revolutionaries from Santa Marta, Cabañas—with a special shout-out to Armando and the extended Leiva Alvarenga/Alvarenga Leiba families as well as the next generation, who continue to struggle for justice: Santa Marteños have my deepest respect, as well as my heart. You are truly inspiring, salt-of-the-earth, bona fide revolutionary heroes of history who dared to fight for justice and dignity, not just for yourselves but for all the poor in El Salvador.

Photo-Ethnographic Testimony of a Salvadoran Military Scorched-Earth Operation (November 1981)

Philippe Bourgois

In November 1981, I was an anthropology graduate student beginning fieldwork on human rights violations and the political mobilization of small farmers in Central America. Convulsed by effervescent revolutionary movements, the region was full of hope. Unfortunately, it was the height of the Cold War. The United States was obsessed with "international communism" taking over its Central American and Caribbean client states "one-by-one" in a "domino effect" and responded by weaponizing the region's right-wing military dictatorships.[1]

I had made multiple trips to refugee camps near La Virtud, Honduras, and was impressed by the utopian vision of social justice of Salvadoran refugees. Most had fled into Honduras in March 1981, when the Salvadoran military launched a large-scale scorched-earth invasion against isolated rural hamlets in Cabañas. Jesuit priests had been teaching literacy and organizing cooperatives in the region for over a decade. Many refugees were "delegates of the word," whose families hosted liberation-theology Bible-study groups. Inspired by the dialogical empowerment pedagogy of Paulo Freire, they referred to themselves as *concientizados* (those who had seized consciousness). Merging faith and critical thinking, they demanded "social justice for the poor."[2]

Targets of military and death-squad repression, most of the rural population welcomed the recently unified FMLN guerrillas into their communities. Two delegates of the word arranged for me to cross into El Salvador for a two-day visit to an FMLN-controlled northern corner of Cabañas Province. I hoped to obtain permission to conduct dissertation fieldwork on daily life among "revolutionary peasants." Three days later, I found myself trapped with about 1,400 civilians in a scorched-earth invasion. Encircled by both the Salvadoran and Honduran militaries, we could not flee as refugees across the border into Honduras.

As an anthropologist, I kept field notes and a personal diary, in two separate two-and-a-half-by-four-inch notebooks stuffed into my T-shirt pocket. We were under fire for eleven days, hiding and fleeing. Terrified, I attempted to calm my racing mind by scribbling down field notes. I wanted to document, as a social scientist, what we were enduring, but I also vented my terror. I thought most of us would be killed and wrote goodbye letters to my loved ones. More usefully, I wrote down the names of the dead and wounded, hoping my notebooks might serve as a human rights document recorded in real time. I asked about a dozen of the young men and women I befriended during the flight to send those notebooks and letters to my mother's address if I was killed and they survived.

I also carried a small 35mm camera, and this photo-ethnographic testimony includes seven photos from a roll of thirty-six I took during the scorched-earth operation, along with four photos taken before and after the invasion in the refugee camps.

TERRAIN OF CABAÑAS SCORCHED-EARTH INVASION OF NOVEMBER 10–20, 1981

Taken after the civil war, somewhere near the site of the massacre of Santa Cruz (which occurred on the fifth day of the scorched-earth operation), this photo shows the rugged terrain through which we fled. The government military foot patrols and air force circulated only during daylight hours, so we ran mostly at night, hiding immobile after sunrise. Family members, friends, neighbors, and other good Samaritan heroes carried the wounded, babies, and the elderly or infirm who could not run.

Referred to as a *zona liberada* ("liberated zone" or, more neutrally, "FMLN-controlled zone"), the territory consisted of a dozen dispersed hamlets. All were wiped off the map during this scorched-earth operation. Six years later, in 1987, several hundred refugee families returned to Cabañas from the Mesa Grande refugee camp in Honduras at great risk in the midst of the full-blown conflict, and they consolidated all twelve hamlets into one large centralized village, Santa Marta. Most survivors and their progeny still live in Santa Marta in 2022 (as we go to press). They regularly commemorate lost loved ones from the war and their revolutionary social justice ideals.

It could have been somewhere in this picture, on any of these many hill-sides with only steep footpaths—no roads or bridges—that three-year-old Armando was kidnapped by a soldier and forced to shout out innocently for his mother, exposing all those who responded to the soldiers' bullets and grenades (see pp. xxx-xxxi).

DAY 1: OUTSIDE OUR CAVE, AWAITING THE NEXT BOMBARDMENT

I took this photo during a lull in the bombardments on the first full day of encirclement. It shows some of the companions with whom I was hiding, outside our cramped cave shelter (called a *tatu*) dug into the cliffside. We were straining our ears for incoming aircraft and mortars. In classic doublespeak, the US and Salvadoran military cynically referred to these initial bombardment phases of scorched-earth operations as "softening up the guerrillas" for "land invasion" (i.e., burning thatched houses and granaries, killing livestock, and trampling crops).[3] Worse yet, the Huey helicopters strafing us were officially categorized as "non-lethal" military assistance by the US government.[4]

The woman on the far right is the little boy's mother, and the entrance to our cave is the dark hole barely visible to the right of the head of the woman in the back. She was pregnant and feeling sick. Whenever the air force attacked or mortars pounded, all four of us, along with additional neighbors from our hamlet—crammed into the tiny, squat cave. Not even the toddler could stand up in it.

Moments before I took the picture, I scribbled into my pocket diary:

Morning of first full day, November 11, 1981
Just my luck to have gotten stuck in an invasion. Squatting with sulfur burps and dysentery in a muddy cave with a 2-year-old boy, his mother, a [wounded] 14-year-old boy, a developmentally challenged 30-year-old man....
    The 2-year-old—screeching because a Fouga Magister plane above us is dropping bombs—just took a shit. The mosquitoes are biting in the dampness. A piece of shrapnel fell not 15 yards from us.

My next entry a few hours later was more desperate:

It's midday now and I'm stretched out scared in the cave again, 'cause the mortars are falling close now. They make an almost splitting noise when they strike. The worst is that you hear them when they're shot and it takes about 30 seconds for them to reach their target. So you wait holding your breath hoping you are not the target. And, man, do they hit hard.

Later that same day, before sunset, my brain spinning from terror, I described another aerial attack in real time again:

I'm crouched in the cave again. They have tightened the circle around us and the sun is setting. Above, one of my country's helicopters is spewing forth machine gun bullets. Occasionally a mortar explodes below.
    Now the helicopter is circling back towards us and my companions and I cram closer together inside the cave.
    Bummer! The noise is getting louder and louder. Reminds me of mosquitoes buzzing in my ears when I try to sleep. Except this mosquito kills!
    How are we gonna get out of here and what is going to happen to us all?

I tried to assuage my spiraling anxiety by adapting and singing lyrics from a Bob Dylan song that reminded me of missing my hometown:

Oh momma, could this really be the end?
Stuck inside of Salvador
With the New York Blues again.

But I failed to cheer myself up.
    Everyone in this picture survived the guinda. They even had the courage to reenter El Salvador into a neighboring FMLN-controlled zone in

Chalatenango to continue cooking in support of the struggle and to accompany husbands who were guerrilla fighters. They endured the Guinda de Mayo of 1982, described in several testimonies by Liz's Pro-Búsqueda companions in this book. It was even worse and more prolonged than this Cabañas guinda of November 1981.

SAME CHILD SURVIVOR IN HONDURAN REFUGEE CAMP
ONE YEAR LATER

The mother of the little boy (visible in the previous photo in front of the cave) took this picture of us together again in the refugee camp of Mesa Grande, Honduras, about a year and two months later. Her now three-year-old son was just recovering from hepatitis A. (I fell sick with hepatitis one month later.) They endured at least three military invasions (March and November 1981 in Cabañas and May 1982 in Chalatenango).

DAYS 2 AND 3: BABY-FACED GUERRILLA FIGHTER PROTECTING US

This photo was taken on the second day of the invasion, and this adolescent was running to our periphery to prevent the government troops from entering on foot and killing us face-to-face. He was one of several dozen (fewer than one hundred) full-time FMLN fighters. He paused to let me photograph him. I was heartened by the size of his large automatic weapon, because the guerrillas were shockingly outgunned by the Salvadoran military. In fact, it seemed irresponsible to me that the FMLN had so effectively gained the support of local residents but had hardly any decent weapons to protect the civilians supporting them from the military repression. There were not nearly enough guns or ammunition for everyone who wanted to fight. It was too late, however; we were all in this together, targeted for extermination.

The category of "child soldier" was not salient in human rights discourse during the late 1970s and early 1980s. It tugs at my heart now to see so many baby faces among the guerrilla fighters protecting and dying for us. Some fighters, I am told now, were only thirteen or fourteen years old. This boy was fifteen. He had joined at twelve as a "messenger," taking extraordinary risks to deliver crucial military logistical information and casualty reports across FMLN-controlled zones. Child (and also adult) messengers ran nonstop, sometimes for days, to seek ammunition and reinforcements. They sprinted through the broken terrain both at night and in broad daylight, hoping that the Salvadoran Air Force (which strafed and bombed "anything that moved" in pro-FMLN zones) would not see them.

Like virtually everyone in northern Cabañas, the armed child in this picture was from a small farming family. Many, if not most, of the young adults and adolescents living here were part-time fighters, referred to as *milicianos* (militia members). They had only minimal training in how to load, unload, and clean a range of military weapons, beat-up hunting rifles, and small pistols. *Milicianos* did not have designated weapons or even uniforms. Anticipating the likelihood of dying, they dressed in their Sunday-best clothes when deployed into combat, with freshly washed, tight-fitting blue jeans. Many had only a small pistol stuffed in their back pocket with instructions to save their last bullet as a "*tiro de gracia* (mercy shot)" for themselves to avoid the likelihood of interrogation under torture if captured or of prolonged suffering if catastrophically wounded.

Two guerrilla organizations operated in Cabañas and coordinated, as far as I could tell, amicably. This well-armed fighter was in the Fuerzas Armadas de la Resistencia Nacional (FARN; Armed Forces of National Resistance). My visit had been organized by the Fuerzas Populares de Liberación (FPL; Popular Liberation Forces). I asked the local FPL commander in my hamlet why this FARN fighter was so much better armed than those under his command. He explained the FARN had successfully collected ransoms of multinational executives in recent years and had purchased a shipment of Belgian FALs (the weapon in this picture). FALs were easily available to the highest bidder in the international arms market.[5] A *miliciano* armed with only a pistol was following him three to five meters behind, ready to recuperate the scarce semiautomatic weapon if his companion stepped on a land mine or was shot down. I photographed the *miliciano* as well, but my camera's light-exposure washed out the tiny pistol bulging from his back pocket.

On my first return visit to Santa Marta in 1994, I gave the now-adult former adolescent guerrilla fighter a copy of this picture. We lost touch, but on my most recent visit, in October 2017, he called out to me as I passed by a slash-and-burn *milpa* (corn and bean fields are called milpas throughout Central America). He was weeding his beans, and I no longer recognized him at age fifty. Hard work under the torrential rains and burning sun of Cabañas had aged him.

Worried now in retrospect about how blind I had been to FMLN child-recruitment practices, I asked him what he actually understood about politics back then. Appreciating my concern, he answered thoughtfully, "I think about that a lot now. I joined at twelve, when *la tyra* [short for 'the tyranny'] killed my father. He was a delegate of the word. I can remember clearly that I understood everything that was happening. It amazes me now too. Strangely, it seems to me as if our minds back then matured faster than teenagers do today." Tears welled in his eyes, and in mine, so he shifted to talking in detail about the FMLN's utopian vision of "*la revolución*": land to the tiller, marketing and purchasing cooperatives, and respect for the poor. He was soft-spoken, with a gentle demeanor, and resolutely proud of having been a revolutionary child fighter.

Both of us fell silent, embarassed. He then forced a shy smile and waved his machete across his milpa on the rocky hillside in front of us, asserting in a louder, confident voice, "I fought for the right to plant corn and beans without having to pay some landlord a percentage of my crop." That Sunday, I met him again in the town plaza, and he enthusiastically took up our conversation right where we had left off. He described the cooperatively farmed extra communal milpas they continued to plant each agricultural cycle to provide food for the elderly and infirm—"just like during the revolution."

DAY 4: BOY HUGGING MORTAR FRAGMENT, MORNING
BEFORE MASSACRE OF SANTA CRUZ

Mortar fire caused most civilian casualties during the initial encirclement and bombardment stage. Blasts hit day and night, roving steadily across the entire territory in waves. They pounded cooking fires and housing infrastructure especially hard. By the end of the fourth day, so many civilians had been wounded that we feared it would be impossible to carry them with us if we delayed our escape. In the late afternoon, consequently, the political organizers announced we would break through the military cordon (*"romper cerco"*) that night and go into flight (*guindear*). Our hope was that we would find a spot outside the combat zone capable of hiding all thousand or so of us without the air force or roving foot patrols finding us and slaughtering us point-blank while the military completed this scorched-earth operation inside the FMLN territory.

I took this photo of an adorable little boy hugging a piece of military shrapnel as a safety talisman on the morning before we set off on the guinda. Poor boy! His mother (standing behind him in the dark-green dress) told me he would not put the shrapnel fragment down. He was terrified by his inexplicable luck over not having been killed by it. The explosion from which it flew had killed a playmate two years older who had been running to hide behind a boulder one hundred meters away. The boy's mother, younger brother, and adolescent cousin, all in the picture, had seen the explosion, cowering together. The young woman on the far left (in a dangerously bright pink dress) was coming to give me a bowl of bean soup and plate of tortillas to share with a militia fighter (off camera) who had just returned from an overnight stint guarding our periphery.

These women were revolutionary *tortilleras* (the rural term for "cook"). They prepared corn or sorghum tortillas, the staple food across rural Central America. They may have also been *milicianos*, but their most crucial contribution to our survival and to the struggle for justice and self-defense was food preparation. They fed the full-time fighters and anyone without family support, like me. During the guindas, they prepared food for all the civilians in flight. Cooking was especially dangerous because of the visibility of the smoke from cooking fires to air force and artillery. During momentary ebbs in the bombardment, they bravely ran to smoldering cooking fires a few hundred yards away to resume the essential task of emergency food preparation for all, at great risk to themselves.

I have shown this picture to hundreds of survivors in Santa Marta, but no one remembers the women, which probably means they did not survive. They were newcomers. The mother had introduced herself to me as the girlfriend of a recently arrived new commander, who, I heard, was killed. Sadly, no one remembers their *nombres de guerra* (war names) or their real names. They are just two more unsung heroes, along with the two little boys, who would not let their mother and their older cousin out of their sight. They were probably shot or blown up, next to one of their mother's cooking fires, either during this scorched-earth operation or during the next one in Chalatenango during May 1982.

DAY 5: FAMILY GRIEVING RIGHT AFTER MASSACRE
OF SANTA CRUZ

I took this picture a few hours after the massacre of Santa Cruz (which lasted about four hours, from 3:00 a.m. to daybreak on November 15). We had all run together helter-skelter through the military cordon, blasted by grenades and machine guns. We were too stunned and grief-stricken to comprehend what we had just endured under fire that night—people dying all around us.

The story of these four people, however, is particularly tragic. I had forced myself to calm down enough to reenter fieldwork mode and was attempting to objectively document the human rights catastrophe. I approached this young father, a few years younger than I, obviously overwhelmed, squatting sadly next to his two-year-old son, whose hand is caressing his father's neckline for reassurance. The woman standing next to him, coddling the newborn, is not the mother. A grenade blew up the baby's mother as she sprinted through the line of fire. Despite having been in her mother's arms, the newborn somehow survived, her forehead grazed by a fragment of shrapnel from the explosion that killed her mother. Presumably the blast propelled the newborn into the air, but the rags that serve as diapers among the rural poor must have softened her body's landing and spared her fragile newborn neck and cranium from damage. The shrapnel did graze her deeply enough, however, to leave a lifetime scar on her forehead.

Two grandparents, several aunts and uncles, and multiple young cousins died instantly in that same explosion. The father was not killed with his wife that night because he was part of the guerrilla decoy attack attempting to distract the enemy into shooting and pursuing them instead of the civilians. The only survivors from his nuclear family and his wife's extended family were the sister-in-law, holding his baby in this picture, and an uncle (off-screen) who had been carrying his two-year-old son. The sister with the baby in this photo was also nursing her own, only slightly older, baby (not in the photo). She was worried about the survival of her own baby because her breast milk was drying up from fear, hunger, and dehydration. She was trying to teach her newborn niece to suckle on a bottle of sugar water to calm her hunger cries and her disorientation at no longer being in her mother's arms.

I recontacted everyone in this photo on my first return visit to Santa Marta in 1994. I have stayed in that sister's house on subsequent visits and have become a close friend of her family. I rarely see her smile, despite the hundreds of hours I have spent among them. In fact, when I first arrive, we both usually have to suppress tears, overwhelmed by the emotions that the sight of one another initially precipitates. For this reason, I have mixed feelings about the dignified, but somewhat overly celebratory, term *survivor* to refer to those of us who were not killed in this scorched-earth tragedy. I fear it inadvertently erases the irresolvable grief, rage, and amorphous guilt that trauma generates. Sadly, the sister died prematurely in 2018 of high blood pressure and kidney disease despite being slim—a casualty of Big Corporate Food having penetrated the rural retail markets of Mexico and Central America.

The father squatting in the photo suffers today from agoraphobia. When I visit, he sends a younger daughter (born after the war, when he remarried) to fetch me. She discreetly explains, "He very much wants to talk to you but doesn't like to walk through town, so will you please let me take you to him now?" The toddler in the photo (the newborn's older brother) was murdered at eighteen, when a fellow road-crew worker smashed him in the head with his pickax. His death may have been caused by his refusal to join one of the legendarily violent gangs of El Salvador. The tormented life story of Pedro, one of Liz's Pro-Búsqueda companions, documents the brutal demographic collateral disaster of gangs produced by the civil war—but also made in the USA.

The baby girl in this picture is still alive but has not fared well in adulthood. Abandoned by her boyfriend after becoming pregnant as a teenager, she followed him, hoping to reunite in a shantytown in Ilobasco, an industrial market town about an hour and a half outside of the capital of El Salvador. He then abandoned her again, leaving her stranded in his grandparents' overcrowded zinc shack. She used to send me carefully written, polite letters requesting financial help. Ashamed of not being able to cover her share of her in-laws' rent and food, she referred to herself as an *"arrimada,"* the derogatory word for unwanted squatter. I used to send her money each time, but it was never enough to resolve her survival quandaries, and she no longer contacts me.

Our first temporary hiding place, where I took this picture, was a couple kilometers outside the guerrilla-controlled zone, and it was a life-saving stroke of temporary good luck. Called "La Quebrada Huiscoyol [The Huiscoyol Stream]," it was the source of the Huiscoyol River at the bottom of an inaccessible, steep ravine. Preciously clean water bubbled from its muddy walls feeding a small stream. Dehydrated and exhausted from running all night under fire, we quenched our thirst and slept.

DAY 5 AGAIN: "NON-LETHAL" US HUEY HELICOPTER USED TO STRAFE CIVILIANS

This US-made, Huey UH-1H helicopter veering away from me on one of my visits to the Mesa Grande refugee camp when the civil war was still underway flashed me back into being strafed in the Quebrada Huiscoyol hiding place right after the massacre of Santa Cruz. Outrageously, the US State Department claimed in 1981 that these Huey helicopters were "non-military, human rights assistance" when Congress (temporarily) forbade military aid after Archbishop Óscar Romero was assassinated by one of Major Roberto D'Aubuisson's death squads.[6] The only difference between "non-lethal" helicopters and military-grade ones was the removal of the external machine-gun parapet with its 360-degree pivot. Instead, the gunners had to open their side door when strafing civilians from their "human rights" helicopters during this Cabañas invasion.[7]

Incidentally, these same Huey helicopters are used for traffic control and weather reports, as well as police pursuits in sprawling megacities like Los Angeles. They often target adolescent gang members—some of them second-generation Salvadoran refugees—embroiled in internecine conflicts and exchanging automatic-weapon fire. I live in Los Angeles and often startle from the drone of a Huey suddenly overhead on my block. Adrenaline momentarily grips my chest just as it did on that first sunrise huddled in the Quebrada Huiscoyol right after the massacre of Santa Cruz. This is how I described that Huey helicopter in my diary in real time, totally freaked out:

Morning of the fifth day [November 15, 1981]:
What a horrible nightmare!...I was sure I was dead dying wounded tortured. I had decided to commit suicide. And it has only begun....

Machine gun bullets from helicopter just struck inches away from me—This is a real nightmare.

...I would almost rather be dead. I was stupid to come here....

I think I'm going to die soon. As long as I'm not wounded I don't mind. I'm sad about leaving my family—mother, father, sister, Alexa, Tony, my friends. I'm sad to leave them as a "disappeared." That is frustrating. Reduces the political value of my massacre....

It's not really that hard to die though. It's almost a relief....As long as I am not wounded.

If I'm wounded I will try to slit my wrists with the Swiss Army knife my mother gave me. Life becomes easier when you die....I hope they find my body. Is that just for political reasons?

To clarify the moment described in this note: The helicopter had arrived at daybreak and was hovering immediately on top of us, shooting into an extended family of about eighteen people exposed above the ravine, which was too steep for them to run down. The family included half a dozen infants, one or two infirm elders, and a wounded father. They had not been able to descend into the ravine with us. Moments before the helicopter arrived, I had climbed up a tall tree, thinking it might protect me from the mortar and bomb shrapnel pounding us for the past four days inside the territory. My tree perch, however, had brought me that much closer to the murderous eyes of the helicopter's gunner. He was only twenty or thirty meters directly above me, and I could see him clearly as he leaned out the wide open side door to maximize his machine gun's swivel range. One of the spent casings from his machine-gun bullets (killing the family above us) glanced off my baseball cap. I can still remember hearing what seemed to me at that moment to be a surreally pretty tinkling noise as the bullet casings daintily bounced off leaves, branches, and stones before tumbling into the mud. It all seemed to be in slow motion.

Again, in surreally slow motion, the helicopter suddenly lifted upward and veered into the distance. Everything resumed normal speed. In the distance, we heard the helicopter strafing intermittently at whatever signs of movement it detected on the ground below. I could not believe the gunner had not seen us, crammed like sardines immediately below in the narrow ravine's streambed. It seemed impossible to still be alive, because propeller backwind had furiously blown the leaves of my treetop every which way. In fact, I could practically see through the helicopter pilot's Ray-Ban aviator glasses. Had we been spotted, all seven hundred or so of us huddled below would have been killed instantly, simply by the gunner lobbing a handful of grenades and pounding us into unrecognizable human "hamburger" (as I unforgivingly kept describing our likely fate in my diary).

DAY 6: BORN IN FLIGHT UNDER FIRE

This photo of a newborn, taken right after sunrise on our second day in the Quebrada Huiscoyol ravine, is still hard for me to believe. Two babies were actually born in the middle of that second night of the guinda. I was sleeping among the *sanitarios,* the name for young men and women with slightly better literacy skills who had been trained as "barefoot doctors." I had been advised to stay with them and carried medications for them in my backpack. In the middle of the night, I heard one of the *sanitarios* being woken up to assist with a birth. I managed to fall back asleep, dismissing it as a nightmare. The next morning three smiling women and a newborn were right next to me.

The newborn's mother is on the far right. The *sanitario* midwife I had heard being awakened is in the center, holding two water bottles she had just filled from the clean water bubbling from our ravine's walls. The woman with the baby in her arms smiling widely is a guerrilla fighter who had heard that her sister (the midwife) had helped two women give birth and had come running to congratulate her. Amazingly, both babies born that night survived. They did not reach a refugee camp for another six months, however, because both mothers were so dedicated to the revolution that they were among those who reentered the neighboring Chalatenango zone of control, right after we crossed into Honduras on the twelfth day of this ordeal. Consequently, they also endured the infamous 1982 Guinda de Mayo. Sadly, the guerrilla fighter smiling widely in this picture died in May 2022 of liver disease from hepatitis C. She did not drink alcohol and never injected narcotics. She was probably infected because syringes were scarce in combat zones in El Salvador and were sometimes reused during medical emergencies. She was a guerrilla fighter for several years and would have suffered multiple medical emergencies.

The noise of crying babies posed our greatest risk of detection, and I was thankful that our ravine was deep enough to prevent the cries of the newborns from being audible to patrols passing on top of the ravine. Unfortunately, on our second night, we had to flee again because our concentrated crowd had fouled the mud with our excrement. We had also eaten all our tortillas and were starving.

DAYS 7, 8, AND 9: EXHAUSTED, STARVING, THIRSTY TODDLER CLUTCHING SUGARCANE FRAGMENT

I took this photo the next morning before collapsing, weary from another night-flight hiking to this good-enough hiding place. My companions chose the spot because it was by a sugarcane field with a stream. It had trees and thick-enough underbrush to more or less conceal us from air force patrols. Unfortunately, the bright white pith from the sugarcane we devoured reflected sunlight dangerously.

The poor little girl fell asleep hugging her equally exhausted mother, still clutching in her tiny hand the hunk of sugarcane she had been sucking. We had hoped to stay here until the scorched-earth operation ended. Unfortunately, after two uneventful days we had chopped too much of the sugarcane and feared an aircraft might see our mounds of white pith. The guerrilla fighters also monitored the military's radio channel and could hear soldiers receiving unusual orders. In previous invasions the soldiers had usually rushed over the zone fast, smashing houses, haphazardly looting possessions, and killing any humans or animals still alive, before immediately retreating to the safety of their military garrisons. This time, however, they were deployed into smaller patrols and stood guard on strategic promontories to hold the territory.

We had fouled up the stream again. Diarrhea was overwhelming all of us and the malnourished children were at high risk of rapid dehydration. Consequently, the next night we fled to an abandoned farm with a larger, cleaner stream, with brush to hide us. That third hiding place was also, thankfully, near a field of abandoned sorghum. We cooked the sorghum tortillas at night to hide the smoke, but the next day the team monitoring the military radio transmissions alerted us that the military had detected our cooking fires. We fled immediately in broad daylight, completely exposed to the skies. Luckily, only one air force patrol passed, and we hid under a big cement bridge just in time. We crossed back into the former FMLN-controlled zone, wary of the new mobile patrols and guard posts. We were desperate to reach the Lempa River and cross into the Honduran refugee camps, but the Honduran military was still amassed at that border crossing.

DAYS 10 AND 11: FIVE-YEAR-OLD GIRL SHOWING
SHRAPNEL WOUND ON SIDE OF THIGH

I took this photo on the first or second day after we reentered our former FMLN-controlled zone. For the next two and a half days, we zigzagged, searching for better hiding places, more food, and potable water. The Salvadoran troops were now aware of our presence, so we decentralized across multiple valleys to increase survival chances during strafings and bombardments for at least some of us.

The girl is showing me a shrapnel wound on her thigh, barely visible as a dot because of the bright sunlight. Her father had decided not to carry her through the line of fire in Santa Cruz because she had been bleeding too heavily. They were among the two hundred to three hundred people who fled back into the territory and then separated into fragmented family groups to hide. They were even more disheveled, exhausted, starving, dehydrated, and disoriented than we were because the Salvadoran Army's new US Special Forces scorched-earth strategy of rapid mobile patrol units rampaging throughout the zone had forced them to hide in quasi-solitary confinement in bug-ridden thickets.

Writing this forty years later has clarified to me our bad luck at being caught in a transition moment in US-Salvadoran military tactics. This was one of the first military invasions in which a few dozen newly trained officers from Fort Bragg, Georgia, of the soon-to-be infamous Atlacatl Battalion, assisted rank-and-file Salvadoran military troops in killing civilians more systematically. We survived only because the US Congress had temporarily put restrictions on military aid to El Salvador. Unfortunately two months later, in January 1982, President Jimmy Carter reversed course and reauthorized what became under President Ronald Reagan a more massive flow of military aid, including the even more efficiently murderous A-47 Dragonfly attack jets.[8] In December 1981, the entire Atlacatl Battalion completed its counterinsurgency training at the US Military's School of the Americas in Fort Benning, Georgia. They were fully indoctrinated into the same failed US counterinsurgency scorched-earth techniques that had produced the Vietnam War humanitarian disaster (1954–75).

The FMLN commanders did not yet know how to keep a step ahead of these new rapid flexible Atlacatl patrols and their onsite US Green Beret Special Forces advisers. The very next month (December 1981), in El Mozote, Morazán, the Atlacatl massacred over nine hundred civilians on their first deployment as a complete battalion. They meticulously separated the men into a school building and packed the women and children—many of them newborns and toddlers—into a church, which they then exploded with grenades, followed by point-blank automatic-weapons fire.[9] For years US diplomats cynically ridiculed human rights denunciations, even when they were corroborated by multiple credible eyewitness survivors. Finally, an international team of forensic anthropologists used state-of-the-art technologies of cadaver excavation and genetic identification to conduct a rigorous body count. In addition to the systematic sex and age segregation of victims, they documented the atrocity of military gang rape. The US government fell silent on the subject of El Mozote and has never acknowledged this crime against humanity under the tutelage of US military training and more than a decade of ongoing Green Beret oversight inside El Salvador.[10]

The only reason so many of us survived the November 1981 Guinda of Cabañas was because a US television film crew from NBC's *The Today Show* had accompanied Nicaraguan celebrity Bianca Jagger on a human rights visit to inspect Central American refugee camps in Honduras.[11] Hearing the terrible bombardments occurring just over the border in El Salvador, they bravely insisted on hiking to the Lempa River crossing point with Cabañas. The Honduran military immediately retreated, fearing the international scandal of a primetime US television camera crew filming them preventing civilian Salvadoran refugees from seeking safety.[12]

As soon as we heard the coast was finally clear, we ran to the border and swam across the river. The healthiest and youngest of us made it out first at sunrise before the Salvadoran Air Force started patrolling again. Slower runners, especially those carrying children, the wounded, or the infirm elderly did not make it out until later that day and even into the next night. They were subject to more pursuit and strafing.

ONE YEAR LATER: CHILD SURVIVORS AT MESA GRANDE REFUGEE CAMP, HONDURAS

I took this photo on one of my return visits to the Mesa Grande refugee camp in Honduras, some forty kilometers from the Salvadoran border. Refugees from several different FMLN-controlled zones in Chalatenango and Cabañas were relocated there, including survivors of the two 1981 guindas in Cabañas (in March and November) as well as the 1982 Guinda de Mayo in Chalatenango. All these children had to run for their lives or were carried by relatives during one, two, or all three of those guindas. As the photo reveals, children are the majority of the population in rural El Salvador. Accordingly, they constituted the bulk of the casualties during the hundreds of scorched-earth operations and thousands of aerial bombardments of the twelve-year civil war. The day after the Cabañas 1981 scorched-earth operation, the FMLN estimated total civilian casualties at "about 200." A Salvadoran military captain admitted to the press that one hundred peasants were killed attempting to cross the Lempa River. As I noted in the foreword, in 2019, Catholic Church documentarians estimated the Santa Cruz massacre death toll at 270.[13] Untold more people were killed or wounded during the days before and after our flight.

To share an example of the incomprehensible and unspeakable horrors these children endured, I will describe the preparations for the guinda and the first hour of the Santa Cruz massacre, which occurred at the beginning of our seven-day flight. The afternoon before we set off, I accompanied the *sanitarios* who were visiting families of the wounded, helping them prepare loved ones for transport in hammocks or by piggyback. They also dispensed diazepam (Valium) pills to mothers nursing babies or toddlers, hoping the sedative would keep the cries of babies from revealing our location as we ran through the military cordon and when we hid afterward. Tragically, mothers were being told to keep a rag handy to muffle their crying babies. In the months afterward, I learned that under fire during scorched-earth operations, loving mothers may have inadvertently suffocated their babies crying from hunger or fear, to keep patrols from killing them and everyone hiding with them.

As time passes, mothers (and sometimes fathers) seek me out during return visits to tell harrowing, outraged accounts of refusing pressure from fighters or other individuals hiding next to them, demanding they smother their crying infant to death. No one claims to have suffocated a baby, but, when speaking about being pressured to do so, they talk in voices that are brittle with pain, loudly accelerated and breathless, or sometimes eerily emotionally detached, as if disassociating from the pain of the memory. I have collected multiple accounts of families hiding for days, thirsty and starving, and of mothers putting urine in their baby's bottle to stop their cries. One described having to helplessly watch a neighbor's wounded child die slowly and silently of exhaustion and dehydration. Many of the worst stories come from those who suffered through the stifling hot days of the even more prolonged Guinda de Mayo.

At approximately three in the morning on November 15, 1981, I was among the first waves of civilians to reach the military cordon at the hamlet of Santa Cruz. Machine-gunning and RPG grenade explosions suddenly burst out on all sides of us. About two hundred meters ahead of us, slightly to our left, a column of guerrilla fighters was attacking the army as a decoy. We were supposed to sprint forward through the cordon at this very moment, taking advantage of the enemy troops being distracted into shooting back toward the guerrilla fighters off to our left. This, however, is how I described the confusing mayhem moment of the massacre in my notes a few hours after surviving it:

> I rolled up my pants above my knees, and took off my [Nike] sneakers and socks to try to wade without getting everything wet across a shallow 50 or 60 yard wide river, called "Copinolapa." Halfway across, several babies, suddenly awakened by the terrifying explosions going off right next to us, started shrieking.
>
> How could I have been so stupid to be worried about staying dry!

The next hail of bullets struck the water right around me. I could see their splashes. Initially, I crouched down into the water too scared to move. But the enemy's bullets were striking right into and around us. They could obviously hear us and probably also saw us because gunfire and explosions lit us up. I realized there was no choice but to run forward through these bullets and somehow hope that, out of dumb luck, none would strike me.

Expecting to feel metal rip into me any second, I sprung forward, scraping my feet, stubbing my toes, and falling face down in the water at least twice, maybe three, maybe four, times on hidden river rocks. It was like in a slow-motion nightmare of wallowing in quicksand. I forced myself to ignore my bruised, torn-up, bare feet and stepped up higher out of the water but instead kept losing my balance. Finally, close enough to the bank, I hurled myself forward in a belly-flop dive, landing prostrate on the mud and gravel. The wind was knocked out of me, and, gasping, I burrowed beneath a pile of rocks but barely made a dent. I spun over flat on my back, hoping I was under the line of fire. I could see the bullets striking into the middle of the river where the fleeing crowd was flailing. We were unsure over whether to run forward or backward.

Furious at myself for wasting precious minutes amid these flying bullets, I unrolled each pant leg by bending my legs to my chest, one at a time to avoid sitting up, because the line of fire seemed to be only inches above me. I threw away my socks and slipped on my soggy sneakers and wasted yet more precious seconds tying my shoelaces tightly. I could not believe my luck thus far at not being struck by bullets or shrapnel, because I could see wounded people around me. I swore to keep my sneakers on until I was safe again—even while sleeping. My raw, throbbing feet were finally well protected again, so I forced myself to crouch and sprint forward during a momentary lull in the firing.

Everything seemed to be exploding every which way, harder than ever.

It was impossible to tell friend from foe. Our call-and-response password combination was useless. The enemy had immediately learned it, and our bleatingly naive calls merely identified us as sitting ducks to be shot in the dark. I hoped the sparks from guns on my left were our guerrilla-fighter companions prying an opening for us to run through. But grenade blasts kept making me hit the dirt. I have no idea why flying shrapnel did not hit me during each explosion. The closest, loudest blasts made a weird, almost dry, painfully loud splitting sound, as if an entire tree trunk had instantly separated lengthwise into two separate halves. I landed once on stinging nettles and several times on thorns.

We were still in the crux of the line of fire, and I was not sure if I should continue sprinting forward blindly in the dark, straight into what seemed like a nonstop barrage of machine guns and grenade explosions. Thank God! The loud, brave voices of guerrilla fighters, who evidently saw us paralyzed by terror, burst into heroic clear shouts from a hill to our side: "¡Avance! ¡Avance! ¡Rápido! ¡Agáchense! ¡Adelante! [Advance! Advance! ... Fast! ... Crouch! ... Forward!]."

I sprinted forward 50 more meters until, out of breath, I saw a large boulder and eagerly threw myself behind it to rest. But a woman was already occupying the spot and whispered desperately to me, "¡Vete! ¡Vete de aquí! [Scram! Get away from here!]." I couldn't understand how someone could heartlessly beg me to run back into the flying bullets from this well-shielded spot. Then I realized her baby was shrieking. She was trying to save my life, as well as her baby's and her own. I had startled the baby awake, and there was no way she could calm it down with me there panting loudly. So I held my breath and sprinted forward again. Soldiers were shooting purposefully directly into the sound of crying babies in the darkness of the night. The cries were their priority targets. I hope she and her baby survived, but I have no idea—and I doubt they did. Too many loud explosions were erupting all around us, nonstop. I thank that mother now in these pages for saving my life, and, four decades later, I feel sick at the thought that I possibly caused her and her baby's deaths. It was too horrible to be believed in the moment.

Another unmanageable memory is the wounded who were festering in agony. They were writhing in pain and frothing at the mouth, or knotting their brows, immobile and gritting their teeth. One little girl with a bloodied dangling foot, piggyback on her brother, was intermittently passing out and reawakening with distress etched across her face. I just uselessly sprinted past those heroic suffering people, too terrified to help. It was beyond cruel. The wounded looked like they were going to die slowly in prolonged anguish—unless a big set of bombs finally blew us up. I caught myself hoping a well-aimed grenade explosion would simply wipe me out painlessly in one big burst. I wanted the horror to finally be over. Worried I was going crazy, I tried, unsuccessfully, to push these thoughts out of my head. I feel guilty for having been so uselessly terrified—not brave or strong enough to help.

Suddenly, an even louder series of explosions and splitting bursts from a promontory a stone's throw ahead of us erupted. I sprawled on my stomach, expecting metal and more explosions to follow. Instead, however, the night fell wonderfully silent, followed by loud confident calls for us to run forward—fast. I jumped to my feet, sprinting forward faster, no longer bothering to crouch. I passed right through the center of the hamlet and saw people running ahead of me up a very steep hill and followed them.

Later I found out those big explosions were from inside the one-room schoolhouse of Santa Cruz, where the military had installed a machine-gun nest. Several hundred of us had been pinned down right in the line of fire by those machine guns. Our lives were saved by a teenage fighter named Luis Hernández. According to another former guerrilla-fighter friend of mine: Luis "snuck up right next to the schoolhouse wall and shot a *bazukaso* [portable RPG grenade launcher] through its window. That calmed things down a little, allowing some of *la gente* [the civilians] to make it through."

Luis Hernández was a true hero. Unfortunately, heroes and good Samaritans were the first to die, and Luis died later that night, still determined to protect us. Enemy reinforcements arrived an hour or so later and reinitiated the momentarily interrupted massacre. My guerrilla-fighter friend says she had to run right over the hero's body. His courageous sacrifice enabled me and many of the slower runners carrying babies, toddlers, and the wounded, to survive.

I was moved to see, years later, the name and date of the Santa Cruz massacre inscribed on a commemorative metal wall in a rundown park in downtown San Salvador. It occupies an entire designated line among the names of dozens, maybe hundreds, of bigger and smaller massacres, as well as over seventy-three thousand individuals also listed by name on the long wall. The wall is modeled after the Vietnam War Memorial in Washington, DC, and this parallel architectural memorial reference between the tragedies of two useless wars is sadly appropriate. The same US military and intelligence personnel who lost the Vietnam War six years before the initiation of the Salvadoran Civil War also advised and weaponized the Salvadoran military and its intelligence agencies, with just as disastrous results. The United States imposed the same morally bankrupt and failed counterinsurgency scorched-earth strategy on El Salvador that radicalized the Vietnamese peasantry into a massive national liberation movement, whose underdog army defeated the much better-armed and better-financed US military machine. Like many who visit, grieving, to commemorate murdered loved ones and to reflect on this brutal era in Salvadoran history, all I could do was run my fingertips gently across the engraved letters, "Masacre de Santa Cruz," one by one, and cry.

APPENDIX B **Refugee Children's Drawings of the Salvadoran Civil War**

Elizabeth Barnert and Philippe Bourgois

We present six illustrations of the Salvadoran Civil War drawn by elementary school children in United Nations refugee camps in Honduras during the early 1980s. Philippe collected hundreds of these drawings on multiple visits to the camps (located in La Virtud, Mesa Grande, and Colomoncagua, Honduras) between 1981 to 1984, and circulated them to human rights and social services organizations in the United States and Europe. The drawings reveal the profound vulnerability of children in the conflict zones of the war. Through art, the children express their outrage over the cruelties they suffered, and they call for help and solidarity from the international community.

On his visits, Philippe brought colored pencils, markers, crayons, and eight-by-eleven-inch white paper to the elementary schools, which were always short of supplies. The students were eager to draw their experiences from the war, and their teachers were eager to facilitate the process. The drawing sessions were spontaneous events and not formally organized as therapy, but both Philippe and the teachers could see that the process of drawing and observing the adults' emotional reactions to their artwork helped the children to process the traumas they had endured.

Energized, they applied themselves assiduously to the task, and most did not stop drawing until their supply of paper ran out.

The children used multiple colors in every picture. Red and orange were consistently in highest demand to convey the bleeding wounds and mangled bodies of their neighbors and family members. The older children, despite only limited literacy skills, confidently annotated their work with descriptions of exactly what was happening. They tell us who the victims are (e.g., *"el pobre campesino"* [the poor farmer]) and denounce the perpetrators (military units, helicopters strafing, US government, "Ronan Riga" [Ronald Reagan]). It is as if the children understood that most viewers living in peace could not possibly imagine the horrors occurring on a routine basis in their isolated, rural hamlets and needed to be educated. Their notes and self-descriptions of their ages and classroom levels express an idealistic hope for international solidarity.

The children, like those in the last photograph of appendix A, had survived the first Salvadoran military scorched-earth invasion of Cabañas in March 1981, and many probably also lived through the one in November 1981, with a few of them possibly also enduring the more prolonged and brutal May 1982 invasion of Chalatenango (Guinda de Mayo). The survivors of the Cabañas and Chalatenango invasions had to cross either the Lempa or the Sumpul River. Many people drowned or were shot while being strafed by Salvadoran helicopters at these border crossings before they could make it to the refugee camps in Honduras.

At the time, the Salvadoran government had no tolerance for even the most minimal reforms or the most apolitical human rights documentation of any of the events pictured here. Simply living in a territory reputed to be supportive of the FMLN was enough to warrant murder by the Salvadoran military, whether one was an innocent child, an unarmed small farmer, an armed guerrilla fighter, or an outsider caught in the crossfire. The care and precision with which the children detailed the horrors inflicted during the war, and the innocence with which they tried to explain them to a public that had no idea of, or denied, what was going on in El Salvador renders their artwork a powerful objective documentation of the joint US and Salvadoran governments' crimes against humanity committed against the rural poor during the early to mid-1980s of the civil war.

Several of the children's drawings not presented here similarly depict soldiers shooting at families. One child's caption identifies the name of the Special Forces corps attacking the civilians: "The whole hunting battalion killing [*todo el batayo casador ascesinando*] children, women, and elderly people." Online military archives confirm that the *Batallón de Cazadores* (spelled "batayo casador" by the nine-year-old child) was an official military unit dating back to the 1898 Spanish-American War. It was attached to larger military units for "special operations" (presumably scorched-earth invasions). The battalion was discontinued in 1988, rendered redundant by the new, even more murderous, US-trained BIRIs (Rapid Reaction Infantry Battalions, such as Atlacatl, Belloso, Atonal).[1] Several child artists emphasized the devastation caused by US Huey H1 helicopters strafing them by annotating the flying bullets striking people hitting the ground: "helicopter machine-gunning." The letter *h* is often silent in Spanish, and the rural Salvadorans generally pronounce *helicóptero* as "alicoptero." Most of the children misspelled "helicóptero" with a phonetic alliteration of "alicoptero." Another child identified the institutional perpetrators for viewers unfamiliar with US-Central American power politics, "sent by the United States ambassador and the North American government of Ronan Riga [Ronald Reagan]." Another child was careful to specify "farmers assassinated by the Salvadoran military." He added, for more emphatic precision, in another shade of colored pencil "and by the intervention of the United States."

Drawing by nine-year-old Salvadoran refugee girl, showing Salvadoran military troops shooting a woman while a military helicopter flies above. Meanwhile, another helicopter sets a farmer's thatched-roof home on fire, and a ground soldier patrols nearby. The child artist explains, "The poor peasant. They burned his house."

Drawing by nine-year-old Salvadoran refugee girl, showing Salvadoran soldiers led by an officer with a larger visored cap shooting at a family in flight: a mother carrying a baby, a daughter, and a son in front, who is being struck by bullets. The helicopter is strafing the mother and baby from behind. On the far left, a supine body under a tree may be dead or dying. On the right, a person, possibly a child, appears to be hiding under a tree.

Drawing by twelve-year-old Salvadoran refugee, showing either of two classic terror tactics regularly deployed during the early years of the war, before the guerrillas could keep the military from entering "FMLN-controlled zones" at will. On the far left is a bloodied, beaten man (visible from his upper body and the top of his head outlined in red to indicate blood in contrast to the dark marker of his lower body, as well as from his swollen and misshapen figure). He is being restrained or held up on his feet by two smiling soldiers wearing berets (probably the individuals who bloodied him and who appear to be from one of the US-trained BIRIs, suggested by the distinct insignias on their berets). They are likely either forcing the man to lead them to the next hamlet to identify other families to kill or forcing him to watch a grinning rank-and-file solider (identifiable by his round helmet) torture his son, who is so young he is light enough to be lifted into the air by the back of his neck. The child's face is outlined in red, as is the blood flowing from his mouth, while the rest of the child's body is drawn in yellow marker. A military airplane surveills above.

Drawing by twelve-year-old Salvadoran refugee, showing a soldier with the top third of his bayonet covered in blood (indicated by contrasting red and yellow marker on the bayonet), dragging a woman by her hair while cutting her up. She is bleeding profusely (red and orange marker on her hair, down her backside, and at her wrists, where her hands have been severed off). In the background, a man is strewn on the ground with his right arm, left hand, and feet chopped off (red flowing from the extremities). Blood or vomit also spew from his mouth (in orange marker). The soldier on the right is shooting a woman in the chin and has already sprayed bullets across her chest and into her chin (in red marker) as she flings her arms open, presumably praying to God or begging for mercy.

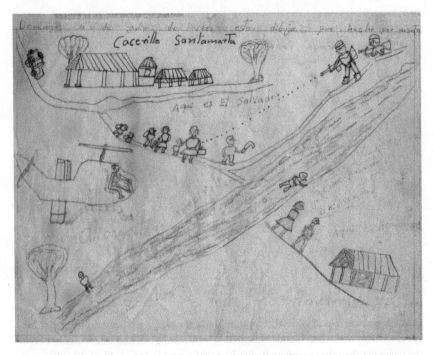

Drawing by Salvadoran refugee child, showing families fleeing from the hamlet of Santa Marta, pursued by ground soldiers, with a military helicopter above. Automatic weapons fire is striking a mother holding her young child's hand. The families are carrying their possessions on their back and have no weapons to defend themselves, except for the father in front, who waves his curved scythe (called a *cuervo* and used for weeding). This could have occurred during either of the two major guindas of Cabañas, when hundreds of families fled into Honduras, with many drowning or shot in the Lempa River, at the border with Honduras. Dead bodies are visible underwater, represented by yellow shadowy forms. Either a corpse or a man swimming is arriving on the Honduran bank. The child artist's identifying caption (on top) communicates collective solidarity with his classmates: "Sunday, July 10, 1983. This drawing was done by us." His annotation below the river delineates, "Santa Marta Hamlet [*Cacerillo* Santamarta]," with additional geographic detail shown in multiple distinct colors for international viewers unfamiliar with local geography.

Drawing by thirteen-year-old Salvadoran refugee boy, showing a helicopter strafing farmers, one dead and bullets striking into another. These last two drawings probably depict the March 1981 Cabañas invasion, when people crossed in broad daylight, and many were killed or drowned in the Lempa River (represented by decapitated heads floating down the river). The safety of the refugee camp outside La Virtud in Honduras beckons. This child artist asserts his credibility as a witness of these events by listing his grade level: "These drawings were made by Orlando Lopez. I am 13 years old. I study in the second level schools of refugee camp 5."

Notes

AUTHOR'S NOTE

1. Elizabeth Barnert, Eric Stover, Gery Ryan, and Paul J. Chung, "Long Journey Home: Family Reunification Experiences of the Disappeared Children of El Salvador," *Human Rights Quarterly* 37, no. 2 (2015): 492–510; Elizabeth Barnert, Nathalie Lopez, Philippe Bourgois, Gery Ryan, Paul J. Chung, and Eric Stover, "My Child's Journey Home: Perspectives of Adult Family Members on the Separation and Reunification of the 'Disappeared' Children of El Salvador," *Human Rights Quarterly* 41, no. 1 (2019): 91–114.

2. Asociación Pro-Búsqueda, home page, accessed May 16, 2022, www.prob usqueda.org.sv/.

FOREWORD

1. Caitlin Dickerson, "Parents of 545 Children Separated at the Border Cannot Be Found," *New York Times*, October 21, 2020, www.nytimes.com/2020/10 /21/us/migrant-children-separated.html; "Detention Statistics," Freedom for Immigrants, accessed June 6, 2022, www.freedomforimmigrants.org/detention -statistics.

2. Dickerson, "Parents of 545 Children"; "Family Separation: A Timeline," Southern Poverty Law Center, March 23, 2022, www.splcenter.org/news/2022 /03/23/family-separation-timeline.

3. Tomas Andreu, "Canonización de monseñor Óscar Romero: 'Mi hermano Roberto d'Aubuisson estuvo en la planeación del crimen de monseñor Romero en El Salvador,'" *BBC News Mundo*, March 18, 2018, www.bbc.com/mundo/noticias -america-latina-43517465; Douglas Farah, "D'Aubuisson: Death Comes from the Executioner," *Washington Post*, February 23, 1992, www.washingtonpost.com/ar chive/opinions/1992/02/23/daubuisson-death-comes-to-the-executioner/df5839 ff-fe39-4a51-ac3c-7f4e38e0d5f2/.

4. Leonardo Boff and Clodovis Boff, *Introducing Liberation Theology* (Maryknoll, NY: Orbis Books, 1987); Carolyn Forche, *What You Have Heard Is True: A Memoir of Witness and Resistance* (New York: Penguin, 2019).

5. Michael Taussig, *Law in a Lawless Land: Diary of a "Limpieza" in Colombia* (New York: New Press, 2003).

6. Michael T. Taussig, *Walter Benjamin's Grave* (Chicago: University of Chicago Press, 2006), http://public.eblib.com/choice/publicfullrecord.aspx?p=53 0448. Taussig memorializes the philosopher Walter Benjamin's call for solidarity with the everyday emergency faced by the poor during the rise of fascism in 1930s Nazi Germany. Poignantly, Benjamin, a Jewish Marxist refugee, committed suicide while trapped at the French/Spanish border, attempting to flee Hitler's genocide.

7. Philippe Bourgois, Seth M. Holmes, Kim Sue, and James Quesada, "Structural Vulnerability: Operationalizing the Concept to Address Health Disparities in Clinical Care," *Academic Medicine* 92 (2017): 299–307.

8. Carlos Salinas Maldonado, "El Mozote: 40 Years after the Worst Military Massacre in the Americas, Victims Still Calling for Justice," *El País*, December 16, 2021, https://english.elpais.com/usa/2021-12-16/el-mozote-40-years-after -the-worst-military-massacre-in-the-americas-victims-still-calling-for-justice .html; Mark Danner, *The Massacre at El Mozote: A Parable of the Cold War* (New York: Vintage Books, 1994); Belisario Betancur, Reinaldo Figueredo Planchart, and Thomas Buergenthal, "Report of the UN Truth Commission on El Salvador," United Nations Security Council, April 1, 1993, www.derechos.org/nizkor/salvad or/informes/truth.html.

9. *Guinda* is Salvadoran slang for "fleeing during a scorched-earth military campaign" (i.e., running desperately for one's life). *Guinda* literally means "hang." Like the strategic abbreviation of the cryptic moniker "Pro-Búsqueda" (literally Pro-Search), it is a popularly recognized euphemism that reveals the resonance of resistance to repression in El Salvador.

10. Pierre Bourdieu, *Pascalian Meditations*, trans. Richard Nice (Stanford, CA: Stanford University Press, 2000).

11. Nancy Scheper-Hughes and Philippe Bourgois, "Introduction: Making Sense of Violence," in *Violence in War and Peace: An Anthology*, ed. Nancy Scheper-Hughes and Philippe Bourgois (Oxford: Blackwell, 2004), 1–27.

12. Bourdieu, *Pascalian Meditations;* Scheper-Hughes and Bourgois, *Violence in War and Peace.*

13. Jared M. Diamond, *Guns, Germs, and Steel: The Fates of Human Societies* (New York: Norton, 1999); Bartolomé de Las Casas, *A Short Account of the Destruction of the Indies* (New York: Penguin, 1992).

14. Eduardo Galeano, *Open Veins of Latin America: Five Centuries of the Pillage of a Continent* (London: Monthly Review, 1997).

15. Jeffrey L. Gould and Aldo A. Lauria-Santiago, *To Rise in Darkness: Revolution, Repression, and Memory in El Salvador, 1920–1932* (Durham, NC: Duke University Press, 2008).

16. Philippe Bourgois, "Lumpen Abuse: The Human Cost of Righteous Neoliberalism," *City and Society* 23, no. 1 (2011): 2–12.

17. Luis Gonzalez Serrano, "El Salvador Tragic: 10 Roque Dalton Poems from 3 Books," *Cordite Poetry Review*, January 31, 2013, http://cordite.org.au/translations/serrano-dalton/; Roque Dalton, "Five Poems by Roque Dalton," *Bomb Magazine*, April 1, 1984, https://bombmagazine.org/articles/five-poems-15/.

18. Juan-Jose Dalton, "'Muerte de Roque, el error más grande de mi vida': Entrevista con Joaquin Villalobos," *ContraPunto: Diario Digital El Salvador*, May 12, 2017, www.contrapunto.com.sv/cultura/archivoRD/muerte-de-roque-el-error-mas-grande-de-mi-vida-villalobos/3622.

19. Jorge Arias Gómez, *Farabundo Martí: La biografía clásica* (Coyoacán, Mexico: Ocean Sur, 2010).

20. Roque Dalton, *Miguel Mármol: Los sucesos de 1932 en El Salvador* (San José, Costa Rica: Editorial Universitaria Centroamericana, 1972); Thomas P. Anderson, *Matanza: El Salvador's Communist Revolt of 1932* (Lincoln: University of Nebraska Press, 1971); Gould and Lauria-Santiago, *To Rise in Darkness.*

21. Boff and Boff, *Introducing Liberation Theology.*

22. Forche, *What You Have Heard.*

23. John B. Quigley, *The Ruses for War: American Interventionism since World War II* (Amherst, NY: Prometheus Books, 2007); Brian Loveman, *No Higher Law: American Foreign Policy and the Western Hemisphere since 1776* (Chapel Hill: University of North Carolina Press, 2010).

24. "US Intervention in Salvadoran Elections Continues," North American Congress on Latin America, July 10, 2008, https://nacla.org/news/us-intervention-salvadoran-elections-continues.

25. Allan Nairn, "Behind the Death Squads: An Exclusive Report on the US Role in El Salvador's Official Terror," *Progressive*, May 1984, 17.

26. Chris Herlinger, "Marisa de Martínez, Sister of Roberto D'Aubuisson, Speaks of Óscar Romero and Her Own Spiritual Calling," *National Catholic Reporter*, March 16, 2020, www.ncronline.org/news/people/marisa-de-mart-nez-sister-roberto-daubuisson-speaks-scar-romero-and-her-own-spiritual.

27. Nairn, "Behind the Death Squads"; Alan Riding, "El Salvador Regime Accused on Rights," *New York Times*, January 22, 1979, www.nytimes.com/1979/01/22/archives/el-salvador-regime-accused-on-rights-interamerican-commiss ion-says.html; Forche, *What You Have Heard*; Inter-American Commision on Human Rights, "Annual Report, 1979–1980," 1980, www.cidh.oas.org/annualrep /79.80eng/chap.5c.htm.

28. Larry Rohter, "4 Salvadorans Say They Killed U.S. Nuns on Orders of Military," *New York Times*, April 3, 1998, www.nytimes.com/1998/04/03/world/4-sal vadorans-say-they-killed-us-nuns-on-orders-of-military.html.

29. Betancur, Planchart, and Buergenthal, "UN Truth Commission."

30. For President Bukele's relationship to organized crime and gangs see: Phillips, Tom. "'Each Day Is Agony': The Lives Swept up in El Salvador's Mass Arrests." *The Guardian*, July 3, 2022, sec. World news. https://www.theguardian.com/wor ld/2022/jul/03/el-salvador-arrests-gangs-nayib-bukele; Martinez, Carlos. "Audios de Carlos Marroquín revelan que masacre de marzo ocurrió por ruptura entre Gobierno y MS." *El Faro*. May 17, 2022. https://elfaro.net/es/202205/el_salvador /26175.; Martinez, Carlos. "Audios de Carlos Marroquín Revelan Que Masacre de Marzo Ocurrió Por Ruptura Entre Gobierno y MS." El Faro Audio. May 20, 2022. Accessed August 2, 2022; https://open.spotify.com/episode/34msfa85tQrpaUTj wDpAFo; EFE. "Presidente Bukele dice en Twitter que es 'el dictador más cool del mundo.'" *El Tiempo*. September 21, 2021, sec. mundo. https://www.eltiempo.com /mundo/latinoamerica/presidente-bukele-dice-que-es-el-dictador-mas-cool-del -mundo-619795.

31. David Gerard, "El Salvador Is Printing Money with Bitcoin," *Foreign Policy*, June 15, 2021, https://foreignpolicy.com/2021/06/15/el-salvador-bitcoin-offic ial-currency-printing-money/; Rodrigo Campos, "World Bank Rejects El Salvador Request for Help on Bitcoin Implementation," Reuters, June 17, 2021, www .reuters.com/business/el-salvador-keep-dollar-legal-tender-seeks-world-bank -help-with-bitcoin-2021-06-16/.

32. Emmanuel Levinas, "Useless Suffering," in *The Provocation of Levinas*, ed. Robert Bernasconi and David Wood (London: Routledge, 1988), 156–67; Veena Das, "Sufferings, Theodicies, Disciplinary Practices, Appropriations," *International Social Science Journal* 49, no. 154 (2010): 563–72.

33. Veena Das, "Moral Orientations to Suffering," in *Health and Social Change*, ed. Lincoln C. Chen, Arthur Kleinman, and Norma C. Ware (Cambridge, MA: Harvard University Press, 1994), 139–67; Primo Levi, *The Drowned and the Saved* (New York: Summit Books, 1988); Deborah Thomas, *Exceptional Violence: Embodied Citizenship in Transnational Jamaica* (Durham, NC: Duke University Press, 2011).

34. Levinas, "Useless Suffering." My concern with rendering suffering less useless is inspired by anthropologist Veena Das's reflection on the provocative declaration by the philosopher of ethics, Emmanuel Levinas, a Jewish prisoner of war captured by the Nazis, who provocatively asserted that *all* suffering must

always be recognized as useless. In response, Das urged anthropologists to "register the pain of the other... [so that] anthropological text may serve as a body of writing which lets the pain of the other happen to it" (Das, "Sufferings," 572). Participant-observation ethnography on war crimes represents a first step toward historical accountability that could hopefully remediate the uselessness of suffering and advocate for a peace with accountability that respects human rights.

35. Patricia Ynestroza, "El Salvador declara 'Bien Cultural' a lugares donde ocurrieron masacres durante guerra civil," *Vatican News*, May 30, 2019, www.vat icannews.va/es/mundo/news/2019-05/el-salvador-bienes-culturales-lugares-ma sacres.html.

36. James S. Corum, "The Air War in El Salvador," *Airpower Journal*, Summer 1998, 27–44.

37. Ralph Sprenkels, *Historias para tener presente* (San Salvador: Asociación Pro-Búsqueda de Niñas y Niños Desaparecidos/UCA Editores, 2002).

38. Commission on Human Rights, *Written Statement Submitted by the Commission on the Churches on International Affairs* (New York City: United Nations, 1982); Betancur, Planchart, and Buergenthal, "UN Truth Commission."

39. Daniel Valencia Caravantes, "Investigación señala responsabilidad de Coronel Ochoa Pérez en Masacre en Cabañas," *Elfaro*, April 26, 2015. https://www.elfaro.net/es/201504/noticias/16904/Investigaci%C3%B3n-se%C3%B1ala-re sponsabilidad-de-coronel-Ochoa-P%C3%A9rez-en-masacre-en-Caba%C3%B1as .htm.

40. Jeremy J. Sarkin and Elisenda Calvet Martinez, "The Global Practice of Systematic Enforced Disappearances of Children in International Law: Strategies for Preventing Future Occurrences and Solving Past Cases," *Catholic University Law Review* 71, no. 1 (2022): 74.

INTRODUCTION

1. Walter La Feber, *Inevitable Revolutions* (New York: Norton, 1993); Joe Fish and Cristina Sganga, *El Salvador: Testament of Terror* (New York: Olive Branch, 1988).

2. La Feber, *Inevitable Revolutions*; Fish and Sganga, *El Salvador*.

3. Steven Roberts, "Congressmen Find Optimism at Home on Economy but not Foreign Policy," *New York Times*, April 7, 1983, www.nytimes.com/1983/04 /07/us/congressmen-find-optimism-at-home-on-economy-but-not-foreign-poli cy.html.

4. La Feber, *Inevitable Revolutions*.

5. Óscar Romero, "Text of Archbishop Romero's Telegram to US President (1980)," National Security Archive, accessed May 17, 2022, https://nsarchive2 .gwu.edu/NSAEBB/NSAEBB339/doc04.pdf.

6. Fish and Sganga, *El Salvador*.

7. La Feber, *Inevitable Revolutions.*

8. Raymond Bonner, *Weakness and Deceit: U.S. Policy and El Salvador* (New York: Crown, 1984).

9. Fish and Sganga, *El Salvador.*

10. Ibid.

11. Mark Danner, *The Massacre at El Mozote: A Parable of the Cold War* (New York: Vintage Books, 1994).

12. Ralph Sprenkels, *El día más esperado: Buscando a los niños desaparecidos de El Salvador* (San Salvador: Asociación Pro-Búsqueda de Niñas y Niños Desaparecidos/UCA Editores, 2001).

13. Ibid.

14. Ibid.

15. Ibid.

16. United Nations, *From Madness to Hope: The 12-Year War in El Salvador* (New York: United Nations, 1993).

17. Ibid.

CHAPTER 1. ARRIVING

1. "El Salvador Poverty Rate, 1980–2022," Macrotrends, accessed May 16, 2022, https://macrotrends.net/countries/SLV/el-salvador/poverty-rate.

2. "Justice Delayed but Not Denied: Transitional Justice in El Salvador," United Nations, April 2, 2020, www.ohchr.org/EN/NewsEvents/Pages/Transiti onalJusticeElSalvador.aspx.

3. Luis Noe-Bustamante, Antonio Flores, and Sono Shah, "Facts on Hispanics of Salvadoran Origin in the United States, 2017," Pew Research Center, September 16, 2019, www.pewresearch.org/Hispanic/fact-sheet/u-s-hispanics-facts -on-salvadoran-origin-latinos.

4. Jon Cortina, personal communication to author, San Salvador, June 2005.

5. Andrea Lampros, Montserrat Martínez Gómez, Cristián Orrego Benavente, and Patricia Vásquez Marías, "Disappeared, Not Lost: Finding El Salvador's Children," in *Silent Witness: Forensic DNA Evidence in Criminal Investigations and Humanitarian Disasters*, ed. Henry Erlich, Eric Stover, and Thomas J. White (Oxford: Oxford University Press, 2020).

6. Ralph Sprenkels, *Historias para tener presente* (San Salvador: Asociación Pro-Búsqueda de Niñas y Niños Desaparecidos/UCA Editores, 2002).

7. Lampros et al., "Disappeared, Not Lost."

8. Christopher Dickey, "U.S. Tactics Fail to Prevent Salvadoran Civilian Deaths," *Washington Post*, June 10, 1982, www.washingtonpost.com/archive/pol itics/1982/06/10/us-tactics-fail-to-prevent-salvadoran-civilian-deaths/ecfb3e03 -5bf6-4285-a3ef-1668004b2bf6/.

CHAPTER 2. GUARJILA WITH FATHER JON

1. Milton Aparicio, *Con Jon Cortina Dios Pasó por Guarjila* (San Salvador: Asociación Pro-Búsqueda de Niñas y Niños Desaparecidos/Trócaire, 2006).

2. "Guernica... Bombing of Guernica," Public Broadcasting Service, accessed May 19, 2022, www.pbs.org/treasuresoftheworld/guernica/glevel_1/1_bombing .html.

3. Aparicio, *Con Jon Cortina*.

4. Sean Salai, "Interview: The Life and Martyrdom of Jesuit Rutilio Grande," *America: The Jesuit Review,* March 12, 2021, www.americamagazine.org/arts-cu lture/2021/03/12/jesuit-rutilio-grande-salvador-martyr-biography-240210.

5. Ralph Sprenkels, *El día más esperado: Buscando a los niños desaparecidos de El Salvador* (San Salvador: Asociación Pro-Búsqueda de Niñas y Niños Desaparecidos/UCA Editores, 2001).

6. "This Is the Homily Óscar Romero Was Delivering When He Was Killed," *America: The Jesuit Review,* October 12, 2018, https://www.americamagazine .org/faith/2018/10/12/homily-oscar-romero-was-delivering-when-he-was-killed.

7. Aparicio, *Con Jon Cortina*.

8. Danny Hajek, "'I Miss Them, Always': A Witness Recounts El Salvador's 1989 Jesuit Massacre," National Public Radio, November 16, 2019, www.npr.org /2019/11/16/774176106/i-miss-them-always-a-witness-recounts-el-salvador-s-19 89-jesuit-massacre.

9. Sprenkels, *Día más esperado*.

10. Walter La Feber, *Inevitable Revolutions* (New York: Norton, 1993).

11. Sprenkels, *Día más esperado*.

12. Ibid.

13. Ibid.

14. Ibid.

15. United Nations Commission on the Truth for El Salvador, *De la Locura a la Esperanza: La Guerra de 12 Años en El Salvador* (San Salvador: Arcoiris, 1993); Americas Watch, *El Salvador: Accountability and Human Rights: The Report of the United Nations Commission on the Truth for El Salvador* (New York: Human Rights Watch, 1993), www.hrw.org/reports/pdfs/e/elsalvdr/elsalv 938.pdf.

16. Sprenkels, *Día más esperado*.

17. Ibid.

18. Inter-American Court of Human Rights, *Case of the Serrano-Cruz Sisters v. El Salvador,* March 1, 2005, www.corteidh.or.cr/docs/casos/articulos/ser iec_120_ing.pdf.

19. Sprenkels, *Día más esperado*.

CHAPTER 3. AT THE NUNNERY

1. Inter-American Court of Human Rights, *Case of the Serrano-Cruz Sisters v. El Salvador,* March 1, 2005, www.corteidh.or.cr/docs/casos/articulos/seriec _120_ing.pdf.

CHAPTER 4. GUERRILLERAS

1. Charles Brenner, "Forensic Mathematics," accessed May 19, 2022, http:// dna-view.com.

CHAPTER 5. MORAZÁN

1. Mark Danner, *The Massacre at El Mozote: A Parable of the Cold War* (New York: Vintage Books, 1994).

CHAPTER 7. SONSONATE WITH CECI AND LUCIO

1. Walter La Feber, *Inevitable Revolutions* (New York: Norton, 1993); Marjorie Miller, "Salvador Rebels Expand War, Destroy Coffee-Making Plans," *Los Angeles Times,* January 10, 1986, www.latimes.com/archives/la-xpm-1986-01-10 -mn-843-story.html.

CHAPTER 18. FATHER JON'S LEGACY

1. Milton Aparicio, *Con Jon Cortina Dios Pasó por Guarjila* (San Salvador: Asociación Pro-Búsqueda de Niñas y Niños Desaparecidos/Trócaire, 2006).

CHAPTER 21. EL NORTE

1. Luis Noe-Bustamante, Antonio Flores, and Sono Shah, "Facts on Hispanics of Salvadoran Origin in the United States, 2017," Pew Research Center, September 16, 2019, www.pewresearch.org/hispanic/fact-sheet/u-s-hispanics-facts -on-salvadoran-origin-latinos/; Aaron Terrazas, "Salvadoran Immigrants in the United States in 2008," Migration Policy Institute, January 5, 2010, www.migrati onpolicy.org/article/salvadoran-immigrants-united-states-2008.

2. "Personal Remittances, Received (% of GDP): El Salvador," World Bank, accessed June 3, 2022, https://data.worldbank.org/indicator/BX.TRF.PWKR .DT.GD.ZS?locations=SV.

CHAPTER 22. ANGELA'S PHONE REUNION

1. Elizabeth Barnert, "Searching for Lost Children: Hundreds Are Still Missing in El Salvador," *San Francisco Chronicle*, April 9, 2006, https://www.sfgate.com/opinion/article/Searching-for-lost-children-Hundreds-are-still-2520222.php.

CHAPTER 29. ANGELA'S EL SALVADOR

1. Nancy Newton Verrier, *The Primal Wound: Understanding the Adopted Child* (Baltimore: Gateway, 1993).

CHAPTER 30. ONWARD

1. Tracy Wilkinson, "Gunmen Torch Vital Records of Rights Group in El Salvador," *Los Angeles Times*, November 14, 2013, www.latimes.com/world/worldnow/la-fg-wn-gunmen-torch-records-rights-group-salvador-20131114-story.html.

2. Jonathan Van Ness, "How Does Traumatic Family Separation Affect Children? With Dr. Elizabeth Barnert," July 17, 2018, in *Getting Curious with Jonathan Van Ness*, podcast, 38:24. www.earwolf.com/episode/how-does-traumatic-family-separations-affect-children-w-dr-elizabeth-barnert/.

3. Romero, quoted in James Brockman, *Romero: A Life* (New York: Orbis Books, 2005).

AFTERWORD

1. Elizabeth Barnert, Eric Stover, Gery Ryan, and Paul J. Chung, "Long Journey Home: Family Reunification Experiences of the Disappeared Children of El Salvador," *Human Rights Quarterly* 37, no. 2 (2015): 492–510; Elizabeth Barnert, Nathalie Lopez, Philippe Bourgois, Gery Ryan, Paul J. Chung, and Eric Stover, "My Child's Journey Home: Perspectives of Adult Family Members on the Separation and Reunification of the 'Disappeared' Children of El Salvador," *Human Rights Quarterly* 41, no. 1 (2019): 91–114.

2. Pauline Boss, *Ambiguous Loss: Learning to Live with Unresolved Grief* (Cambridge, MA: Harvard University Press, 1999).

3. Geoffrey L. Grief, "Ambiguous Reunification: A Way for Social Workers to Conceptualize the Return of Children after Abduction and Other Separations," *Families in Society: The Journal of Contemporary Human Services* 93, no. 4 (2012): 305–11.

4. Anne Frank, *The Diary of Anne Frank, 1929–1945* (New York: Doubleday, 2003).

5. Adam Carlson, "'Families Are Torn Apart': Wrenching Anne Frank Diary Quote Goes Viral after Immigration Raids in Mississippi," *People*, August 13, 2019, https://people.com/politics/anne-frank-diary-quote-twitter-mississippi -immigration-raids/.

6. Lindsey Cramer, Margaret Goff, Bryce Peterson, and Heather Sandstrom, "Parent-Child Visiting Practices in Prisons and Jails," Urban Institute, April 13, 2017, www.urban.org/research/publication/parent-child-visiting-practices-pris ons-and-jails; Bruce Western and Becky Pettit, *Collateral Costs: Incarceration's Effect on Economic Mobility* (Washington, DC: Pew Charitable Trusts, 2010), www.pewtrusts.org/~/media/legacy/uploadedfiles/pcs_assets/2010/collateralc osts1pdf.pdf; Nia Heard-Garris et al., "Health Care Use and Health Behaviors among Young Adults with History of Parental Incarceration," *Pediatrics* 142, no. 3 (2018): e20174314.

7. Child Welfare Information Gateway, *Foster Care Statistics, 2019* (Washing-ton, DC: U.S. Department of Health and Human Services, 2021), www.childwel fare.gov/pubPDFs/foster.pdf.

8. Elizabeth S. Barnert et al., "Using DNA to Reunify Separated Migrant Families," *Science* 372, no. 6547 (2021): 1154–56.

9. Ibid; "DNA Bridge/Puente ADN." DNA Bridge. 2022. https://www.dna bridge.org/.

10. *Convention on the Rights of the Child*, United Nations, November 20, 1989, www.ohchr.org/en/professionalinterest/pages/crc.aspx.

11. Ralph Sprenkels, *Historias para tener presente* (San Salvador: Asociación Pro-Búsqueda de Niñas y Niños Desaparecidos/UCA Editores, 2002).

APPENDIX A

1. "President Eisenhower Delivers Cold War 'Domino Theory' Speech," His-tory, April 7, 1954, www.history.com/this-day-in-history/eisenhower-gives-fa mous-domino-theory-speech; James S. Corum, "The Air War in El Salvador," *Airpower Journal*, Summer 1998, 27–44.

2. Carolyn Forché, *What You Have Heard Is True: A Memoir of Witness and Resistance* (New York: Penguin, 2019); Leonardo Boff and Clodovis Boff, *Intro-ducing Liberation Theology* (Maryknoll, NY: Orbis Books, 1987).

3. Dan Williams, "El Salvador Intensifies Its Air War against Guerrillas," *Los Angeles Times*, July 17, 1985, www.latimes.com/archives/la-xpm-1985-07-17-mn -7813-story.html.

4. Karen DeYoung, "Carter Decides to Resume Military Aid to El Salvador," *Washington Post*, January 14, 1981, www.washingtonpost.com/archive/politics

/1981/01/14/carter-decides-to-resume-military-aid-to-el-salvador/16084fe6-8174
-49dc-be5f-a5a147566f96/.

5. "Abduction Leads to Placing of Ad," *New York Times*, December 2, 1978, 7,
https://timesmachine.nytimes.com/timesmachine/1978/12/02/110977109.html.

6. Corum, "Air War in El Salvador."

7. DeYoung, "Carter Decides to Resume."

8. Corum, "Air War in El Salvador"; Williams, "El Salvador Intensifies";
DeYoung, "Carter Decides to Resume."

9. Carlos Salinas Maldonado, "El Mozote: 40 Years after the Worst Military
Massacre in the Americas, Victims Still Calling for Justice," *El País*, December 16, 2021, https://english.elpais.com/usa/2021-12-16/el-mozote-40-years-after
-the-worst-military-massacre-in-the-americas-victims-still-calling-for-justice
.html; Mark Danner, *The Massacre at El Mozote: A Parable of the Cold War* (New
York: Vintage Books, 1994); Belisario Betancur, Reinaldo Figueredo Planchart,
and Thomas Buergenthal, "Report of the UN Truth Commission on El Salvador,"
United Nations Security Council, April 1, 1993, www.derechos.org/nizkor/salvad
or/informes/truth.html.

10. James Goldston and Jemera Rone, *A Year of Reckoning: El Salvador a
Decade after the Assassination of Archbishop Romero* (New York: Human Rights
Watch, 1990); Betancur, Planchart, and Buergenthal, "UN Truth Commission";
John Beverley, "El Salvador," *Social Text*, no. 5 (1982): 55–72; Danner, *Massacre
at El Mozote*; Forché, *What You Have Heard*.

11. "Jet Set Celebrity Bianca Jagger Arrived from Honduras Wednesday,"
United Press International, November 19, 1981, www.upi.com/Archives/1981/11
/18/Jet-set-celebrity-Bianca-Jagger-arrived-from-Honduras-Wednesday/551637
4907600/.

12. Raymond Bonner, "Salvadoran Refugees Suffer as War Spills into Honduras," *New York Times*, November 23, 1981, www.nytimes.com/1981/11/23/world
/salvadoran-refugees-suffer-as-war-spills-into-honduras.html.

13. Ibid.; Ynestroza, "El Salvador Declara."

APPENDIX B

1. "El Salvador: Information on the Atonal Immediate Reaction Battalion
(BIRI) in 1989, and on the 3rd Brigade's Cazador (Hunter) Battalion in 1991,"
Immigration and Refugee Board of Canada, December 1, 1993, www.refworld
.org/docid/3ae6ac115c.html; "The Spanish American War," *Spanish American
War Centennial Website*, 1996, www.spanamwar.com/index.html.

Index

Contact Information

Were you separated from your child during the war in El Salvador? Pro-Búsqueda can help you.

ASOCIACIÓN PROBUSQUEDA DE NIÑAS Y NIÑOS DESAPARECIDOS

HUMAN RIGHTS CENTER
BerkeleyLaw
UNIVERSITY OF CALIFORNIA

¿donde están?

Text FIND to 99000 / Call to 510.643.2709
Write to: info@probusqueda.org.sv / Go to: www.probusqueda.org.sv

To initiate a search or for information about the disappeared Salvadoran children, contact:

Pro-Búsqueda
Colonia Layco, 27 Calle Poniente, Casa N° 1329,
   San Salvador, El Salvador
Website: www.probusqueda.org.sv/
Email: info@probusqueda.org.sv
Telephone: (503) 22 35 10 39
Skype: Asociacion.probusqueda

UC Berkeley Human Rights Center
Forensic Program, Human Rights Center, Berkeley Law,
   2224 Piedmont Avenue, Berkeley, CA 94720
Website: https://humanrights.berkeley.edu/programs-projects/forensic
   -project
Email: hrc@berkeley.edu
Telephone: (510) 642-0965

Author contact: lizziebarnert@gmail.com